Isaiah by the Day

A New Devotional Translation

Alec Motyer

CHRISTIAN
FOCUS

Dedication

To the worshipping fellowship at St George's and St Martin's churches, Poynton;
specially to our leaders Rob McLaren and Andy Livingston;
and in particular to my friend and colleague in the blessed ranks of the retired,
John Briggs.

Copyright © J. A. Motyer 2011

hardback – ISBN 978-1-84550-654-4
epub – ISBN 978-1-78191-377-2
mobi – ISBN 978-1-78191-378-9

10 9 8 7 6 5

Published in 2011
Reprinted in 2012, 2014, 2016 and 2017
by
Christian Focus Publications,
Geanies House, Fearn, Tain, Ross-shire,
IV20 1TW, Scotland, U.K.
www.christianfocus.com

The translation of Isaiah is © 2011 by the author, J. A. Motyer.
Unless otherwise stated, all Scripture translations are the author's.

A CIP catalogue record for this book is available from the British Library.

Cover design by Paul Lewis
Printed and bound by Bookwell Digital, Finland

100%
From well-managed forests
FSC® C133773
FSC
www.fsc.org

CONTENTS

Author's Preface

Welcome to Isaiah! I send you this invitation as one who loves everything about him – the way he writes, his mastery of words, the rhythmic beauty of his Hebrew and, above all, the magnificent sweep of his messianic vision, taking in the glory of Jesus as God and King, the wonder and fullness of the salvation he accomplished, and the shining hope of his coming again. I want to share all this with you so that you may become as indebted to Isaiah as I feel myself to be. His book is as much the crown of the Old Testament as the Epistle to the Hebrews is of the New Testament – and for the same reason. Isaiah saw the coming King, Saviour and Conqueror; Hebrews knew him as Jesus. May the Lord God bless you richly as you read this tremendous portion of his Word.

Alec Motyer,
Poynton, Cheshire

Introduction

Please read the following carefully.

1. Isaiah wrote a book!
In a Bible with only chapter divisions it is hard to grasp a clear idea of the whole. It just seems like one thing after another. So here is an outline map.

Chapters 1–5. Isaiah's preface
Using a selection of messages he had preached over the years Isaiah paints a picture of the situation in which he was called to be a prophet.

Chapters 6–37. The Book of the King
In chapters 6–12, against the background of the failed monarchy of the house of David, Isaiah shares the vision of the great David who is yet to come (e.g., 9:6–7; 11:1–10) who will have a universal and endless reign. But is this realistic? David's historical kingdom was tiny. Will his promised descendant really rule the world? The answer is given in chapters 13–27 in which Isaiah uses the nations of the world as he knew them to describe the ongoing course of history right up to the promised End. So far so good, but is the vision just 'pie in the sky' or really possible? In chapters 28–35 Isaiah picks out a historical situation in which the three nations which he had used to depict the final glory (19:24–25) come face to face. Tiny Judah was caught in the middle of a squabble in which the then world's superpowers (Assyria and Egypt) came face to face, and in which the God of Israel showed himself to be in sovereign charge of the nations, their history and their destiny. And chapters 36–37 record how completely sovereign he was and how totally subservient to him was (even) Assyria.

Chapters 38–55. The Book of the Servant
Chapters 38–39 record how King Hezekiah turned disastrously from the way of faith to the way of works. In a personal crisis of health he had been given a double promise – of healing for himself and of deliverance for his city. But, having been healed, and having received a huge sign in confirmation, he turned from trusting the Lord's promises to seeking deliverance from Assyria by making an alliance with Babylon. In response, Isaiah in effect said – since

you have chosen Babylon, to Babylon you shall go. Was that then to be the end? Were all the promises of a great coming David forfeited by one false choice (however serious)? Can the sin of man annul the promises of God? The immediate message of 'comfort' (40:1) says 'No'. The Lord's answer to sin is the revelation of 'the Servant of the Lord', portrayed from 42:1 onwards, culminating in the great sin-bearing work of Isaiah 53.

Chapters 56–66. The Book of the Conqueror
The Servant's work of sin-bearing included his victory over every foe (53:11–12). For this the Lord's people are called to wait in obedient and righteous living (56:1). Like the Servant, the coming Conqueror is revealed in four special passages, starting in 59:20 and culminating in the spine-tingling climax of 63:1–6.

It would be worth your while to read through this outline as many times as it takes to fix it firmly in your memory, so that as we read Isaiah together you will always know where you are on the map.

2. Using the translation
Isaiah wrote very stylish Hebrew. Even his prose writing has a poetic, rhythmic quality, and his poetry is stately, beautiful, often rhyming and invariably impressive. It is hard to resist the temptation to go beyond a basic 'literal' translation into one that tries to offer some comparably stylish English – so to speak, to 'go for' a poetic rendering. My aim, rather, has been to bring you as near to the Hebrew as I can, as far as possible even following the Hebrew order of words (which is generally important to get the emphasis right) and, again as far as possible, using the same English translation for all Isaiah's main vocabulary.

The translation is set out in short lines for a practical purpose: as a rule we read our Bibles too quickly, failing to pause to take in the Bible's thoughts as they come. Try to follow Isaiah line by line. He's worth it!

3. A few points of detail
(a) Hebrew is an 'and' language
Hebrew tends not to make use of a wide system of subordinate clauses but simply to add on each new thought as it comes. This leads to a proliferation of 'ands', and in almost all cases I have left it like that. You will soon realize that in Hebrew 'and' has a wide variety of nuances and I feel it is your privilege to sort them out for yourself. But occasionally, where 'and' expresses a contrast with whatever has preceded and nothing would serve except 'but', I have added an asterisk (*) just to let you know that it is our old friend the conjunction.

(b) Asterisks again

I have also used the asterisk to mark one of the nouns for 'God'. In Isaiah – as throughout the Old Testament – the God of Israel has one *name* and two or three *nouns*. If we were to ask him 'What are you?' he would reply with the *noun*: I am 'God'. If we were to ask him 'Who are you?' he would reply with his *name*, 'Yahweh'. Would it help you if I said that 'God' is his surname and 'Yahweh' is his forename or Christian name? English translations have tended to follow the ancient scruple that the Divine Name was too holy for human use, and therefore they adopted the convention of representing the Hebrew 'Yahweh' by 'the LORD', using upper case letters. Oh dear! We have to have our wits about us when we read our Bibles! Genesis 4:25 shows that 'Yahweh' was used from the earliest times, but its meaning was revealed through Moses (Exod. 3:13–15; 6:2–8). 'Yahweh' is henceforth known specifically as the God who redeems his people and judges his foes.

There are two main *nouns* meaning God. The most common is *elohim*, a plural of 'amplitude' indicating that this God possesses all and every divine attribute; he is totally and completely God. The other noun is *el*: God in his transcendent majesty, glory, and strength. In order to keep you on the ball *elohim* is always translated 'God', and *el* is 'God*' -- the asterisk again.

I have retained the great title 'God/Yahweh of Hosts'; first because I like it and secondly because you, the reader, should drill yourself to remember what it means rather than be spoon-fed with some interpretative equivalent. He is 'Yahweh who is Hosts', possessing in himself every potentiality and power; not a 'bare One' but a 'One' incorporating a multiplicity of attributes, capacities and powers. The addition 'of Hosts' is part of the Old Testament's anticipation of the New Testament revelation of God as the holy Trinity.

(c) 'Thus says Yahweh'

This time-honoured translation of the claim made by all the prophets that they were reporting the Lord's own words lies well within the scope of the perfect tense of the Hebrew verb used, but I have come to the conclusion that 'This is what Yahweh has said' is better. The words originated with Yahweh, were (somehow) shared by him with his chosen agents and faithfully passed on by them.

(d) Nouns and adjectives

Even where Hebrew has an adjective with the required meaning ('holy mountain') writers often prefer to express the adjectival idea by an attached noun ('mountain of holiness'). It seems to me that the attached noun often expresses a fuller and deeper meaning than the simple adjective and I have very often retained it in translation.

(e) The word 'behold'
'Behold' has such an antique ring to it that it is a great problem to modern translations – some even solve the problem by leaving it out! Others try representing it by words of emphasis like 'indeed'. But nothing has quite the same force as 'Behold'. 'Look at this!' was intended to claim attention for something important to the writer.

(f) Daily portions.
I have tried to provide daily portions that match natural divisions in Isaiah. This means that they are not of equal length. If you should find any day's portion too long, take two days over it! The important thing – indeed the main purpose of this whole exercise – is to grasp what Isaiah is saying, what he means at any given point, why this portion follows on from yesterday's. His whole book is a planned development. Make sure, above all things, that you are following it through.

Enjoy!

PART ONE

Backdrop to Isaiah's ministry
(Isaiah 1–5)

Day 1   Isaiah 1:1–9

Isaiah's 'preface'

Like books today, Isaiah starts his book with (a) its title (1:1) and (b) an 'Author's preface' (1:2–5:30), in this case outlining the situation in which he ministered.

Title

1:1.   The vision[1] of Isaiah, son of Amoz,
    which he perceived concerning Judah and Jerusalem,
    in the days of Uzziah, Jotham, Ahaz, Hezekiah,
    kings of Judah.[2]

Backdrop to Isaiah's ministry (1): You are not what you ought to be (1:2–31)

Isaiah starts by looking at the evidence before his eyes. A devastated land (vv. 2–9), a failing church (vv. 10–20), and a corrupt society (vv. 21–26), this last merging into a surprising view of the future (vv. 27–31).

The state of the nation

2.   Hear, O Heavens,
    listen, O Earth,
    for Yahweh has himself spoken:
    Sons I have nurtured and reared
    and they – they! – have rebelled[3] against me!

3.   An ox knows its owner,
    and a donkey its master's trough;
    it is Israel who does not know!
    My people who have no discernment!

4.   Ah, sinning nation,
    a people heavy with iniquity,

1   'Vision...perceived'. The verb *chazah*, can mean actually to 'see' a vision but it is usually broader – 'to see truth', 'to perceive meaning' – in this case by revelation from the Lord.

2   Respectively 790–740, 750–732, 744–715, 729–686 BC. The overlapping years were co-regencies by which the 'old' king secured the succession for the son he chose. The years 745–701 BC were ones of constant threat from the imperialistic expansion of Assyria.

3   The three great words in the 'sin'-vocabulary are 'sin' (*chat'a*, v. 4), the actual item of wrongdoing; 'iniquity' (v. 4, from *'awah,* to be bent), the 'warp' in the fallen human nature; and 'rebellion' (*pash'a*), wilful, deliberate disobedience.

seed of evil-doers,
sons acting corruptly.
They have forsaken Yahweh,
spurned the Holy One of Israel,
turned themselves back into foreigners.[4]

5. What use is it to continue stubborn? –
you will only be beaten again!

6. The whole head is disease-ridden[5];
from the sole of the foot to the head
there is no soundness in it –
bruise and scar and fresh wound;
untreated, and unbandaged, and unsoothed with ointment.

7. Your land a desolation,[6]
your cities burnt with fire,
your country –
in front of you foreigners are eating it up,
a desolation,
like something overturned by foreigners.[7]

8. And the daughter of Zion is left over
like a shed in a vineyard,
like a hut in a cucumber patch,
like a blockaded city.[8]

9. Were it not that Yahweh of Hosts[9] himself
had left over for us a tiny remainder,
we would have matched Sodom,
we would have resembled Gomorrah.

4 Lit., 'have estranged themselves backwards'.

5 Lit., 'for sickness', 'given over to/ the property of'.

6 Very often in Isaiah illustration (v. 6) is followed by explanation (v. 7), cf., v. 26 following v. 25; or again, 8:7b explains v. 7a, etc.

7 'Overturned' (*mahpekah*) is virtually a technical term for what God did to Sodom, e.g. Deut 29:23; Isa. 13:19. 'By foreigners', i.e., with such thoughtless callousness as only foreigners could show.

8 Images in turn of the flimsy, the temporary, and the threatened.

9 Isaiah uses this title of Yahweh over sixty times. Yahweh is not a bare unit but is, within his own nature, a 'host', with every possible potentiality and power. The title is part of the Old Testament preparation for the New Testament revelation of the complex nature of God as the holy Trinity.

Thought for the day: Isaiah 1:2–9

'I don't seem to be able to help it. It's in my nature.' Well, yes, that is certainly one way of looking at our sinful ways: it's doing what 'comes naturally', and different weaknesses and flaws in different people come out in different ways. But as an excuse, it goes nowhere! What 'nature' are we talking about? Our 'old nature' before we knew Jesus, or the new nature that is God's gift to us in Christ? It is still possible to find old school buildings with 'Boys' carved in the stonework over one door, 'Girls' over another, and over a third 'Mixed Infants'. This side of heaven, we are all 'mixed infants', the Spirit fighting the flesh, and the flesh the Spirit (Gal. 5:17), the mind serving the law of God and the flesh the law of sin (Rom. 7:25). It is all there in Isaiah 1:4. On the one hand the four nouns of privilege: we are his people and nation – the redeemed (Exod. 6:6; 12:13); the chosen 'seed' (Gal. 3:9, 16); his sons (Gal. 4:4–7). On the other hand, the four descriptions of shame: sinning, iniquity, evildoers, acting corruptly. There's a war on, but, says Isaiah, in this war it is strictly unnatural for the Christian to choose the way of sin and leave the path of privilege. Look at the beasts. The ox naturally turns to its owner, and the donkey naturally eats its owner's food. It is living according to its true nature. So what about us? Which nature do we choose to make dominant? Which master do we love to be with? What food are we nourishing ourselves on? Where are we turning for shelter and vitality? One further thought: Proverbs 14:34 relates righteousness and national prosperity, sin and public shame. How does Isaiah see this working out in his people? Is it relevant today?

Day 2　Isaiah 1:10–20

The people were spared the fate of Sodom and Gomorrah (v. 9) but sadly the spirit of Sodom and Gomorrah lives on among them (v. 10), and is seen specially in their religion.

The state of the church

1:10. Hear the word of Yahweh,
　　　chiefs of Sodom!
　　　Listen to the teaching[1] of our God,
　　　people of Gomorrah!
11.　What use to me is the abundance of your sacrifices?
　　　Yahweh keeps saying,
　　　I am sated with burnt offerings of rams,
　　　and the fat of well-fed beasts.
　　　And in the blood of bulls, and lambs, and he-goats
　　　I find no pleasure.
12.　When you come to appear before me[2]
　　　who sought this from your hand[3] –
　　　a trampling of my courts!
13.　Stop bringing empty gifts;[4]
　　　it is an abhorrent incense[5] to me.
　　　New moon festival, and Sabbath,
　　　calling conventions –
　　　wickedness[6] coupled with religious duty is too much for me!
14.　Your new moon festivals, and your special occasions
　　　my soul hates.[7]
　　　I am tired bearing them.
15.　And when you spread out your palms,[8] I hide my eyes
　　　from you.

[1]　'Law', *torah*, means 'teaching', not 'legislation'. Such instruction as passes between a caring parent and a loved child (Prov. 4:1). God's 'law' is the loving instruction for life that he has revealed to his redeemed.

[2]　Or 'to see my face'. cf., Exod. 34:24; Deut. 31:11. The variation in translation arises from different ways of adding vowels to the Hebrew consonants.

[3]　'Hand' stands for personal action; also for available resources (Deut. 16:17), which would refer here to the cost of providing the sacrifices. It might also be a reference to the ceremony of laying the hand on the beast to be killed (e.g., Lev. 1:4), the symbol for designating a substitute (Lev. 16:21).

[4]　Lit., 'Gifts of emptiness': gifts which give nothing; or 'of falsehood' – which pretend what they do not mean.

Even though, indeed, you multiply prayer I am not
even listening.
Your hands – they are full of bloodshed![9]

16. Wash! Make yourselves clean!
Remove your evil practice from before my eyes!
Give up wrong-doing!

17. Learn well-doing!
Seek judgment!
Reform the oppressor!
Deal justly with the orphan!
Take up the case of the widow!

18. Come, then, let us argue the point with each other,
Yahweh keeps saying.
Though your sins[10] be like scarlet,
Like snow they will be white!
Though they be red as crimson,
Like wool they will be!

19. If you are willing and listen,
the goodness of the land you will eat;

20. and if you refuse and prove contentious,[11]
by the sword you will be eaten!
For Yahweh's mouth itself has spoken.

---

5   Contrast Gen. 8:21; Lev. 1:9; etc.

6   *'awen*, a very broad word, difficult to translate even though it is frequent in the Old Testament. Basically that which is out of place in any given context; what makes for trouble/mischief; unacceptable or false worship. Here a life discordant with a religious practice and profession. Mischievous law-making (10:1), a 'fault/failing' (29:20), mischief/mischief-making (59:6–7) etc.

7   We would say, 'I hate with all my heart.' 'Soul' is often used of the essential inmost reality of a person. cf., 42:1.

8   *kaph*, the palm of the hand. Here the extending of the empty hand, palm up. Contrasted with the common word for 'hand' (*yad*), *kaph* is the 'cupped' hand or the hand as 'gripping'.

9   'Bloods'; the plural is used of shed blood, violently shed blood, grievous bodily harm, social disruption.

10   See 1:2.

11   Isaiah uses four main words for the general idea of 'rebellion'. For convenience the same translations are used throughout: *pash'a*, 'rebel' – of wilful rebellion against an overlord; *marad*, 'to revolt'; *marah*, as here, 'to be/prove contentious/refractory'; *sarar*, 'to be stubborn, stubbornly rebellious'.

Thought for the day: Isaiah 1:10–20

Every time we try – rightly – to form a spiritual habit we find ourselves walking a tightrope! Simply because the habit can come to be seen as valuable for itself, and the benefit it was designed to bring gets forgotten. Isaiah saw this all round him. People were congratulating themselves on religious habits; they never failed to bring the sacrifices the Lord commanded, the right animal for the right occasion. They were never missing from the Lord's courts. Why, they never once failed to pray. But slowly and surely they forgot what the sacrifices were actually for, and what manner of people they should be if they desired to lift up hands and voices to God. The habit had become all-important. They loved religion but they did not shun sin; they prayed but they did not bother about sin and holiness. And all this is not 'far off forgotten things and battles long ago'. Isn't there a disciplined habit to be cultivated if we are to get to know our Bibles like Jesus knew his? Yes, indeed. But isn't it easy for the habit to become an end in itself, a pride in moving the book-marker on the requisite number of pages per day? But no pondering the Word, no making sure its truth is reaching from the page to the mind and so to the heart, no concern for the Word to change us into the likeness of our Saviour. Or again, we rightly love the Lord's Table, and Sunday is unthinkable without the Breaking of Bread. But be careful here too! The precious habit can take over and the bread and wine pass from hand to hand without any feasting in mind and heart on the Christ of Calvary. Over everything the Bible would inscribe the words: 'These things I write to you so that you may not sin' (1 John 2:1).

Day 3   Isaiah 1:21–31

Isaiah's final topic in his review of the state of affairs is social breakdown. Standards have collapsed; when they are paired 'righteousness' points to moral principles, and 'judgment' to moral practice (v. 21). Leadership is corrupt (v. 23a) and care of the vulnerable has disappeared (v. 23b). Judgment surely must come but judgment does not have the last word.

The state of society[1]

1:21. Ah! How she has become a harlot –
    the trustworthy town!
    Full of judgment,[2]
    righteousness used to lodge[3] in her,
    but now murderers!

22.   Your[4] silver has become dross,
    your liquor diluted with water,

23.   your princes stubborn,[5]
    and in league with robbers.
    Each and every one loves a bribe,
    and pursues all sorts of graft.[6]
    They do not provide justice for the orphan,
    and the widow's case does not come before them.

24.   Therefore –
    (This is the word of the Sovereign,
    Yahweh of Hosts,
    Potentate[7] of Israel) –
    oh, I will relieve myself of my adversaries,
    and I will avenge myself on my enemies,

25.   and I will bring back my hand[8] upon you,
    and I will refine, as with a cleansing agent, your dross,
    and I will remove all your base metal.

1   Verses 21–26 form a complete poem in its own right. Note how vv. 21 and 26 'match' each other. Here Isaiah uses his poem to review the society he ministered in (vv. 21–23) and to bridge over into a message about the future (vv. 24–26), a theme expanded in vv. 27–31.

2   See 2:4

3   *lin*, to be a temporary guest, stay overnight. 'Righteousness' cannot be assumed. It must be invited to stay.

4   In vv. 22, 23, 25, 26 the possessive pronouns are feminine singular, referring to the 'trustworthy town'.

5   'Princes' were the administrative arm of government, civil servants. 'Stubborn' belongs in the 'rebellion' vocabulary of Hebrew, mulish rebellion (see 1:20).

6   'Graft' is in the plural, expressing a distributive, 'every manner of'.

26. And I will bring back your judges as at the first,
and your counsellors as at the start.[9]
Afterwards, you will be called
City of Righteousness,
Trustworthy Town.

The surprising future

27.[10] Zion, with justice, will be ransomed,[11]
and her returning ones[12] with righteousness.[13]
28. And shattering for those who are rebelling, and the sinful,[14]
all at once!
And those who forsake Yahweh are finished.
29. For they will reap shame
from the fine trees which you have desired,
and you will be dishonored by the gardens
which you have chosen.
30. For you will be like a great tree withering in its foliage,
and like a garden which has no water.[15]
31. And the strong will be tinder,
and what he has made a spark,[16]
and they will burn, both of them together,
with no one to put the fire out!

---

7 Heb. *'abir*, used of 'sheer strength', here the absoluteness of divine power. cf. 49:26; 60:16.

8 'To bring back the hand' is usually a description of a back-handed blow of judgment (Ps. 81:14). Here, it is a message of hope, a thing which Isaiah frequently introduces with an element of surprise. Instead of a punishing blow, a work of restoration.

9 'First … start', i.e. the return of David. He was the first to capture and hold Zion, and make it his capital (2 Sam. 5: 6–10; 1 Chron. 11:4–9).

10 Verses 27–31 comment on the foregoing poem. The topics of judgment and restoration (vv. 24, 25–26) are repeated, in reverse order, in vv. 27–28. Verses 29–31 round the section off by exposing the failure and self-destructiveness of false religion.

11 *padah*, 29:22; 35:10; 51:11, focuses on the price paid in order to redeem. Hence the rendering 'ransom'.

12 'Returning', i.e., to Yahweh, the standard way to express repentance.

13 Justice and righteousness, i.e., in the work of ransoming, Yahweh's absolute standards are safeguarded: 45:21; Rom. 3:26.

14 See 1:2

15 'Fertility' religions were concerned with productivity (in man, animals, land – in general, economic prosperity). They saw trees dying and reviving and thought some principle of renewal lived there. Particularly they venerated evergreens with their seemingly undying character. Hence, trees, coppices and gardens were the locus of such religious rites. But, Isaiah notes, trees and gardens have no inherent life but depend on irrigation. Take away the water and they die! The species of trees he refers to can no longer be identified.

16 i.e., the worshipper and his man-made gods, inherently self-destructive.

Thought for the day: Isaiah 1:21–31

Paul puts our proper testimony in our mouths when he writes, 'I am the chief of sinners' (1 Tim. 1:15), and describes our condition exactly with the words that 'in me (that is, in my flesh) nothing good dwells' (Rom. 7:18). In our most realistic moments we not only accept this estimate in our minds, but also feel how true it is. Isaiah expressed the same reality, but much more vividly: the silver had become dross, the drink diluted. The first picture is of a transforming contamination: the precious had become the worthless; sin's dire power to corrupt had reached into every art and part of the personality. The second picture is of compromise: the liquor had admitted a foreign body, and every part was not only contaminated but in conflict. Quite a picture! What a truth! But, however true, it is not the end of the story – 'I will refine … your dross' (v. 25). Very likely this could be translated (NKJV, NIV), 'I will … purge away your dross'. This, of course, is true enough. The Lord's power to save does work to rid our lives of impurities. But it misses the link between 'dross' in verse 22 and in verse 25. The silver had become dross; the Lord's hand would turn the dross back into silver. He will totally undo what sin, Satan and our own wilfulness have achieved. His ransom-price will leave nothing in the hand of the kidnapper of all that he sought to grasp. Isaiah will presently tell us at what cost this will be done, bringing back as sons those who wandered off as sheep (53:6), and bestowing the Lord's gift of righteousness (54:17), but in this early passage it is for us to fill in the gaps in the story. The returning hand of judgment (v. 25) fell on the Son of God, the Just died for the unjust (1 Pet. 3:18), and the 'It is finished' at Calvary (John 19:30) meant and means exactly what it says.

Day 4   Isaiah 2:1–4

Backdrop to Isaiah's ministry (2): You are not what you were meant to be (2:1–4:6)

What did the Lord expect from his people? The glorious vision of 2:2–4 gives the answer. The elect people was meant to be a magnet to all the earth, drawing all others into the knowledge of the Lord. The reality has proved to be very different, with his people religiously (2:5–21) and socially (2:22–4:1) sadly conformed to the world rather than being the point of its transformation; but the future will see the ideal restored (4:2–6).

Heading

2:1. The word which Isaiah son of Amoz perceived concerning Judah and Jerusalem:

The great 'might-have-been'

2.   And it shall be, at the end of the days,
   the mountain of Yahweh's house will be secured
   as the head of the mountains
   and it will be lifted up more than the hills
   and all the nations will stream to it.

3.   And many peoples will come,
   and they will say:
   'Come,
   Let us go up to the mountain of Yahweh
   to the house of the God of Jacob,
   so that he may teach us something of his ways,
   and that we may walk in his paths'.
   For out of Zion will go forth teaching,
   And Yahweh's word out of Jerusalem.

4. And he will set things to rights between the nations,[1]
    and arbitrate[2] between many peoples,
    and they will hammer their swords into ploughshares,
    and their spears into pruning knives.
    Nation will not take up the sword against nation,
    and they will not, any more, learn war.

---

1   The verb 'to judge' (*shaphat*) has the basic meaning of 'making an authoritative pronouncement which decides issues'. Likewise its noun (*mishpat*/'judgment') points to a society in which such a rule prevails (1:21); in 1:27 'judgment' is the precept of right or legality which such a pronouncement voices and, for example in 42:1, 3, 4, *mishpat* is the pronouncement itself, the revelation of the Lord's truth (cf., Deut. 5:1). 'To judge', therefore, does not have the meaning of 'to condemn', to pass an adverse sentence, but to make whatever decision settles a particular issue – or all issues (Ps. 98:7–9), to 'put things to rights'.

2   *yakach*, 1:18; 11:3–4; 29:21; 37:4. The general idea is of arguing a point out so as to reach a decision, therefore 'to reach a thought-out conclusion'. The noun *tokechah*, 37:3 – 'a day when things have reached their (grim) conclusion', like 'crisis'.

Thought for the day: Isaiah 2:1–4

How would you answer the question, What is the church? Think about it! A building? A distinct organisation with agreed forms and norms? People who 'come on Sunday'? Isaiah can be our teacher in these few, wonderful verses. The church is a worldwide company, from every nation and people, drawn together by the magnetic power of the Word of God. Isn't that what he says? There is such a supernatural power at work as would make streams go uphill! We know, of course, that the power does not lie in the printed page, but in the Spirit of God. Nevertheless, it is the magnetic quality of revealed truth – God's own teaching, his Word (v. 3) – that is at work. This is the way that, particularly the Old Testament, thinks of mission. As a broad comparison (not to be pushed to extremes) the New Testament stresses 'outreach', and the Old, 'ingathering'. The New sends missionaries; the Old thinks of a magnet. How very careful we need to be! We have all inherited from the past our cherished 'traditions', our received preferences. They are certainly not to be undervalued or discarded lightly, but they must always be kept in review: have they become more important than the Word of God? Do they best present what the Bible teaches today? In some cases, are they scriptural at all? Is our church known locally primarily as a place where God's Word reigns supreme? If asked, would a non–member describe us as 'those people who love the Bible'? And there is another side to it. Isaiah, so to speak, overhears people talking (v. 3). They express their desire to learn God's Word. It is only as we, each of us, yearns for the Word that the whole company will bear the mark of the Word, and experience its power to draw others in.

For further thought: When we cherish his Word, the Lord will teach us Christlike ways (v. 4).

Day 5   Isaiah 2:5–21

Contrary to the ideal of verses 2–4, far from drawing the nations in, the Lord's people have become like them (vv. 6–9); they have made their own gods and must come under divine judgment (vv. 10–21).

The actual Jerusalem: (1) Worldliness and man-made gods

2:5.   House of Jacob,
      come,
      let us walk in Yahweh's light.

6.   For you have abandoned your people,
      the house of Jacob,
      because they are full from the east,[1]
      and go fortune telling like the Philistines.[2]
      And with the children of foreigners they shake hands,[3]

7.   and their[4] land has become full of silver and gold,
      and there is no end to their treasures,
      and their land has become full of horses,
      and there is no end to their chariots,

8.   and their land has become full of no-gods,[5]
      to the work of their hands they bow in worship,
      to what their fingers have made!

9.   And humankind is humiliated,
      and each individual is demeaned[6] –
      impossible that you should forgive them![7]

10.   Go into the rock,
      and hide yourself in the dust,
      because of apprehension of Yahweh,
      and from the splendour of his eminence.

11.   Humankind's haughty looks[8] will be demeaned
      and the cockiness of individuals[9] brought down,
      and Yahweh alone will be exalted in that day.

1   i.e., the worldly source of light, contrasted with Yahweh's light, v. 5.

2   The Philistines were not noted as fortune-tellers, but as prime examples of the unenlightened people of the world. The desire to be 'like the Philistines' is worldliness supreme!

3   Presumably, make agreements and treaties with, as if Yahweh was not sufficient for his people's needs

4   'Their', vv. 7–8, is lit. 'his', referring to the singular 'Jacob'.

5   *'elil* means 'a nothing'. The plural *'elilim* sounds like the plural for 'God', *'elohim*, and is used by Isaiah as a dismissive mockery. cf., vv. 18, 20; 10:10–11; 19:1, 3; 31:7.

6   'Humankind … each individual' is respectively the generic word *'adam* and the *'ish*, the word for

12. For Yahweh of Hosts has a day
    against everything eminent and lofty,
    and against everything uplifted,
    and it will be demeaned:

13. Against all the cedars of The Lebanon,
    those lofty and uplifted ones,
    and against all the oaks of The Bashan,[10]

14. and against all the lofty mountains,
    and against all the uplifted hills

15. and against every tall tower,
    and against every fortified wall

16. and against all the ships of Tarshish,
    and against all coveted craft.[11]

17. And the haughtiness of humankind will be humiliated,
    and the cockiness of individuals will be demeaned,
    and Yahweh alone will be exalted in that day.

18. And the no-gods[12] will totally pass away.

19. And they will go into the caves in the rocks,
    and into the holes in the dust
    because of apprehension of Yahweh
    and from the splendour of his eminence
    when he rises to terrify the earth.

20. In that day
    humankind will throw away
    each his no-gods of silver and his no-gods of gold,
    which they made each for himself in order to bow in worship,
    to the mice and to the bats,

21. to go into the tunnels in the rocks
    and into the clefts in the cliffs,
    because of apprehension of Yahweh
    and from the splendour of his eminence,
    when he rises to terrify the earth.

---

the individual person. Isaiah
may have meant 'ordinary
folk … great/well-known
individuals', but either way
the intention is 'all alike'.

7   Lit., 'Do not bear away for them.'
    'Bear away' understands 'sin'
    as its object, and is a standard
    idiom for 'forgive', as on the
    Day of Atonement (Lev. 16:22).
    Hebrew uses the imperative to
    express an absolutely certain
    outcome – here in the negative,
    the impossibility of forgiveness.

8   Lit., 'The eyes of the
    haughtiness of humankind'.

9   'Humankind … individuals';
    see v. 9, note 6.

10 These place names always
    have the definite article.

11 The word (*sekiyyoth*) only occurs
    here. It may mean 'works of
    art' or 'ships'. 'Craft' includes
    both, though my preference
    would be for 'works of art'.

12 See v. 8.

Thought for the day: Isaiah 2:5–21

Where is our trust placed? We claim that we are trusting Jesus, but in daily practical reality is it really so? What wisdom do we live by? Do we ever let the wisdom of the world take the place of the light of the Word of God (v. 6a)? Do we read our horoscope on the quiet (v. 6b)? What are we trusting for security, the support systems this world offers – insurance and assurance policies (v. 6c), money and investments (v. 7a), military capability (v. 7b)? And do we never make our own gods according to our own fancies (v. 8)? In post-Christian countries, the no-gods are those of folk religion, nice, heart-warming assumptions: trouble-free life after death, a 'god' they never thought of life-long who is only too delighted to welcome them into a cushy heaven. Grandma watching over us, still with us though long dead. Isaiah's definition of a 'no-god' is self-reliance. The idolater had 'done it all himself' with his strong hands and skilled fingers. So have you never met someone whose commitment to Christian works has become a pathological zeal? They just can't stop. Devotion has become the hard taskmaster called Duty and, though they would sternly deny it, the onlooker wonders if somewhere along the line justification by faith with its glorious restfulness has been swallowed by salvation by works. Dutifulness has killed off joyfulness. It truly is a point at which sensitive and constant alertness is the order of the day. Our most precious possession is 'Yahweh's light' (v. 5), 'the light of the gospel of the glory of Christ, who is the image of God … the light of the knowledge of the glory of God in the face of Jesus Christ' (2 Cor. 4:3, 6). Ever and always, as our outstanding priority, 'Turn your eyes upon Jesus; look full in his wonderful face' – not, of course, by way of inner vision, but by way of the printed page – the Emmaus way (Luke 24:31–32), the only way the risen Lord allowed.

Day 6 Isaiah 2:22–4:1

Isaiah continues to compare the actual Jerusalem with the ideal of 2:2–4. Far from Jerusalem being the stable city magnetic to the world, it is itself falling apart. Isaiah 3:1–7 gives the evidence of the disintegration; 3:8–15, its cause; and 3:16–4:1 a case in point, the daughters of Jerusalem encapsulating the spirit of their mother.

The actual Jerusalem: (2) Social collapse and its cause

2:22.[1] For your own good give up on humankind,
    in whose nostrils is but breath,
    for at what worth is it to be reckoned?

3:1–2. For behold:
    The Sovereign, Yahweh of Hosts,
    is going to remove from Jerusalem and from Judah
    prop and pillar,[2]
    the entire prop of bread and the entire prop of water,
    soldier and man of war,
    judge and prophet and fortune-teller and elder,

3.   prince of fifty and prominent person[3]
    and counsellor and one wise in magic arts and the
    clever sorcerer.

4.   And I will appoint youngsters as their princes,
    and capriciousness will rule over them,

5.   and the people will oppress each other[4] –
    person against person,
    friend against friend;
    young will behave arrogantly against old,
    and the despicable against the honoured.

6.   For a man will grab hold of his brother in his father's house:
    'You have a suit of clothes; you must be our chief!'

[1] 2:22 is a 'bridge' verse. In the preceding verses man-made gods have failed; in the following verses human society has failed. There is no point in trusting humankind for security.

[2] In the Hebrew, the masculine and feminine forms of the same word – an idiom expressing totality by means of contrast.

[3] i.e., minor public official and, lit., 'uplifted of face', someone well known in public life.

[4] 'Oppress' is a word used of Egyptian servitude, Exod. 5:5 – the Lord's people behaving like pagans towards each other.

7.   He will protest,[5] in that day, saying:
     'I will not become a healer,[6]
     and in my house is neither bread nor clothes.
     You must not make me the people's chief.'

8.   For Jerusalem has stumbled,
     and Judah has fallen,
     because their tongue and their actions,
     as regards Yahweh,
     are designed to prove contentious[7] to the eyes of his glory.

9.   The very look of their faces itself answers against them,
     and their sin[8] – like Sodom they publicise it!
     They do not conceal it!
     Woe to their souls!
     For they have repaid evil[9] to themselves in full.

10. Say of the righteous that all's well,
     for the fruit of their actions they will eat.

11. Woe to the wicked!
     Evil!
     For full repayment of their hands[10] shall be done to each.

12. My people!
     Their chief taskmaster[11] is infantile!
     And it is women who rule over them.[12]
     My people!
     Your directors are misleaders,
     and the road of your paths they have swallowed.[13]

13. Yahweh has taken[14] up position to contend;
     he is standing to argue his people's case.

14. Yahweh himself comes to judgment[15]
     against the elders and princes[16] of his people.
     'It is you who have grazed the vineyard bare.
     Plunder from the downtrodden[17] is in your houses.

15. What business of yours is it to crush my people,
     and to grind the faces of the downtrodden?'
     This is the word of the Sovereign, Yahweh of Hosts.

16. And Yahweh said:
     'Because the daughters of Zion[18] are haughty,

5   Lit., 'He will lift up', an ellipsis for 'lift up his voice'.

6   'Bandager', one tending the wounds in the body politic, cf., 1:6.

7   See 1:20.

8   See 1:2.

9   'Evil' (r'a) ranges in meaning from a bad taste to full moral wrong. It frequently, as here, means 'trouble' or 'calamity' (cf. v. 11).

10   For 'hands' see 1:12.

11   'Taskmaster' is here the plural, understood as a plural expressing greatness or completeness. 'Taskmaster' is used in the history of Egyptian bondage, Exod. 3:7, but here of oppressive rule by the current king. 'Infantile' is an uncertain translation but the word seems to be related to that for an 'infant'.

12   i.e, presumably the ladies of the royal harem.

13   The double description 'road … path' suggests what should be unmistakeably clear. 'Swallowed', obliterated for their own advantage.

14   Isaiah describes this inset courtroom scene as if he

and go along with their necks stuck out –
ogling with their eyes,
tripping along like children – so they walk –
their feet tinkling with ankle-bangles –

17. the Sovereign One will cover with scabs
the scalps of the daughters of Zion,
and Yahweh will expose their foreheads.'[19]

18. In that day, the Sovereign One will remove
the beauty of bangles, and the headbands, and the
moon-charms,

19. the pendants and the bracelets and the drapes,

20. the head-scarves and the ankle-chains and the sashes,
and the high collars and the lucky mascots,

21. the rings and the nose-jewels,

22. the fine clothes and the wraps and the cloaks and the purses,

23. and the mirrors[20] and the stoles and the hats and the shawls.

24. And this will happen:
Instead of scent, there will be a rotten smell,
and instead of a belt, a rope,
and instead of styled hair, baldness,
and instead of tailored clothes, sack-cloth tied on;
branding instead of beauty.

25. Your[21] menfolk by the sword will fall,
and your military force in the war,

26. and her gates will moan and mourn,
and on the ground, bereft, she will sit.

4:1. And seven women will grab at one man in that day,
saying, 'Our own bread we will eat
and our own clothes we will wear.[22]
Only let your name be pronounced over us.
Remove our disgrace!'

15 'Judgment', see 2:4. Here
'to settle the issue'/'put
the matter to rights'.

16 See 1:23

17 Noun 'aniy from 'anah,
'to be low(ly)', regularly of
those at the bottom of life's
heap – the downtrodden.

18 Isaiah offers a 'case in point'.
Note how the topic of 'the
daughters' becomes, in vv. 25 to
4:1, truth about Zion herself. The
frivolous womenfolk encapsulate
the spirit of their 'mother'.

19 Uncertain translation, possibly a
vulgar word for the private parts.

20 Possibly 'gauzes', see-through
garments. But like many of the
articles here, there is an element
of guesswork in translating.

21 'Your' is feminine singular.
Isaiah turns from the 'daughters'
to the 'mother', Zion herself.
In v. 26 'her' refers to Zion.

22 Contrast Exod. 21:10

Thought for the day: Isaiah 2:22–4:1

There is such a thing as divine hostility; indeed, candidly considered, the Bible would teach us that it is a much more serious thing to fall out of the power of the Lord than to fall into the power of Satan! To fall out of the power of the Lord is to lose his protection and be exposed to his hostility: the Lord standing up like a prosecuting lawyer in court (v. 13), the Lord hitting out at our welfare (v. 17), taking away our enjoyments (v. 18). So what provokes him to anger? Isaiah replies, 'their tongue and their actions' (v. 8). Sins of speech are one of the most lightly regarded of all sins today, and one of the most serious in the Bible's estimation. Likewise, Isaiah does not leave us ignorant of God-displeasing actions: leadership willing to destroy the national economy for self-interest (v. 14) and careless of the needs of the uninfluential 'bottom end' of the social scale (vv. 14–15); and people devoted to frivolity and shallow indulgence (vv. 16–23). The Bible would not object to the 'daughters of Zion' having nice things or wanting to look nice, but, as Isaiah shows, it does object to defining what life is all about in terms of wealth and possessions, and making outward show our chief desire.

On the importance of the tongue, look up Isaiah 59:2–3, 13 with Romans 3:8, 13–14; Psalm 120:3–4; Proverbs 6:16–19; Matthew 12:36–37; James 3:2–8; 1 Peter 3:9–10.

To think about: If the Lord's anger is roused by the faults mentioned above, then the Christian's best contribution to social stability is the way we speak, our care for the needy, and the clear evidence of life lived on the basis of a true sense of values. Our local church fellowship is the primary arena for all this.

Day 7 Isaiah 4:2–6

Isaiah concludes his sad record of failure by predicting that the Lord's purpose cannot be thwarted and that the intended glory will yet come.

The greatness that is yet to be

4:2. In that day,
    the Branch of Yahweh will become an adornment, and
    a glory;
    and the fruit of the earth eminence and beauty
    for those who escape of Israel.

3. And it shall be, whoever is left in Zion,
    and whoever remains over in Jerusalem,
    'Holy' will be said of him:
    everyone who is listed for life[1] in Jerusalem,

4. whenever the Sovereign will have washed away
    the filth of the daughters of Zion,
    and rinsed off the blood-guiltiness of Jerusalem from
    its midst,
    by the Spirit of Judgment,
    and by the Spirit of Burning.[2]

5. And Yahweh will create
    over the whole establishment of Mount Zion,
    and over its gatherings[3]
    a cloud by day, and smoke,
    and the brilliance of a fire of flame[4] by night.
    For over all the glory will be a bridal canopy.

6. And a booth there shall be
    for a shade by day from heat,
    and for refuge and for a hiding place
    from flood and from rain.[5]

[1] Lit., 'written unto life', i.e., whose name is on the Lord's list.

[2] 'Judgment', i.e., the cleansing meets the standards of divine justice; 'burning' teaches that it meets also the demands of divine holiness.

[3] The word translated 'conventions' in 1:13. A noun from the verb 'to call', occasions on which the worshipping community was called together.

[4] Cloud, smoke, fire are Exodus symbols of the Lord's presence among his people; e.g., Exod. 19:17–19.

5   Contrast Exod. 40:34–35 where access to the holiest was barred. But now, following
     the cleansing, there is free access into shelter, Heb. 10:18–19.

6   Exod. 13:22.

Thought for the day: Isaiah 4:2–6

We do not, of course, worship the Bible but, under the supreme glory of the Lord Jesus Christ, we can never exalt or prize it too highly. Think that, in Isaiah, 700 years before Jesus was born, he was predicted so accurately in his divine and human natures; both a 'branch', tracing his 'descent' from God, and the 'fruit' of earthly growth (v. 2). And this prediction is not a 'one off', but will continue through Isaiah. (Look up and ponder 11:1–2, 10; 32:1–2; 49:1; 53:1–2.) On the title, 'Branch': in Jeremiah 23:5–6 the 'Branch' which springs from David is also 'the Lord our righteousness'; in Zechariah 3:8–9 the 'Branch' is the Lord's servant and when he comes iniquity will be dealt with instantly; Zechariah 6:12–13 makes the branch both king and priest; in Isaiah 11:1, 10 the Messiah is both the 'shoot' (a different word) and 'root' of David.

The Bible was written over many years, by many authors, yet it has the same message of salvation throughout. The Lord, says Isaiah, preserves those he has 'listed for life', and they are his 'holy' ones (v. 3), because he has cleansed them individually (v. 4a) and collectively (v. 4b). His cleansing satisfies both his justice and the fire of his holiness (v. 4c). See also 45:21, 25; Romans 3:24–26; Ephesians 1:3–7; Titus 3:4–7.

And here is a third strand of truth in our marvellous Bibles – the glory that will be (vv. 5–6). The Exodus symbols[6] of cloud and fire (v. 5) picture the Lord's ceaseless presence with his people (Rev. 21:22–23); Isaiah's 'bridal canopy' will one day celebrate the marriage of the Lamb (Rev. 19:7); the Lord's tent, once shut to those who thought to enter (Exod. 40:34–35), will be an available refuge (v. 6; Heb. 10:19–22); and the broken-down Zion which Isaiah saw all round him will become Zion as it was always meant to be (Heb. 12:22–24; Rev. 21:2–5).

Day 8   Isaiah 5:1–7

Backdrop to Isaiah's ministry (3): You are not what you might have been (5:1–30)

In Isaiah's famous song of the Vineyard (vv. 1–7), verse 4 supplies the keynote to this final section of his review of the situation he faced when he became a prophet: Did the Lord leave anything undone of all that was required for his people to be what he wished? 'Was there more to do for my vineyard that I have not done in it?' The failure to produce the 'judgment' and 'righteousness' the Lord sought is spelled out in a series of six 'woes' (vv. 8–12, 18–23; the dire consequences are stated in vv. 13–14, 24–30). Unlike the first two sections of Isaiah's 'backdrop', this third section ends without a note of hope – what else, if the Lord has nothing more to do?

The song of the vineyard: Nothing left undone

5:1.   Please let me sing about my Beloved,
> my Loved One's song about his vineyard:
> My Beloved had a vineyard
> on a very fertile spur.[1]

2.   He dug it over,
> and cleared it of stones,
> and he planted it with Soreq Vine.[2]
> And he built a tower in the centre of it,
> and also he carved out a wine-vat in it.
> And he confidently expected it to produce grapes
> and it produced stink-fruit.[3]

3.   Now then, resident of Jerusalem and man of Judah,
> Please pass judgment between me and my vineyard:

4.   What was there more to do for my vineyard
> that I have not done in it?

1   Lit., 'a horn, son of oil/fatness'. 'Horn' (*qeren*) does not occur elsewhere in Isaiah, nor anywhere in the Bible in the meaning required here. Vineyards were situated on slopes where they would catch the sun. 'Horn' is used in the sense of uprising ground. 'Son of' is a regular idiom for describing the condition something or someone is in. cf., Gen. 12:4, lit., 'son of 75 years'.

2   'Soreq'. See Judg. 16:4, apparently also the name of a noted type of vine.

Why, when I confidently expected it to produce grapes,
did it produce stink-fruit?[3]

5. Now then, please let me inform you what I am going to
do to my vineyard:
remove its hedge – and it will be for grazing;
break down its fence – and it will be a trampling ground.

6. And I will make it into a ruin[4] –
unpruned, uncultivated –
and it will grow high with thorns and briers,
and the clouds I will command
not to rain (any) rain on it.

7. For the vineyard of Yahweh of Hosts is the house of Israel,
and the man of Judah the plantation of his delight.
And he confidently expected judgment[5]
but – behold! – violence![6]
righteousness but – behold! – a shriek!

---

3 Only found here (vv. 2, 4), *be'ushim*, derives from *ba'ash*, 'to stink'.

4 Meaning uncertain.

5 On 'judgment' see 2:4; 26:8. 'Judgment' (*mishpat*) and 'righteousness' (*zedeq*) coming together usually mean, respectively, right practice and right principles: 1:21, 27; 9:7; 16:5; 32:1, 16; 33:5; 56:1; 59:9.

6 The translation 'violence' is uncertain. The words 'judgment … violence' and 'righteousness … shriek' form a pair of rhymes in Hebrew. It does not seem possible to reproduce this in English without some violence to the meaning: 'He looked for the lawful and behold the awful; the rightful and behold the frightful.'

Thought for the day: Isaiah 5:1–7

Put into one word what the Lord looks for in his people, and that word is obedience. When he brought his redeemed people (Exod. 6:6) out of Egypt by the blood of the Lamb (Exod. 12:13), he led them straightaway to Sinai (Exod. 3:12; 19:1), for the Lord's law is not a ladder by which the unsaved seek to climb into his good books, but a pattern for the life of obedience, so that those already in his good books, by redemption, may live according to the will of their Redeemer, and experience his covenant blessings. This link between obedience and blessing reaches back to Eden, where Adam and Eve enjoyed the riches of the Garden by simply obeying one single rule (Gen. 2:16–17). Isaiah taught this same great truth in the Song of the Vineyard. Provided only that his people lived according to his revealed 'judgment' (compare Deut. 5:1), and held to his principles of 'righteousness', the vineyard was safe behind its protecting wall, and no marauding beast could enter and trample it. When the Lord says 'What more...? (v. 4) he is anticipating the 'every blessing' of Ephesians 1:3. Within his vineyard every needful blessing and supply awaits the obedient life – a cardinal truth expressed by Peter when he spoke of 'the Holy Spirit whom God has given to those who obey him' (Acts 5:32). The Word of God is our constantly available domestic and personal 'means of grace'. Publicly and corporately we have Christian fellowship and the Lord's Table; at home, in the family, and in the quiet time we have our Bibles; we can daily learn the pathway of obedience and so live in the protected enclave of sufficiency. When we read a command, let us keep it; a promise, let us believe it and rest on it; an example, let us follow it. 'Lord,' says the hymn, 'be thy Word my rule; in it may I rejoice.'

Day 9   Isaiah 5:8–30

Isaiah now spells out what he meant by the 'stink-fruit' which the vineyard produced. He does so in two series of 'woes': two 'woes' (vv. 8–12) followed by two 'therefores' (vv. 13, 14–17); four 'woes' (vv. 18–23) followed by two 'therefores' (vv. 24, 25–30).

5:8. Woe to those who link house to house,
         keep joining field to field,
         till space is exhausted,
         and you must live by yourselves in the middle of the land![1]

9.   In my hearing!
         Yahweh of Hosts! –
         I swear,
         houses, however many, will come to desolation,
         great ones and good ones without occupant!

10.   For ten yokes of vineyard will produce a single bath,
         and a homer of seed will produce an ephah.[2]

11.   Woe to those getting up early in the morning
         so that they may pursue intoxication,
         delaying on in the evening
         so that wine may inflame them!

12.   And the fact is that harp and lyre, tambourine and flute –
         and wine! –
         are what make a banquet for them![3]
         And the activity of Yahweh they fail to notice,
         and the works of his hands they never see.[4]

13.   Therefore,[5]
         my people go captive through lack of knowledge;
         their 'quality'[6] famine stricken,
         and their masses[7] parched with thirst.

1   Small houses bought up and linked to become a 'stately home', all the surrounding land gradually acquired to become a huge empty estate around the mansion.

2   A 'yoke' was a land measure based in some way on what oxen could plough; a 'bath' was eight gallons, here a negligible yield; a 'homer' was ten ephahs (80 and 8 gallons dry measure respectively) so that the yield was a tenth of the sowing.

3   i.e., All they desire is music and binge-drinking.

4   'Notice' is imperfect tense, signifying a recurring characteristic; 'see' is perfect describing a permanent trait, hence 'fail to' and 'never'.

14. Therefore,
    Sheol[8] keeps its throat enlarged,
    and gapes open its mouth without restriction,
    and down go their splendour and their masses,
    and their noisy crowds,
    and each among them who exults.
15. And humankind is humiliated,
    and each individual demeaned,[9]
    and the eyes of their haughtiness are brought low,
16. and Yahweh of Hosts will be exalted in judgment,
    and the holy God*[10] will reveal his holiness in righteousness.[11]
17. And sheep will feed as if in their pasture,
    and the desolations of the fat ones squatters will eat.[12]
18. Woe to those dragging iniquity with cords of falsehood,
    and, as with cart-ropes, sin;[13]
19. such as say,
    'Let him quickly hasten his work in order that we may see it,
    and let the plan of the Holy One of Israel approach
    and happen
    so that we may know it!'
20. Woe to those calling[14] evil good,
    and good evil,
    making darkness to be light,
    and light to be darkness,
    making bitter to be sweet
    and sweet to be bitter!
21. Woe to the wise in their own eyes,
    and, from their own point of view,[15] discerning!
22. Woe to the heroes at drinking wine,
    men of ability for mixing intoxicants,
23. who acquit the guilty for a bribe,
    and as to the innocence of the innocent parties
    they take it away in each case.
24. Therefore,
    like a tongue of fire eats up stubble,
    and dry grass sinks down into the flame,

5 Here and in vv. 24ff, the first 'therefore' shows how the punishment fits the crime; the second 'therefore' stresses the totality of the coming judgment.

6 Certainly up to the time of the Second World War, 'the quality' was a term used in this sense of the wealthy 'upper' classes.

7 From a verb 'to growl, roar, be boisterous', the noun first means 'noise', 'hub-bub', then a 'crowd' such as makes a noise or murmuration.

8 'Sheol': the name of the 'place' to which all the dead go, and in which they live on.

9 See 2:9.

10 'God' is here: 'el, i.e. God in his transcendent strength. An asterisk after 'God' signifies the use of 'el.

11 On 'judgment... righteousness' see 5:7.

12 Verse 17 might sound like a scene of pastoral serenity, but actually describes the former 'manicured' lawns now turns over to sheep, and produce formerly providing luxury living for 'fat' plutocrats now available to any passing incomer. 'Squatters' here translates ger, an overnight guest, asylum seeker, refugee.

13 See 1:2.

14 Lit., 'saying to'.

15 Lit., 'in front of their faces'.

their root will become just mustiness,
and their blossom go up like dust.
For they have scorned the teaching of Yahweh of Hosts,
and the utterance of the Holy One of Israel they
have spurned.

25. Therefore,
Yahweh's exasperation[16] burned against his people,
And he stretched out his hand against them:
The mountains trembled,[17]
and their corpses were like rubbish in the streets.
In spite of all this his exasperation has not receded,
And still his hand is stretched out.

26. And he will raise a banner for nations afar,
and whistle for them each from the end of the earth.
And, behold, at speed, swift, each comes.

27. None wearies and none stumbles among them;
not one slumbers and not one sleeps;
no belt at any waist is opened,
and no one's shoe-lace is undone.

28. His arrows are sharpened,
and all his bows strung.
His horses' hooves are reckoned hard as flint,
and his wheels like a whirlwind.

29. He has a roar[18] like a lion,
and he roars like full-grown lions,
and he snarls and seizes prey,
and escapes safely and none can deliver.

30. And he[19] will snarl over it that day
like the snarling of the sea.
And should one look to the land –
behold, darkness, adversity.
The light, even, has grown dark with its rain-clouds.

16   Isaiah uses a large vocabulary of 'anger'. Up to a point the individual words can be given distinct meanings: *'aph,* from the verb 'to snort', is personally felt and expressed anger, hence 'exasperation'; *qetsep,* 'impatience'; *chemah* (vb. 'to be hot'), 'rage'; *chemah* (vb. to burn), 'fury'; *ka'as,* 'vexation'; *za'am,* 'indignation'; *'ebrah,* (vb. 'to pass over, go beyond'), 'outburst', outbursting anger'; *za'ap,* 'storm of anger'.

17   A regular pictorial way of expressing earth's reaction to the presence of the Holy One (e.g., 6:4); or the divine anger (e.g., Ps. 18:7).

18   Specifically (*she'agah*) the lion's pouncing roar, intended to paralyse its prey with fright.

19   Isaiah's habit is to use an illustration and then explain it. Here the invincible foe of vv. 26–28 becomes the invincible lion of v. 29, but, says v. 30, this is no ordinary lion: it is Yahweh setting himself in opposition and in consequence all hope is extinguished.

Thought for the day: Isaiah 5:8–30

It's a pretty sobering thing to weigh up Isaiah's 'woes' and to find them so much in evidence all round us – sobering indeed when we consider that when the Lord saw them he considered it was time to put the light out (v. 30). Possessions (v. 8) and pleasures (v. 11), a God-excluding worldview (v. 19), denial of absolute, objective moral values (v. 20), exaltation of self and its opinions (v. 21), a frivolous lifestyle (v. 22), the collapse of the judicial system (v. 23). If you see these things present and on the increase – and can you deny it? – then watch out for the tongue of fire (v. 24) and the light being switched off. Surely – are we not bound to say it? – the remaining time must now be short. But, however short, or, indeed, however prolonged by a God of mercy whose patience gives time for repentance (2 Pet. 3:8–9), Jesus' way contradicts the way of the world, and the urgency of the times summons us to show the difference.

1) Jesus and possessions and pleasures: Matthew 6:19–21, 25–34.
2) Seeing God in everything: creation (Ps. 95:3–5; Isa. 40:12); events (Isa. 40:23–24; 45:7); it is he who determines our experiences (1 Cor. 10:13), sends our blessings (James 1:17–18).
3) The Bible reveals God's 'truth unchanged, unchanging', including his moral values (Ps. 119:8 9). The world feels free to make up the rules as it goes along (v. 20a) and to consider that one man's meat is another man's poison (v. 20b). Not so with the Word of God (Isa. 40:8).
4) The proper administration of justice, exactness in sentencing, making the punishment match the crime, is God's recipe for a sound and purged society (Deut. 19:18–21).

Our holiness is our primary environmental contribution – for was it not when sin entered that the environment corrupted (Gen. 3:17–19)? And our holiness is our primary social testimony (Matt. 5:13–14).

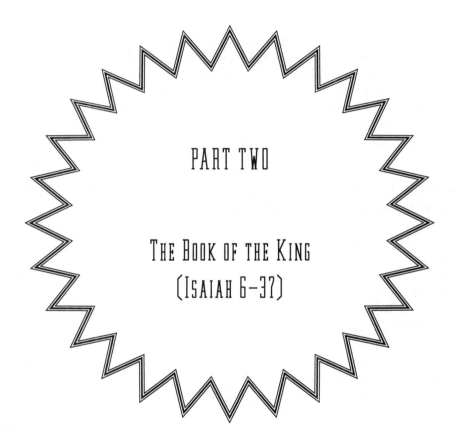

PART TWO

THE BOOK OF THE KING
(ISAIAH 6–37)

Day 10   Isaiah 6:1–13

Having set the scene in chapters 1–5, Isaiah now takes up the task of setting out the fruits of his prophetic ministry. The first major section of his book, starting with his calling to be a prophet, focuses on Jerusalem, the Davidic monarchy and the coming messianic king. The Prologue (ch. 6, Isaiah's personal experience of salvation) is balanced by an Epilogue (ch. 12, the Song of the Saved Community). In between, first Judah (7:1–9:7) and then Israel/Jacob (9:8–11:16)[1] come under review.

The Light that shines beyond the coming darkness: The expected King and the triumph of grace (Isaiah 6–12)

Prologue: A sinful individual cleansed and commissioned

6:1. In the year of the death of King Uzziah,[2]
      I saw the Sovereign,
      sitting on a throne,
      exalted and uplifted,[3]
      and his robes were filling the temple.

2.   Seraphim[4] were standing in attendance on him.
      Each had six wings:
      With two he was covering his face,
      and with two he was covering his feet,
      and with two he was flying.[5]

3.   And one kept calling to another and saying:
      'Holy, Holy, Holy[6] is Yahweh of Hosts;
      that which fills all the earth is his glory.'[7]

4.   And the posts of the threshold trembled
      because of the voice of him who was calling,
      and the house itself began to be filled with smoke.[8]

5.   And I said:

---

1   See 1 Kings 12 for the division of David's kingdom into Judah (in the south) and Israel/Jacob (in the north).

2   Also called Azariah (2 Kings 15: 1–7). 2 Chron. 26 gives a fuller account and also explains (vv. 16–23) how pride led him to trespass into priestly privileges, in consequence of which the Lord struck him with leprosy from which he never recovered. Isaiah alone of the prophets dates parts of his ministry by reference to death (cf. 14:28). Uzziah's death picks up the fading light imagery of 5:30 – when sin ends in death, has the Lord nothing further to say?

3   cf., the same words in 52:13; 57:15. Each case is best understood as referring to the Lord.

'Woe is me!
For I am silenced.[9]
For a man unclean in lips am I,
and among people of unclean lips I am living.
For my eyes have seen the King,
Yahweh of Hosts!'

6. And one from among the Seraphim flew to me,
   and in his hand a glowing ember
   he had taken with tongs from upon the altar.

7. And he touched it to my mouth,[10]
   and said:
   'Behold!
   This touched your lips
   And your iniquity went.
   And as for your sin[11] – the price is paid!'[12]

8. And I heard the Sovereign's voice,
   as he was saying,
   'Whom shall I send?'
   and,
   'Who will go for us?'
   And I said:
   'Behold me![13] Send me!'

9. And he said,
   'Go,
   and say to this people:
   Hear and hear again and do not discern;
   and see and see again and do not know.

10. Make this people's heart unperceptive,[14]
    and their ears insensitive,[15]
    and glue their eyes shut,
    lest they see with their eyes,
    and hear with their ears,
    and discern with their heart,
    and turn back,
    and one heal them.'

11. And I said,

4   Only here meaning 'Burners/
    Burning Ones'– named to
    describe their appearance and
    their burning ministry (v. 6).

5   Singular verbs and pronouns
    ('he... his') describing 'each'.
    Possibly 'they' would be more
    natural in English, or 'they each'.

6   Hebrew uses repetition to express
    both what is superlative and what
    is the total truth about something.
    cf., Gen. 14:10 where 'full of pits'
    is lit., 'pits pits'; in 2 Kings 25:15
    'solid gold' is 'gold gold', i.e., best
    quality gold. The holiness of the
    Lord is the only instance in the
    Old Testament of a superlative
    requiring a threefold repetition.

7   Just as 'grace' means 'God acting
    in his grace' so 'glory' means
    'God in all his glory' – his active
    presence in the full reality of
    deity fills every place and is the
    only thing capable of doing so.

8   Exod. 19:18; cf Gen. 15:17.

9   The verb (damah) means 'to be
    silent', but its use throughout
    the Bible includes meanings like
    'ruin' and the silence of death.
    Here it includes exclusion from
    the heavenly antiphonal 'calling',
    but to be excluded from heaven
    is to be consigned to death.

10 Not 'purification by fire' (which
    is not really an Old Testament
    idea). The coal represents
    the fire in the altar (the fiery
    holiness of God) which has
    spent itself on a substitutionary
    sacrifice and is satisfied.

11 See 1:2

'How long, Sovereign?'
And he said:
'Until whenever cities crash in ruins,
without inhabitant,
and houses, without humankind,
and the land will have crashed in ruins – desolation! –

12. and Yahweh will have removed afar humankind,
and there is wholesale abandonment throughout the land.[16]

13. And should there continue in it a tenth,
it is only consigned for burning yet again.
Like the evergreen and the oak[17]
which, when felled, their stump remains,
so the holy seed is its stump!'

---

12 The verb *kaphar*, whose first meaning is 'to cover' (Gen. 6:14), and then (in the piel formation) 'to pay the covering price', is frequently translated 'to make atonement' but always with a 'price-paying' intention. The derivative noun *kopher* means 'ransom price' (cf. 43:3). The piel mode of the verb in Hebrew is commonly called the 'intensive active' – e.g., the verb 'to break' becomes 'to shatter' – but frequently the modes of the verb develop distinctive significance as here.

13 The conventional answer to a conversational opening (e.g., Gen. 22:7), generally rendered, 'Here am I.'

14 Lit., 'fat', cf., the colloquialism 'a fat-head', slow to comprehend, quick to misunderstand.

15 'Heavy', cf., 59:1, broadly used of slow faculties; cf., Exod. 4:10.

16 More lit., 'and that which has been forsaken is abundant in the midst of the land'.

17 Note the suddenness with which the message of hope intrudes into the gloom! In the case of evergreen and oak, 'while there's life there's hope'. Within the soil of the land there remains the 'stump', and the 'holy seed' will yet prove to be the 'root out of a dry ground' (53:2), the Messiah.

Thought for the day: Isaiah 6:1–13

Hearing the Word of God is a serious business. Remember how Hebrews, calling us to live with ears open to the Word 'today' (Heb. 3:7, 15; 4:7), ends with a sobering reminder of the searching power of the Word and the inescapable God whose Word it is (Heb. 4:11–13). Isaiah would have agreed. We are habit-forming beings; each decision predisposes us one way or another. A right decision makes the next decision in line just that little bit easier and we are on the way to some good, settled habit; a wrong decision makes the next wrong decision that bit easier and we are further down a very slippery slope. Over it all presides the Sovereign God in total justice, holiness and fairness. He alone knows in advance the 'point of no return' – the point where a bad habit (however long or short in preparation) becomes irreversible. Actually he not only knows it, but he decides it. One person experimenting with a drug escapes being 'hooked' for a long time – maybe even for ever; another person is 'hooked' after one experiment. And once 'hooked', whatever they may think about their capacity to break free, such freedom is an illusion, a thing of the past. Isaiah's people had been called to obedience (1:19), to walk in the light (2:5); they had been alerted to the Lord's desire for a harvest of righteousness (5:7) – all to no avail. But the only way to mend such a situation is to send them the Word of God again (6:8), yet if they reject again it will be their last chance. The very word which could save them would blind them (6:10). What a serious thing it is to hear the Word of the Lord! Obedience is the mark of the redeemed. What if the next invitation of grace and summons to righteousness gave us our last chance to clear some cherished sin out of our lives!

Day 11   Isaiah 7:1–17

Darkness and light in Judah and Israel (7:1–11:16)

Isaiah 5:30 was a picture of light disappearing behind gathering storm-clouds. The death of Uzziah (6:1) demonstrated that the wages of sin is death (Rom. 6:23). Yet Isaiah's own experience (6:7) was of the holy God reaching out to save a sinner. Would this gracious salvation operate also on a national level? Looking first at Judah, the kingdom of David (7:1–9:7) and then at Israel (9:8–11:16), the breakaway kingdom of the north (1 Kings 12), Isaiah preaches the same fourfold message to each: each had a moment of decision (7:1–17; 9:8–10:4); in each kingdom refusal of the Lord's Word would bring his judgment (7:18–8:8; 10:5–15). A 'remnant' would be saved (8:9–22; 10:15–34) and, out in the future, lay a stupendous royal hope, the coming messianic King (9:1–7; 11:1–16).

Darkness and light in Judah (7:1–9:7)

The moment of decision

7:1. It happened in the days of Ahaz, son of Jotham, son
    of Uzziah, king of Judah, that Rezin, king of Aram,
    and Pekah,
    son of Remaliah, king of Israel, came up to Jerusalem for war
    against it and were not able for war against it.[1]

2.   And when it was told to the House of David, saying, 'Aram
    is swarming in Ephraim,' his heart and the heart of his people
    were shaken as the trees of a forest are shaken by the wind.

3.   And Yahweh said to Isaiah:
    'Go out, please, to meet Ahaz,
    you and Shear-jashub[2] your son,
    at the end of the aqueduct[3] of the upper pool,
    at the causeway of the Launderer's Field.

[1] Aram (N.E. Palestine) and Israel, ancestral enemies, were driven into each other's arms in a defensive alliance against rising Assyrian power, from 745 BC onwards. They sought to create a western Palestinian 'bloc' by putting pressure on Judah to join their alliance. cf. 2 Kings 15:37 – 16:20; 2 Chron. 28:5–8, 16–20. In Isa. 7, v. 1 summarises the whole story:

4. And say to him:
    "Take care to keep quiet![4]
    Do not be afraid!
    And your heart – do not let it be timid
    because of these two stubs of smouldering sticks,
    the burning exasperation[5] of Rezin and Aram
    and Remaliah's son –
5. because Aram has planned evil against you –
    Ephraim and Remaliah's[6] son – saying,
6. 'Let us go up against Judah.
    Let us split it asunder
    and break it up for ourselves,
    and let us crown a king in it,
    the son of Tabeel!'"[7]
7. This is what the Sovereign Yahweh has said:
    'It will not happen,
    and it will not be!
8   For the head of Aram is Damascus,
    and the head of Damascus is Rezin.
    And within sixty-five years Ephraim will be shattered
    so as not to be a people.
9. And the head of Ephraim is Samaria,
    and the head of Samaria is Remaliah's son.
    If you will not affirm, you will not be affirmed.'[8]
10. And Yahweh spoke again to Ahaz, saying:
11. 'For your assistance,[9] ask a sign,
    direct from[10] Yahweh your God.
    Make the asking[11] deep or make it high above.'
12. And Ahaz said:
    'I will not ask:
    I will not test Yahweh out.'[12]
13. And he said:
    'House of David, please hear!
    Is it too slight a thing to make people weary
    that you should also weary my God?
14. Therefore the Sovereign himself will give you a sign:

a new mustering of alliance forces, their advance and failure. Verse 2 is the moment when news first reached the palace of the impending assault.

2   *Shar-jashub* means 'a Remnant will return' – a message of hope if we stress 'will', of threat if we stress 'remnant'. It all depends on how Ahaz reacts to Yahweh's promise (v. 7).

3   Jerusalem had an impregnable position but was vulnerable because its water-supply ran overground in a conduit from an outside spring. Ahaz was obviously wondering what steps to take against the coming siege.

4   'Take care and keep quiet', not two commands, however, but one as above.

5   See 5:25

6   Is Isaiah deliberately pretending to 'forget' the name of Israel's king – so to speak, cutting him down to size as eminently forgettable – 'Remaliah's lad'!

7   It was a time of dynastic threat – they intended to terminate the 'House of David' by appointing an otherwise unknown 'puppet'.

8   The words translated here 'affirm ... affirmed' are two forms of the same verb (*'amen*). The hiphil means 'to believe, trust' (e.g., Gen. 15:6), and the niphal 'to be made firm, sure, to be affirmed'. Isaiah's somewhat enigmatic statement makes a beautiful and effective rhyme in Hebrew: apart from the way of faith there is no security. Ephraim which chose the way

Behold!
The virgin is pregnant,[13]
and going to give birth to a son.
And she will call his name Immanuel.

15. Curds and honey[14] will he eat
when he knows to spurn the evil and choose the good.[15]

16. For before a child[16] might know to spurn evil and
choose good,
the land of whose two kings you go in dread will be forsaken.

17. Yahweh will bring
on you,
and on your people,
and on your father's house,
days which have not come
since the day Ephraim departed from Judah,
the king of Assyria!'

of collective security (salvation by works) by allying with Aram, and consequently was on its way to elimination; the House of David is called to simple reliance on the promises of v. 7 – to be saved by faith or not saved at all.

9 'For you', a 'dative of advantage', i.e., 'for your good/to help you',

10 The double preposition 'from-with'.

11 This form of the noun 'asking/request' is not found elsewhere, which has suggested to some to make a minute change to read, 'Go deep into Sheol or go high above'. As we might say, Yahweh is ready to 'move heaven and earth' to persuade Ahaz to take the way of faith.

12 i.e., demand that Yahweh prove himself able and willing before trusting him to keep his word. Put him on probation.

13 Isaiah uses a timeless present tense in order to establish a link between the faithlessness of Ahaz and the birth of Immanuel to a lost inheritance.

14 The food of poverty, see v. 22.

15 An indefinite indication of age. Evil and good can indicate the age of moral awareness, but equally they are used of what is nasty and what is nice, the age when a baby begins on solids.

16 'The child', referring to Immanuel; or, treating the definite article as generic, such a child – 'a child'.

Thought for the day: Isaiah 7:1–17

'Promises, promises!!' we say, mockingly, when we know or suspect that the promise is not going to be kept! But when the Lord makes promises he means them, he means to keep them, and he means his people to trust them as they plan the future. He looks to us to obey his commands; he looks to us to trust his promises. Indeed it is as we trust his promises that we find ourselves able to obey his commands: it's called 'the obedience of faith'. Abraham is the father of those who believe (Rom. 4:11). Genesis 15:3–6 tells how he 'simply' believed what God promised: Romans 4:18–22 reveals how totally his faith rested on the word of promise, taking account of everything that stood against it; Hebrews 11:17–19 describes how he held to the promise even when it was challenged by death itself. And he was proved right. Since it is through faith in the Lord's promises that we are saved (Acts 16:31), then surely, if faith is mighty to solve the great and eternal problem of our sinfulness, alienation, and helplessness, is it not the way to tackle every problem – to look up to our almighty, ever-loving God and say 'I trust you'? Poor old Ahaz came a fearful cropper on this very point. It was natural to fear the stronger northern powers; it was logical to want to do something about Jerusalem's water supply. But it was not the reaction of a believer to whom the Lord had said 'it won't happen'. Faith, indeed, would teach a different logic: your enemy sounds impressive (Aram ... Damascus) but what does it amount to? Only Rezin and Remaliah's boy! Apply the same reasoning to Jerusalem and we arrive at the 'House of David', the repository of all God's promises, and behind that the King of all kings who has promised his city's security! Faith is not a 'leap in the dark'; it is a leap into the light, decision on the basis of evidence.

Day 12   Isaiah 7:18–8:8

Coming judgment

The second part of Isaiah's review of Judah's future. To depart from the way of faith (7:1–17) is to enter the arena of judgment. This judgment is on its way at the hand of Assyria.[1]

The coming invasion

7:18. And it will be,

> in that day,
> Yahweh will whistle
> for the fly which is within the border of the streams of Egypt,
> and for the bee which is in the land of Assyria,

19. and they will come and swarm, all of them,

> in the remotest[2] ravines and in the crevices of the cliffs,
> and on all the thorn-bushes,
> and in all the watercourses.

The helpless victim

20. In that day,

> the Sovereign will shave with a razor
> (one hired over the river –
> the king of Assyria)
> the head and the hair of the feet;[3]
> the beard too he will sweep away!

The unvaried diet of the poor survivors

21. And it will be,

> in that day,
> a man will keep alive
> a calf of the herd and two sheep;

22. and it will be,

> through the abundance of milk-production,

---

[1] The irony is that, refusing to trust the Lord, Ahaz acted with political astuteness by appealing over the heads of Aram and Ephraim to Assyria for help (2 Kings 16). In doing so he took a veritable tiger by the tail. The Assyrian war machine rolled over Judah, and never again (until Luke 1:32) did a sovereign king sit on David's throne.

[2] 'Remotest' is uncertain; 'sheerest' is also suggested. But the picture is clear: the whole land 'infested' with invaders.

[3] A euphemism for intimate body-hair

he will eat curds,
for curds and honey each will eat,
everyone who is left within the land.

A once rich land gone to rack and ruin

23. And it will be,
in that day,
everywhere there used to be a thousand vines,
worth a thousand silver coins,
will be consigned to thorns and briers.
24. With arrows and with bow one will go there,
for all the land will be but thorns and briers.
25. And all the mountains
which used to be so carefully hoed –
you would not go there
for fear of thorns and briers.
And it will be a place for turning cattle loose
and a trampling-ground for sheep.

Imminent disaster: a sign to watch for [4]

8:1. And Yahweh said to me:
'Take large placard[5]
and write on it in ordinary lettering:[6]
"TO MAHER-SHALAL-HASH-BAZ".'[7]
2. And I will swear in for myself as reliable witnesses,
Uriah the priest and Zechariah son of Jeberekiah.'[8]
3. And I approached the prophetess[9]
and she conceived, and bore a son.
And Yahweh said to me,
'Call his name
Maher-shalal-hash-baz.
4. For before the child shall know
to call "my father" and "my mother",
he[10] will carry off
the wealth of Damascus,
and the spoil[11] of Samaria,
in the presence of the king of Assyria.'

4   In case the sign of Immanuel (7:14) should be misunderstood, Isaiah offers the conception and birth of his second son as an indication of the imminence of Assyrian invasion.

5   The word translated as 'mirrors' in 3:23. Neither rendering is absolutely certain. The parent verb means 'to lay bare' – here the idea of a large bare surface – space on a hoarding, some large advertising unit – suits the context.

6   Lit., 'with the pen of a man' – here *'enosh*, a 'mere' human.

7   A dedication. The name means '(one who is) hurrying to the spoil, hastening to the booty'. All designed to start onlookers asking questions.

Explanation: Why the coming calamity?

5. And Yahweh spoke yet once more to me, saying:
   'Because this people have spurned
   the waters of the Shiloah[12] which flow gently,
   and are delighted with Rezin and Remaliah's son,
7. therefore –
   behold! –
   the Sovereign is going to bring up against them
   the waters of the River,
   mighty and abundant,
   the king of Assyria and all his glory.
   And it will rise up over all its channels,
   And go over all its banks.
8. And it will come freshly on[13] into Judah –
   sure to flood and spread –
   to the neck itself it will reach.
   And it will be,
   the outspreading of its wings[14]
   entirely fills the breadth of your land,
   Immanuel.'

---

8 2 Kings 16:10ff. A man named Zechariah is mentioned in 2 Kings 18:2.

9 Was Isaiah's wife a prophetess, or was she given a 'courtesy title' as his wife, or was she called 'prophetess' because, bearing Maher-shalal-hash-baz, she was, in literal truth, the bearer of the Word of the Lord?

10 This is called, in Hebrew usage, a 'third singular indefinite'. In English we express the same indefiniteness by 'they'.

11 Heb., *shalal.*

12 The stream from the Gihon Spring which provided water for Jerusalem – a nothing compared with the great Euphrates!

13 'Come freshly on' – as flood waters find a new place to break into. Ahaz had sought Assyrian help against his northern neighbours, Aram and Ephraim, but in fact he brought into his land a flood that could not be stemmed. Imperialists do not come to help; they take over! Judah will be over-run. Immanuel's inheritance will pass into Gentile ownership. Yet the flood reaches only the neck. Judah remains 'alive', even though totally swamped.

14 Is 'wings' a metaphor for the swirling and extending edges of the flood, or is Isaiah typically mixing his metaphors, allowing the picture of the flood to merge with that of an enormous bird of prey lighting on Judah?

Thought for the day: Isaiah 7:18–8:8

Decisions are made by those at the top of life's heap; consequences fall on those at the bottom. King Ahaz and his cabinet called in Assyrian aid, and as a result the land was reduced to subsistence farming and the monotonous struggle for survival. Two centuries earlier (1 Kings 12) Jeroboam the son of Nebat decided to rebel against the house of David, and the ten northern tribes (Israel/Ephraim) followed him. They spurned, says Isaiah, the gently flowing Shiloah (Jerusalem's water-supply) and in the long run, happy with 'Remaliah's lad', brought on themselves the flood waters of Euphrates. It's all very well (in fact it is marvellously well!) that Yahweh is totally in command, but the felt reality is like submitting to an enforced razor, like seeing your home under six feet of water. And – thank you, Ahaz! – the flood swamps Judah too, leaving the impoverished poor just about nose above water, fighting for survival. And this is no 'might-have-been'; it is all only too factual. Isaiah foresaw it, and so it happened – exactly so! Therefore we say – and, oh may we mean it and tremble! – the judgments of God are both inevitable and inescapable. Nations cannot turn their backs on him, or choose the way of self-pleasing or self-salvation – or, as they may call it, collective security – with impunity. God is not mocked. Or again, because the Sovereign remains fully in charge of the historical process, we who believe may indeed rest securely in his care: 'God *is* still on the Throne'. But in its way the most obvious lesson to learn from Isaiah's analysis of the political process is how concerned we should be to make our elections of our leaders a much more prolonged and committed matter of prayer than we usually do, and to be constant and earnest in our prayers for those who are in positions of leadership and influence. It is an apostolic injunction to pray 'for kings and all who are in authority' that we may lead an undisturbed and quiet life in all godliness and seriousness (1 Tim. 2:1–2). It is an easy injunction to overlook, but one we neglect at our peril.

Day 13   Isaiah 8:9–22

The remnant

Even the awful pictures of 7:20–22 and 8:8 are under the Lord's control. He will never fail to preserve a remnant of his people. We met this principle in 1:9, in the promise of 1:26, in the vision of 2:2–4 and 4:2–6. In these present verses Isaiah gives the truth of the remnant fuller expression. Who are they? What marks them out? In what way are they 'in the world' but not 'of the world'?

Immanuel's people

8:9.   Sound the battle-cry,[1] O peoples,
      and be shattered!
      And listen, all distant parts of the earth.
      Arm yourselves – and be shattered!
      Arm yourselves – and be shattered!

10.   Take careful counsel,[2]
      and it will be frustrated;
      speak the word,
      and it will not happen,
      for God is with us.[3]

The sheltered people

11.   For this is what Yahweh has said to me,
      as with strength of hand,[4]
      and he admonished[5] me
      not to walk in the way of this people,
      saying:

12.   'You[6] are not to say "Conspiracy",
      respecting everything of which this people says "Conspiracy".
      And what they fear you are not to fear,
      nor are you to react in terror.

1   No certainty about this rendering. Possibly, 'Do your worst!'

2   Lit., 'Counsel a counsel'. Just as to 'shout a shout' means to shout loudly, 'counsel a counsel' means to 'take careful counsel', plan your strategy well.

3   i.e., 'for Immanuel'. The presence and cherishing of the messianic hope, and the indwelling of the expected Messiah, is the preservative of the remnant.

4   The 'hand' represents personal action. In what was now revealed to him, Isaiah sensed a particular pressure or urgency from Yahweh: 'with compelling power'. 'As' could be developed into 'with what seemed...'

13. Yahweh of Hosts
    is the One you must respect as holy:
    He is what you are to fear;
    he is what causes you terror.[7]

14. And he will prove to be a holy sanctuary[8] –
    and a trip-stone and a stumbling-rock
    to both houses of Israel:
    a trap and a snare for those living in Jerusalem.

15. And many will stumble over them,
    and fall, and be broken up, and snared, and captured.'

The people of the Word of God

16. 'Bind up the testimony,
    and seal the teaching
    among my instructed ones.'[9]

17. And I will wait expectantly for Yahweh,
    who is hiding his face from the house of Jacob,
    and I will wait confidently for him.[10]

18. Behold!
    I and the children whom Yahweh has given me
    are intended to be signs and portents[11] in Israel,
    straight from Yahweh of Hosts,
    who resides in Mount Zion.

19. And when they say to you,
    'Seek the mediums and the "knowing ones"[12]
    who squawk and sigh[13]' –
    is it not their God a people should seek?[14]
    On behalf of the living to the dead![15]

20. To the teaching and to the testimony!
    If they do not speak according to this word,
    The fact is none need expect dawn![16] –

21. he[17] will go through it[18]
    distressed and hungry.
    And it will be,
    when he is hungry
    he will lose patience

5   The very strong verb *yasar,* 'he put me under discipline'.

6   In vv. 12, 13 the second person pronouns are plural, referring to the remnant. It was apparently a 'panicky' time, with suspicious terrors on the increase. The remnant are called to show that they do not share the anxieties of unbelievers.

7   Lit., 'He your fear; and he your terror!'

8   i.e., a place where God dwells in holiness. The picture is of the Lord surrounding his people with his holiness and in that way creating an enclave of security for them in uncertain times.

9   'Bind' or 'wrap up' so as to make it secure from being tampered with; 'seal', give it the mark of authenticity as divine revelation. 'Instructed ones', cf., 50:4; 54:13. 'My disciples' in its true sense of those under instruction.

10 'Wait expectantly' (*chakah,* 30:18; 64:4), and 'wait confidently' (*qawah,* 5:2, 4, 7; 25:9; 26:8; 33:2; 40:31; 49:23; 51:5; 59:9, 11; 60:9; 64:3). The verbs are really synonymous (as is *yachal,* 42:4, translated 'wait in hope' and *sabar,* translated 'await'). All share the ideas of confidence, expectancy and (sure) hope.

11 A sign points; a portent startles into paying attention.

12 From *yad'a* to know, used of occultists who claimed to be 'in the know', possessors of secret knowledge, as in 19:3.

and use his king and his God as a curse.
And he will turn his face upward,

22. and gaze earthward,
and, behold,
affliction and darkness,
a dark fog of pressure,
and into black darkness he is being banished!

---

13   *hagah*, always needing to be translated according to context. Broadly of a 'murmur', but a sad groan (16:7; 38:14); a lion's growl (31:4); a meditation (33:18); of something said 'under the breath' (59:3); the cooing of a dove (59:11).

14   'Seek', not in the sense of searching for something lost, but in the special sense of coming assiduously to where something is known to be; e.g., Deut. 12:5.

15   Highly compressed, an indignant expostulation, meaning, 'On behalf of the living (should people go seeking) to the dead?'

16   A slightly speculative rendering. Isaiah's indignation has made him allusive rather than precise. 'Dawn', the hope that comes with a new day (Ps. 30:5).

17   Isaiah individualises the coming experience of calamity.

18   The trek through the land on the way to captivity? 'It' is feminine, as is the Hebrew word for 'land' *('erets)*.

Thought for the day: Isaiah 8:9–22

The word translated 'a holy sanctuary' in verse 14 (*miqdash*) is found in Exodus 25:8, where the Lord commands, 'Let them make me a sanctuary that I may dwell among them.' This was Israel's privilege and pride: they were allowed to provide a Tent (later a House, 1 Kings 8:12–13) where the Lord himself would come to live. But Isaiah turned the idea on its head: in the calamitous times ahead the Lord would be the 'sanctuary/holy shrine' and his true believers could take shelter with him. As Psalm 61:2–4 develops the thought, he the Rock, he the shelter/refuge, the strong tower, the tabernacle and the sheltering wings. This is the secret of the unworrying people in a worried world: 'fear him, ye saints, and you will then have nothing else to fear' (see v. 13); they are different from the 'world' which sees a new scare round every corner (v. 12). They are 'safe in the shelter of the Lord, beneath his hand and power' (T. Dudley-Smith), and they are nourished by a hope that cannot fail (v. 17). But there is more: sheltering in the Lord, they possess the 'testimony', the 'teaching' (vv. 16, 20), the 'word' (v. 20). This is their light in the darkness. The Lord himself has spoken the 'Word'; in this way he has 'testified' about himself and his truth, and given his true people 'teaching' to hold, understand, and live by. The call to be different, to be 'separate', used to be (so it seems) a greater concern for believers than it is today – and sometimes the way 'separation' was meant to show was pretty silly. Isaiah's model remnant shows a better way. Believers display unanxious peace, nourish their minds and guide their lives by the Word the Lord has spoken, face the uncertain and cloudy future with calm and certain expectation; they flee constantly to the shrine, the Lord himself who waits to welcome them, and centre their lives reverently on his awesome presence.

Day 14   Isaiah 9:1–7

The glorious hope

The fourth element in Isaiah's address to Judah (see Day 11, p. 48, introducing Isaiah 7:1–11:16) defined the believing remnant as the people with hope (8:17). Here is their hope in detail. It reverses the darkness (vv. 1–2), ends oppression, suffering and enmity (vv. 3–5), and centres on a Wonder Child who is God and who ushers in the limitless and unending kingdom of David (vv. 6–7).

9:1. But there will be no darkness
    for the one who experienced distress.[1]
    Round about that former time
    he brought dishonour to the land of Zebulun and the
    land of Naphtali,
    and later
    he determined to bring it honour –
    the road by the sea,
    around the Jordan,
    Galilee of the nations.[2]

2. The people who were walking in the darkness
    have seen a great light;
    those living in a land as dark as death[3] –
    light has flashed out on them!

3. You have multiplied the nation;
    to it you have brought great rejoicing.
    They rejoice before you like rejoicing in harvest,
    just as they exult when they share out spoil.

4. Because the yoke which burdened them,
    and the stick across their back,
    the cudgel of the taskmaster over them[4]

[1] One of Isaiah's exceedingly compressed statements: 'For no darkness to her to whom distress.' Contextually the above rendering is an acceptable elaboration. 'The one who' is feminine, anticipating the feminine 'land' in the following lines.

[2] i.e., the whole area between the Sea of Galilee and the Mediterranean, Northern Transjordan and Galilee north of the Sea of Galilee. The first areas to fall to the Assyrians (734 BC) will be the first to see the messianic light (Matt. 4:12–23).

[3] Only here in Isaiah (see, e.g., Ps. 23:4; 107:10; Amos 5:8), *tsalmaweth* is a compound noun comprising 'shadow' and 'death'.

[4] Lit., 'the yoke of his burden, the stick of his back, the staff of his

you have shattered,
like the day of Midian.[5]

5.   Because every boot that tramps[6] in the ruck,
and clothing rolled in blood,
will be consigned to burning,
fodder for the fire.

6.   Because a child has been born to us,
a son has been given to us,
and the princely rule has been set on his shoulder,
and one has called[7] his name
Wonderful Counsellor,[8]
Warrior God,[9]
Father in perpetuity,
Prince of peace.

7.   To the increase of princely rule and to peace
there is no limit,
on David's throne and over his kingdom,
making it secure and sustaining it,
in judgment and righteousness[10]
from now on and for ever.
The zeal[11] of Yahweh of Hosts will do this.

---

taskmaster'. But the singular 'his' refers back to 'nation' (v. 3), hence 'them' is allowable.

5   i.e., 'as you did that day to Midian', Judges 6–8.

6   'Boot' and 'tramps' are the noun and participle of the same verb (*sha'an*). English would allow 'every foot that foots it', but is not as amenable to assonance and repetition as Hebrew, where the literary effect is pleasing as well as striking.

7   Third singular indefinite, equivalent to 'his name has been called'.

8   Lit., 'a wonder, a counsellor'. The emotive and time-honoured 'Wonderful Counsellor' is possible, but less probable in the light of the fact that each of the following three names consists of two components, suggesting here 'a wonder of a counsellor'. This issue is beyond proof either way.

9   Applied to Yahweh in 10:21.

10   See notes on 2:4; 5:7.

11   *qine'ah*, here in its 'good' meaning of 'keenness, zealousness, commitment' (37:32; 42:13; 59:17; 63:15). Its 'bad' sense is 'animosity, ill-feeling, jealousy' (11:13; 26:11; and the verb, 11:13). The basic idea is strong animated feeling. Hence, 'passionate commitment'.

Thought for the day 14: Isaiah 9:1–7

Of course, the single event of birth of the child did not produce the marvels Isaiah reported. The wonder-child's life and work still lay ahead. But so great was the baby, so mighty in prospect, so completely sufficient for every need, that what he would yet accomplish could be spoken of as already achieved there and then by his birth. Did you notice, as you read, the three 'because' verses (vv. 4–6) – a rising tide of explanation? How has degradation become honour (v. 1), darkness been replaced by light (v. 2) and increase and a joy beyond earthly joy been experienced? Isaiah answers, 'because... because... because'; because the Lord has acted as of old to deliver (v. 4) ... because the enemy has been utterly defeated (v. 5)... because the child has been born (v. 6)! He is, in himself, all that his people need: the 'wonderful counsellor', supernatural in wisdom; God himself come in victorious power, ever fatherly in care; the Prince-administrator of total wellbeing which the Bible calls peace. This is Jesus, who 'from God' is 'for us wisdom... righteousness, sanctification and redemption' (1 Cor. 1:30), whereby we can join Charles Wesley in singing, 'Thou, O Christ, art all I want' (meaning, of course, 'all I need'). Without him we are still under the tyrant's rod, trampled on by our triumphalist foe, held in the kingdom of darkness, under the bondage of sin and death; united with him by the 'love that drew salvation's plan' we have been transferred from the kingdom of darkness to the kingdom of God's dear Son where, even now, we have already been qualified for the inheritance of the saints in light (Col. 1:12–13), and we have the strength to do all things through Christ who empowers us (Phil. 4:13). If David, in his day, was confident that the key to life was 'to behold the beauty of the Lord' (Ps. 27:4), is not our unspeakable privilege to 'turn our eyes on Jesus, look full in his wonderful face'?

Day 15 Isaiah 9:8–10:4

Darkness and light in Israel (9:8–11:16)

Isaiah now turns from Judah to sketch out a parallel experience for the northern kingdom of Israel (see Day 11, p. 44 above, introducing 7:1–11:16). There are here the same four topics: the moment of decision – acceptance or refusal of the Word of the Lord (9:8–10:4); the coming judgment on those who reject the Word (10:5–15); yet, in the judgment, the preservation of a remnant (10:16–34); and, for that remnant, a future, glorious, royal hope (11:1–16).

The moment of decision (9:8–10:4)

National disaster

9:8. A word the Sovereign sent to Jacob,
    and it kept falling on Israel.[1]

9. And the people – all of them – will know,
    Ephraim and the inhabitant of Samaria,
    in spite of arrogance,
    and in spite of greatness of heart[2]
    in saying:

10. 'It is bricks that have fallen;
    and in cut stone we will build!
    It is sycamores that have been cut down;
    and with cedars we will replace them!'

11. And Yahweh has set Rezin's adversaries on high over them,
    and he keeps spurring on[3] their enemies –

12. Aram on the east and the Philistines on the west[4] –
    and they have eaten up Israel by the mouthful.[5]
    In spite of all this

1   Jacob, Israel and Ephraim are all used to designate the northern kingdom.

2   Equivalent here to 'bigheadedness'.

3   'Rezin's adversaries' are the Assyrians, who were expanding their empire westward from 745 BC on, threatening the west Palestinian powers.

his exasperation[6] has not turned back,
and still his hand is stretched out.

Political collapse

13. And the people –
    they have not turned back to him who struck them:
    Yahweh of Hosts they have not sought.[7]
14. And Yahweh has determined to cut off from Israel
    head and tail,
    frond and rush,[8]
    in a single day!
15. The elder and the prominent person[9] – he is the head;
    and the prophet teaching falsehood – he is the tail:
16. those who direct this people have become misleaders,
    and those who are directed are swallowed up.[10]
17. Therefore
    over their prime young manhood[11]
    the Sovereign will not rejoice,
    and for their orphans and their widows
    he will show no compassion,[12]
    for each and every one
    is degenerate[13] and an evil-doer,
    and every mouth is speaking without moral principle.[14]
    In spite of all this
    his exasperation has not turned back,
    and still his hand is stretched out.

Social anarchy

18. For wickedness burns like fire:
    thorns and briers it eats up;
    when it has been kindled in the thickets of the forest,
    they coil themselves up in an uprising of smoke.
19. By the outbursting anger[15] of Yahweh of Hosts
    the land is burnt black,
    and the people have become but food for the fire.
    No one spares his brother:

4   Their present 'best friend' in the face of Assyria – Aram – had always previously been a perpetual thorn in their side! Philistia tended to be a nuisance to everybody; cf., Amos's (1:6ff) reference to their slave-trading.

5   'with (their) whole mouth'.

6   See 5:25.

7   See 8:19.

8   'Head and tail' means 'leader and follower; the high-reaching frond and the low-growing rush; the most and least considered in the people.'

9   'uplifted of face'.

10   For the metaphorical use of this verb, see 3:12. Here it stresses the total dominance of the ruling class over the ruled, and how they use them simply for their own benefit and enrichment.

11   *Bachurim*, an intensive, passive formation from *bachar*, to choose. Therefore, strictly the 'choicest' young men, but used as a general word for young men in their prime (23:4; 31:8; 40:30; 62:5).

12   A big word in the 'pity'-vocabulary of Hebrew. *Racham* provides the noun *rechem* a 'womb' and this gives the clue to the meaning: surging, passionate, maternal concern (cf., 1 Kings 3:26). Throughout we will use 'compassion' and its cognates for this word group.

13   *chaneph*, basically means to 'decline from a standard', e.g., from true religion into irreligion or profanity; from rectitude

20. he carves away on the right, and remains hungry;
    and eats on the left – and they remain unsatisfied.[16]
    Each eats even the flesh of his own arm!
21. Manasseh Ephraim and Ephraim Manasseh[17] –
    they are united only against Judah.
    In spite of all this,
    his exasperation has not turned back,
    and still his hand is stretched out.

Blatant misrule

10:1. Woe to those who are enacting wrongful statutes[18]
    and to the writers who write trouble,[19]
2. designed to turn the poor from (their) rights,
    and to despoil of justice the downtrodden[20] of my people;
    aiming that widows should be their spoil,
    and to loot orphans.
3. And what will you[21] do on the day of reckoning,
    and in the crash which is coming from afar?
    To whom will you flee for help?
    And where will you leave your wealth?[22]
4. Nothing for it but that each crouch down as a prisoner,
    and that down they fall slain.[23]
    In spite of all this
    his exasperation has not turned back,
    and still his hand is stretched out.

14 into some distortion of what is right. Adjective, *chaneph*, debased, profane, degenerate.
    'Without moral principle' is the word, *nebalah*, cf. 32:6, sometimes translated 'folly' but used of failure to recognise moral/spiritual truth/ obligation, e.g., Gen. 34:7; 1 Sam. 25:25 and context.

15 From *'abar*, to cross over, go beyond, *'ebrah* is one of Hebrew's 'anger' words; anger which overflows its banks, bursts out (10:6; 13:9; 13;14:6; 16:6). See 5:25.

16 What is now called 'the rat race' – each using the other simply as a means to self-advantage. Isaiah prefers the picture of carving meat.

17 Manasseh and Ephraim were the main component tribes of the northern kingdom, used here to illustrate the self-seeking 'eating' of brother against brother.

18 Verb (*chaqaq*) and noun (*choq*) match, 'decree decrees'. The basic meaning is to 'engrave' or 'carve out' (22:16; 49:16), to make a permanent written record (30:8). The noun therefore points to the permanency of law, its unchangeable enactments (33:22). On 'wrongful' see 1:13.

19 The legislative branch of government who actually 'frame' the laws, here using their skills to guarantee that their laws can be used for corrupt purposes or are foreseeably hurtful in their application.

20 See 3:14.

21 'You' plural, addressing the corrupt legislators of v. 1.

22 Lit., 'your glory' – the things you gloried in and which gave you status.

23 The details of this translation are uncertain and many alternative suggestions have been made. The substantial meaning, however, is clear.

Thought for the day: Isaiah 9:8–10:4

At the Exodus the Lord's hand was stretched out to defeat his foes and save his people (Exod. 15:1–13), but in Jeremiah 21:5, for example, the outstretched hand is the instrument of the Lord's hostility to his people who have refused his Word. How easy it is for us to rejoice in the former (rightly so!) and to ignore the latter, as if the Lord had changed and our sinfulness, and our neglect of his Word, no longer outraged him. National, political, social and governmental disasters and misdemeanours can all be traced to this one source: the Word of God has been sidelined. Isaiah saw it in his day and, with our eyes opened by him, we see it in ours. The beginning of the remedy lies in our individual hands: our greatest contribution to the good of our nation, to political stability and wholesomeness, to social standards and decency and to proper and just government, is our individual devotion and obedience to God's Word. Recovery starts with me. Isn't this what the Lord Jesus taught in the Sermon on the Mount? When he has set out the basic principles of kingdom-life (in the blessedness/happiness sayings, Matt. 5:2–10, which we put away in the deep-freeze by calling them 'Beatitudes') he immediately transposes the 'they' of general principle into the 'you' of personal discipleship (Matt. 5:11). This blessedness is for you when this is your life-style. But more: when this is your life-style you become the salt of purification and the darkness-dispelling light the world so desperately needs. Not by what we say but by what we are when his Word fashions our lives. The alternative way of life, when we set aside his Word, invites the Lord's displeasure and leaves the world around without any bar to its inevitable corruption, or light to dispel its native darkness.

Day 16 Isaiah 10:5–34

See introductory note on Isaiah 9:8, Day 15, (p. 59). In the present section Isaiah covers the second and third topics of the four: coming judgment (vv. 5–15) and the preservation of the remnant.

Coming judgment (10:5–15)

Assyria is the Lord's instrument of judgment on northern Israel. It is in this way that the (rejected) 'word' of 9:8 will prove its reality as the Word of the Lord. Verses 5 and 15 illustrate the Lord's absolute power to use Assyria as he wills. Verses 6–11 contrast the Lord's motive (just judgment) with Assyria's (world dominion). Verses 12–14 offer contrasting assessments of what is happening: Yahweh sees Assyria's pride which he will punish; Assyria acts according to its assumption of the right to rule the world.

10:5. Ho, Assyria!
  Rod of my exasperation,[1]
  and in whose hand my indignation[2] is the staff!
6.   Against a degenerate[3] nation I dispatch him,
    and concerning a people deserving my outbursting anger[4]
  I command him:
    to take spoil and to seize booty,[5]
    and to make them something for trampling on,
    like mud in the streets!
7.   And, as for him,[6]
    not so does he plan,
    and, in his heart,
    not so does he reckon.

[1] See 5:25.

[2] Or 'animosity'. Another word in Hebrew's 'anger' vocabulary, *za'am*. The verb, *za'am,* 'to be indignant', occurs in 66:14; the noun, in 10:25; 13:5; 26:20; 30:27.

[3] See 9:17.

[4] 9:19. See 5:25.

[5] See 8:1–4. Here nouns and verbs match: to 'spoil spoil and to booty booty' which, in Hebrew, creates a most dramatic effect.

For, to destroy is in his heart,
and to cut down nations not a few.

8. For he keeps saying:
   'Are not my princes[7] altogether kings?

9. Is not Calno just like Carchemish?
   Or is not Hamath just like Arpad?[8]
   Or is not Samaria just like Damascus?

10. Just as my hand has found the kingdoms of the no-gods[9] –
    and their images were more than Jerusalem
    and more than Samaria –

11. is it not the case that,
    just as I did to Samaria and its no-gods,
    so I will do to Jerusalem,[10]
    and to its statues?'

12. And it will be,
    when the Sovereign has finished off all his work
    in Mount Zion and in Jerusalem,
    I will make a reckoning
    with the fruit of the greatness of heart[11] of the king
    of Assyria,
    and with the beauty[12] of the haughtiness of his eyes.

13. For he has said:
    'By the strength[13] of my hand I have acted,
    and by my wisdom,
    for I am discerning:
    I remove the borders of the peoples
    and their treasuries I plunder,
    and, potentate that I am,[14]
    I bring down those who sit enthroned.[15]

14. And, as in a nest,
    my hand has found the resources of the peoples,
    and, as one gathers abandoned eggs,
    I have been gathering even the whole earth,
    and there has not been anyone flapping a wing
    or opening a mouth and squawking!'

15. Does the axe act vaingloriously[16] against the one who
    chops with it?

6 Assyria personified, or the king of Assyria.

7 See 1:23. The king of Assyria would have no one under the rank of king as his underlings and executives!

8 In each of these pairs the first is further south than the second. Thus Assyria records his invincible advance towards Samaria and Jerusalem.

9 See 2:8

10 This Assyrian attack took place in 701 BC. See Isa. 36–37.

11 See 9:9.

12 Here in the 'bad' sense of 'vaingloriousness'. Compare its 'good' sense in 4:2.

13 In Hebrew's 'power' vocabulary, koach, is used of inherent power, ability (37:3; 40:9, 26, 29, 31; 41:1; 44:12; 49:4; 50:2; 63:1).

14 See on 1:24 (occurring again in 49:26; 60:16), the slightly different form here does not affect the meaning (occurring again in 34:7; 46:12).

15 The verb 'to sit/dwell' often has the developed meaning 'to sit enthroned', e.g., 16:5.

16 'Beautify itself', see v. 12.

Or does the saw make itself superior to the one who uses it! –
as if a stick should wield the one who raises it!
As if a staff should raise up what is not wood!

The remnant (10:16–34)
See Day 15, (p. 59), on 9:8ff. In faithfulness the Lord always
preserves the believing 'remnant' among the professing people.

Divine judgment leaves Assyria only a shadow of its former self
16. Therefore,
        the Sovereign, Yahweh of Hosts,
        will dispatch against his[17] stout fellows[18] a wasting,
        and under his glory a conflagration will be kindled,[19]
        like a kindling of fire.
17. And the Light of Israel will become a fire,
        and its Holy One a flame,
        and it will burn,
        and will eat his thorns and briers
        in one day.[20]
18. And the glory of his forest and of his garden-land[21] –
        soul and flesh alike –
        he will terminate.
        And it will be like when an invalid wastes away.[22]
19. And the remnant of the trees of his forest will be a
        mere number
        – a boy could write them down.

Judgment on Israel leaves a remnant
20. And it will be,
        in that day,
        never again will the remnant of Israel –
        those who escape of the house of Jacob –
        be inclined to lean on the one who smote them:[23]
        he will lean on Yahweh, the Holy One of Israel,
        in truth.[24]
21. The remnant will return,[25]

17 Assyria's.

18 Lit., 'fat ones', the invincible
    armies of Assyria.

19 'A kindling will be kindled' =
    'there will be a great kindling'.

20 Fulfilled, Isa. 37:36–38.

21 The idiom of totality expressed
    by contrast: uncultivated,
    natural 'forest' contrasted
    with the planned, tilled
    'garden', i.e., the whole land.

22 It is historically a fact that,
    following Isaiah 37:36–38,
    Assyria entered a period of
    slow decline until it was finally
    extinguished by the rising
    power of Babylon. Nineveh,
    Assyria's capital' fell in 612 BC.

23 Israel (the northern kingdom), in
    the panicky moment when Assyria
    threatened, turned for support to
    Aram, which had been its foe and
    attacker for the previous century!

the remnant of Jacob,
to the warrior God*.[26]

22. But indeed your people, Israel,
will be like the sand of the sea.[27]
The remnant among them will return.
A finished work,
determined upon,
flooding in righteousness.

23. For a finished work – one determined upon –
the Sovereign, Yahweh of Hosts,
is going to do
in the midst of the whole earth.

Jerusalem: Security for the city; destruction for the attacker

24. Therefore,
this is what the Sovereign, Yahweh of Hosts, has said:
'Do not be afraid,
my people, living in Zion,
of Assyria who strikes you with a rod,
and lifts up his stick against you,
the way Egypt did.[28]

25. For within a tiny little time
the indignation[29] will be finished,
and my exasperation,[30]
in their erosion.[31]

26. For Yahweh of Hosts is going to rouse against him a whip,
as in the striking down of Midian at the Rock of Oreb:[32]
his staff will be over the sea
and he will lift it up
the way he did in Egypt.[33]

27. And it will be,
in that day,
his burden will move off from upon your shoulder,
and his yoke from upon your neck –
the yoke will be ruined because of fatness.[34]

28. He has come to Aiath,[35]

24 Genuinely, without pretence,
in true trust, fidelity,
and trustworthiness.

25 See 7:3.

26 This title of Yahweh is part of the
fourfold title of Messiah, 9:6.

27 Some of the wording in vv. 21–23
is ambiguous. Are we to
understand 'a remnant' as 'only
a remnant' – i.e., a veiled threat?
The two forms of *kalah* translated
'a finished work' could mean 'a
total annihilation'. But Isaiah
starts by quoting the promise to
Abraham (Gen. 22:17). This is
the significance of the 'remnant';
it is in this way that the Lord
will begin to keep his promise.
He will act in total accord with
his own righteous nature, finish
what he has determined to do,
and achieve a universal result.

28 Exod. 1:11–14; 5:14–16.

29 See 10:5.

30 See 5:25.

31 Noun only occurring here,
from *balah* (e.g., 51:6), to
become old/worn out.

32 Judg. 7:25.

33 Exod. 14:16, 21, 27.

34 No certainty what this means.
In v. 16 Assyria's crack troops are

traversed Migron;

at Michmash he musters his equipment;

29. they have crossed the pass;

'Geba is our overnight halt'.

Ramah has taken fright;

Gibeah of Saul has fled.

30. 'Scream with your voice, daughter of Gallim;

pay attention, Laishah!'

Anathoth is trodden down;

31. Madmenah is disorientated;

those living in Gebim have taken cover;

32. before today is out, he plans to stay at Nob;

he will wave his hand at the mountain of the daughter of Zion,[36]

the hill of Jerusalem.

33. Behold!

The Sovereign, Yahweh of Hosts,

is about to lop boughs off with terrifying force;[37]

the loftiest are cut down

and the tallest brought low.

34. He will chop down the thickets of the forest with iron;

even The Lebanon,[38] through the majestic One, will fall.

---

called 'fat ones'. Is Isaiah subtly hinting that there is a different 'fatness' resident in Zion, able to disempower every hostile force? Possibly Yahweh himself; or the Davidic monarchy in which divine promises were housed.

35 Vv. 28–32, Isaiah poetically sketches the southward march of invincible Assyria, unaware of the divine 'axeman' (vv. 33–34) awaiting him in Zion!

36 i.e., be within striking distance, so confident of victory that he (so to speak) waves a cheery greeting.

37 Noun only occurring here, related to the verb translated 'terrify' in 2:19. Note how the confidently waving hand of v. 32 is 'modulated' into the picture of branches trembling, breaking, falling.

38 i.e., even if the Assyrian were as extensive, mighty, apparently permanent, as Lebanon, he will fall before the power of real majesty.

Thought for the day: Isaiah 10:5–34

Looking at the world around, or back into the past – or, indeed, imagining the future – all we can see is a tangle of peoples, events, needs unmet, problems ever increasing, and progress and betterment always, it seems, matched (sometimes outstripped) by deterioration, further terror, suffering, injustice. We find our world baffling and worrying, and we need to stand where Isaiah stood, see what he saw, and be fortified by the revelation granted to him. For, looking at an equally tangled, threatening and unjust world, he insisted that 'God is still on the throne', in full managerial, executive, directive rule. First, the awful threat of Assyrian invasion was part of the divine moral government of the world. Assyria was 'dispatched' against a 'people meriting wrath' (v. 6).

Neither Assyria nor Jerusalem saw it that way, but that was the fact of the matter. Then, again, even the dreaded 'super-power' (at that time, Assyria) was but an axe in the hands of the divine Woodman (v. 15) – totally for his use, subservient to his purposes. Assyria did not see itself like that, but that was the fact of the matter. Thirdly, in its seemingly invincible onward march, triumphalist Assyria was actually on its way to putting its head on the block (v. 34). It did not think so, but that was the fact of the matter (and so it turned out, 37:36–38). And finally – and with what choice comfort we may hold on to the truth! – in all the tangle of events, all their inexplicable twists and turns, in all the problems, terrors and calamities that make up life, the Lord's eye never leaves his believing 'remnant'; he never ceases to concern himself with their survival. He made his promises and will keep them (vv. 21–23, 24–27). Jesus said just the same about God's elect (Mark 13:20, 22, 27).

Day 17   Isaiah 11:1–16

The glorious hope (11:1–16)

The fourth part of Isaiah's forecast for northern Israel. See introductory notes Days 11, 15, 16 above (pp. 44, 59, 63).

The King in the new creation (11:1–10)

His ancestry and character

11:1. And there will come out a shoot from the root-stock of Jesse,
and a sprout from his roots will be fruitful.

2. And there will rest on him the Spirit of Yahweh,
the Spirit of wisdom and discernment,
the Spirit of counsel and valour,[1]
the Spirit of knowledge and fear of Yahweh.

3. And his satisfaction[2] will be in the fear of Yahweh.

The nature of his rule

And not by what his eyes see will he judge,
Nor by what his ears hear will he adjudicate.

4. In righteousness he will judge[3] the poor,
and with fairness he will adjudicate for the downtrodden[4]
of the earth.
And he will strike down the earth with the staff of his mouth,
And with the spirit of his lips he will put the wicked to death.

5. And righteousness will be the belt round his body,
and faithfulness the belt round his waist.[5]

The King's realm: Eden restored

6. And the wolf will be a guest with the lamb,
and the leopard with the goat will lie down,
and the calf and the mature lion and the well-fed
beast together,
with a little lad leading them along.

1   'Counsel and valour' occur in 36:5 for, respectively, a 'plan' of campaign and the 'military force' to carry it out.

2   Lit., 'his scenting of a pleasurable odour', the same metaphor as in Gen. 8:21 where it is used of the Lord's satisfaction in Noah's sacrifice.

3   On 'righteousness' and 'judge' see 5:7. 'To judge' often means (as here) 'to set things to rights'.

4   'Poor' are those without resources; 'downtrodden' those without influence to resist stronger interests and pressure-groups.

5   The 'belt' symbolises readiness for action; 'righteousness' is commitment to the Lord's revelation of what is true and right; 'faithfulness' is fidelity or steadfastness in holding to what righteousness requires.

7. And the cow and the bear will pasture;
   together their young will lie down,
   and, like an ox, the lion will eat straw,
8. and the baby will play happily beside the cobra's hole,
   and into the viper's nest
   the toddler will actually reach out his hand.[6]
9. They will not do wrong,
   nor act corruptly,
   in all the mountain of my holiness,
   for the earth will have become full of the knowledge
   of Yahweh,
   like the waters are spread over the sea.

King of the world
10. And it will be,
    in that day,
    the Root of Jesse,[7]
    who is going to stand up as a banner for the peoples –
    to him the nations will seek,[8]
    and his resting-place is glory.[9]

The gathering of the Lord's worldwide Israel (11:11–16)

11. And it will be,
    in that day,
    the Sovereign will again, a second time,
    with his hand,
    take possession of the remnant of his people, which remains,
    from Assyria and from Egypt,
    and from Pathros and from Cush and from Elam,
    and from Shinar and from Hamath and from the remote
    sea-lands.[10]
12. And he will lift up a banner for the nations,
    and he will gather the scattered ones of Israel,
    and the dispersed elements of Judah he will collect
    from the four extremities[11] of the earth.
13. And ill-feeling[12] against Ephraim will go away,

6   It is uncertain what particular snakes are referred to in v. 8. 'Nest' is a contextual rendering. The word (only occurring here) seems to be related to 'light'.

7   The reference to 'Jesse' makes v. 10 link with v. 1. Messiah is both a descendant of Jesse (v. 1) and the root from which Jesse arises. Only the New Testament can explain how this can be. But v. 10 also acts as a bridge into vv. 11–16. It announces the worldwide kingdom and from v. 11 on we see the peoples gathering.

8   'Seek' (as so often in the Old Testament) means not to look for something that has been lost but to come eagerly to where it can be found.

9   i.e., 'his resting place is where the glory is'. The 'resting place' is both where he rests, i.e., his home, and the place of rest into which he invites his people.

10 Isaiah is not drawing a map but using the world-map of his day to picture worldwide regathering – east to Assyria (and beyond), south to Egypt (and beyond),

and Judah's adversaries will be cut down.
Ephraim will not cultivate ill-feeling against Judah,
nor Judah be an adversary to Ephraim.

14. And they will swoop[13] on the Philistine slopes to the west;
together they will take the sons of the east as prey;
Edom and Moab within their outstretched hand,
and the sons of Ammon under orders to them.

15. And Yahweh will remove completely the tongue of the
sea of Egypt,[14]
and he will wave his hand over the River,[15]
with the drying heat[16] of his wind,
and he will strike[17] it into seven watercourses,
and will make a road for sandals.

16. And there will be a causeway for the remnant of his people
which remains, out of Assyria,
as there was for Israel
in the day they came up from the land of Egypt.

---

north to Hamath, and west to
lands beyond the sea. The four
'extremities' of v. 12., 'remote
lands', is *'iyyim*, see 41:1.

11 Lit., 'wings', as outspread
in every direction.

12 See 9:7.

13 Isaiah takes the metaphor of
the coming King seriously.
Kings extend their dominion by
conquest. So the coming King
is the world-conqueror. That he
is also 'Prince of Peace' prepares
for the New Testament's full
revelation of conquest by the truth
of the Gospel; cf., Acts 15:13–18.

14 The barrier of the Red Sea was
broken to secure the Exodus from
Egypt (Exod. 14). For the greater,
worldwide Exodus Isaiah foresees
the sea itself will be dried up.

15 The Euphrates: every barrier to
the re-gathering will be removed.

16 Uncertain translation. For the
idea see Exod. 14:21; 15:10.

17 For this use of 'striking',
see 2 Kings 2:8.

Thought for the day: Isaiah 11:1–16

The Lord Jesus, says Paul, has become 'for us wisdom from God' (1 Cor. 1:30). Isaiah got there first, of course, and it is attractively tempting to think that Isaiah 11 was the apostle's daily Bible reading the day he wrote to the Corinthians! What a portrait the prophet painted of our great royal Messiah! 'Wisdom' is a true understanding of life and how to live it; 'discernment' is seeing right to the heart of any matter, seeing a problem or situation as it really is. Jesus, too, knows how to plan sensibly in every situation ('counsel') and to impart the practical ability ('valour') to get it done; and in him we see, and from him we learn, that true, deep reverence, the 'fear of Yahweh', which is meant to be the governing principle for this 'time of our sojourning' (1 Pet. 1:17). We cannot read Isaiah 11 (and crowds of other passages) without sensing afresh the wonder of our Bibles: such detailed anticipation and accurate forecasting of the Coming One. This is great gain, but even more important it is to take the next step and be uplifted in wonder, love and praise of the one thus foreseen, the Lord Jesus Christ. If he really is like Isaiah foresaw – practical, effective wisdom for every day, power over all the power of the enemy (v. 4), Lord of the beautiful and blessed future he holds in store for us (vv. 6–9) – what fresh commitments we should make to live close and stay near to him. The old hymns often hit the target with exactitude: 'O pilgrim bound for the heavenly land, Never lose sight of Jesus'; or the gentle, beautiful perfection of 'Turn your eyes upon Jesus, Look full in his wonderful face, And the things of earth will grow strangely dim, In the light of his glory and grace.' 'Strangely dim'? Quite so! They will be seen in their proper size, place, proportion and importance when he takes centre stage.

Day 18   Isaiah 12:1–6

See Day 10, (p. 40), where this section of Isaiah began. One individual, participant in national sin and condemnation, was brought 'back to God from the dark paths of sin' through the efficacy of the altar on which the substitutionary sacrifice had been made (6:6–7). The following chapters revealed the whole nation, in both its parts, deep in rebellion, but the Lord never failed to promise a saved remnant who would enter upon a glorious hope. Isaiah ends by allowing us to see the remnant lifted up in praise for its salvation.

Epilogue: The saved community in praise and testimony (12:1–6)

12:1. And you[1] will say, in that day:
    'I thank you, Yahweh;
    you were, indeed, exasperated[2] with me.
    O let your exasperation turn back,
    and do comfort me!

2.   Behold!
    God* is my salvation!
    I trust,
    and I am not apprehensive,
    for my strength and song is Yah,[3] Yahweh,
    and he has become salvation for me.'

3.   And you[4] will draw water with delight
    from the fountains of salvation.

4.   And you[5] will say, in that day:
    'Give thanks to Yahweh;
    proclaim his name;

1. Masculine singular. Isaiah, the saved individual of 6:1–13, finds himself a member of the saved community.

2. 5:25.

3. An abbreviation of endearment of the divine Name.

4. Masculine plural: the saved community. All who come to the fountains will enjoy the same salvation.

5. Masculine plural. Worldwide proclamation is the task of the saved community.

among the peoples make them know his actions;
make them recall that his name is worthy of
highest exaltation;
5. make music to Yahweh,
for he has acted supremely;
this is worthy to be made known in all the earth.
6. With shrill cries,[6] shout aloud,
dweller[7] in Zion,
for great among you is the Holy One of Israel.'

_____

6   Two verbs here: 'Scream out and sing aloud', but 'scream' gives the wrong idea. The verb means 'to ululate'. In 10:30 it is the scream of distress; here and in 54:1 the ululation of excited joy.

7   Female; cf., Miriam leading the women in celebratory song, Exod. 15:20–21. Ps. 68:11 speaks of the 'company of women' announcing victory; cf., 1 Sam. 18:6–7.

Thought for the day: Isaiah 12:1–6

The Bible speaks with one voice: sixty-six books, many authors known and unknown, spread over thousands of years of time, yet a coherent, consistent revelation of one God, one revealed truth, one people of God, one way of salvation. Another ground for awe and wonder before such a unique book. It is that last matter of 'one way of salvation' that emerges in today's reading. What did our earlier brothers and sisters in the family of Abraham believe in this vital matter? First, not only that salvation arises from God but that he is himself 'salvation' (v. 2); it is one way of defining what he is. When we stand before him we stand before salvation. This is our supreme ground of assurance: God, who in other circumstances would be our judge, unapproachable in holiness, is himself our salvation. Secondly, we need salvation because of the wrath of God against sin and sinners (Rom. 1:18) – not because sin damages or mars us (though it does) but because it enrages and alienates him. But, thirdly, Isaiah saw this exasperated anger fade away and be replaced by comfort (v. 2). He does not say here how that seemingly impossible change has come about, because he has already told what had happened. In 6:6–7 he saw the Seraph bring to him the fire from the altar; evidence that the fiery wrath of God had burnt itself out on the body of a substitutionary sacrifice. In the fourth place, salvation is, on our side, by faith: when we 'trust', all fear and apprehension disappear. Fifthly, the salvation into which we enter once for all by faith is constantly available, never exhausted: we enjoy free access to the fountains of fresh supply. And finally, the same wondrous God who is 'salvation' is also our strength for the road and the joy which transforms. Salvation from God; salvation by faith; salvation in endless freshness; salvation ministering strength and delight!

Day 19   Isaiah 13:1–22

Today we begin a new section in Isaiah's 'Book of the King' (chs. 1–37). He introduced 'David' very quietly, without naming him, in 1:26, and then, against the background of failure in Judah and Israel (chs. 6–12), shared the vision of the glorious King yet to come, also seeing the coming David as the world's King (9:7; 11:9, 11–16), and it is to this theme that Isaiah now turns (chs. 13–27), painting a panorama of the whole world brought into one under David's kingship and the Lord's reign (e.g., 19:24–25; 25:6–8). At first sight these chapters are puzzling and complicated, and time spent now getting a clear grasp of the whole will prove to be time well spent. It falls into three divisions, each with five parts.

13:1–20:6. Isaiah reviews the world around him: *Babylon* (13:1–14:27) the 'super-power' which would bring the whole world into one by despotism; *Philistia* (14:28–32) crowing over another blow to the dynasty of David and expecting its total demise (but, says Isaiah, David's throne is rather going to triumph); the Gentile power, *Moab* (15:1–16:14), could find shelter in its hour of need in David and Zion, but is held back by pride (that is, even then 'David' was the key to security in a threatening world if only the Gentile powers would realise it); *Damascus* (Aram) and *Ephraim* (17:1–18:7) share a common fate (Ephraim, the northern kingdom, thought to find security in alliance with Aram, but rather found destruction – this is not the way of security for the people of God); *Egypt* (19:1–20:6) is heading for disaster, but also will one day be joined with Israel and Assyria as one people in one world under one God (19:24–25).

21:1–23:18. Again there are five divisions, matching those of the first section, but now they are given cryptic names (as if, probing further into the future, Isaiah saw the same principles at work in world history as were exemplified in the nations currently around him): the Babylon principle, that there will still be some super-power attempting world-dominion, unity by despotism, but it will share Babylon's fate (21:1–10); the need for patience in a dark world, the long drawn out sequence of day and night, as if the Lord were doing nothing (21:11–12); the Gentile world, still troubled, trying to meet its dangers by collective security, and failing (21:13–17); Jerusalem under threat, taking the road of self-sufficiency, the sin that cannot be forgiven (22:1–25); yet, at the end, the determinedly secular world, typified by commercial Tyre, will be 'holiness to the Lord' (23:1–18).

24:1–27:13. Isaiah now offers no headings. He is gazing right forward to the End, but his vision still follows the same five themes: the global village, the human attempt to hold the whole world in an organised unity, will collapse (24:1–20); but 'after many days', there will be the glory of the Lord's reign in Zion (24:21–23); the Gentile world will not be forgotten but will be gathered to Zion to the great feast (25:1–12), proud Moab alone excluded; the people of God will enjoy the true security of the strong city of salvation (26:1–20); and the trumpet of Jubilee will summon the final gathering to the final harvest (27:1–13).

Finally, looking up key-verses, see how distinct themes unite each of the five sections.

(1) Babylon represents human attempts to unite the world by power. Babylon, the imperialist of Isaiah's day, will fall (13:19–20); the imperialist attempt to make the world one under a super power will fail (21:9); human efforts to create the 'global village' – the whole world organised under human

rule and regulations – lead only to 'the city where nothing makes sense' and its downfall (24:10).

(2) Philistia illustrates the antagonism of the world to David's rule (14:29) but Zion's future is secure (14:32), even though, as time passes, nothing seems to happen (21:11–12). In the long run 'after many days' the Lord will reign in glory in Zion (24:22–23).

(3) The world's need can only be met in David's rule. Moab could have found refuge in Zion (16:4–5) but pride would not allow it (16:6). Yet left to itself, mutual help, collective security, is not the solution (21:15–17). Ultimately all the world will enjoy the Lord's feast in Zion (25:7–9) – except proud Moab (25:10).

(4) And what of the Lord's people? Sadly, they follow the false trails of security in worldly alliances (17:3–4) and self-sufficiency (22:9–11), but only in the strong city of salvation is true peace and safety to be found (26:1–4).

(5) The ideal of one world, one people, one God will be brought into being by the Lord himself (19:24–25; 23:18; 27:12–13).

The first series of five oracles: Who rules the world? (13:1–20:6)

Isaiah blends together the contemporary situation, impending events, and predictions of the End to show that the Lord is in executive charge of his world. He will keep his promises.

Babylon: A peep behind the scenes (13:1–14:27)

The contemporary, rising superpower is seen in relation to the Day of the Lord. History is not shaped by superpowers but by the Lord.

13:1. An oracle on Babylon,
which Isaiah, son of Amoz, perceived.[1]

The Day of the Lord[2] (13:2–16)

Wrath

2. On an exposed mountain,
lift up a banner.
Raise (your) voice to them.
Beckon with (your) hand,
so that they may come
against the gates[3] of the nobles.
3. It is I who have commanded;
also I have called up my warriors for my exasperation,[4]
my magnificent exulting ones.

Worldwide unrest

4. A voice![5]
A hub-bub[6] on the mountains!
Something like people in abundance!
A voice!
A crashing among the kingdoms!
Nations assembled!
Yahweh of Hosts mustering a battle-host!
5. Coming from a land afar,
from the furthest end of heaven,
Yahweh and the instruments of his indignation[7]
to despoil all the earth!

Helpless bewilderment

6. Wail,
for the day of Yahweh is near;
like shambles[8] from Shaddai[9] it comes.
7. Therefore all hands hang limp,
and every heart of frail humanity[10] melts.
8. And they are terrified.
Agonies and pains take hold.

1 See 1:1.

2 Seven aspects of The Day: wrath (2–3), worldwide unrest (4–5), helpless bewilderment (6–8), cosmic disruption (9–10), just visitation of recompense (11), the whole order of creation reversed (12–13), horrific suffering (14–16).

3 i.e., as an attacking force; or 'into the gates' as those who have already conquered.

4 See 5:25.

5 'A voice' is sometimes used as an ejaculation – 'Listen!', cf., 40:3, 6; 52:8; 66:6.

6 See 5:13.

7 See 5:25.

8 Heb., *shod,* destruction, spoliation. The rendering 'shambles' is chosen to try to reflect *shod mishshaddai.*

9 This title first occurs in Gen. 17:1 (cf., Gen. 28:3; 35:11; 43:14;

Like a woman in labour they writhe.
They look at each other in bewilderment;
their faces are faces of flame.[11]

Cosmic disruption

9. Behold!
   The day of Yahweh is coming,
   savage —
   outbursting anger[12] and fury of exasperation[13] —
   to make the earth into a desolation,
   and to destroy sinners out of it.[14]
10. For the stars of heaven and their constellations
    will not gleam with their light.
    The sun is dark at its emergence
    and the moon will not beam with its light.

Just recompense

11. And I will visit evil on the inhabited world,
    and upon the wicked their iniquity,[15]
    and I will bring the pride of the arrogant to an end,
    and the haughty airs[16] of the terrifying I will demean.

The order of creation reversed

12. I will make ordinary humankind[17] scarcer than fine gold,
    and human beings than the gold of Ophir.
13. Therefore,
    even the heavens I will shake,
    and the earth will tremble out of its place,
    through the outbursting anger[18] of Yahweh of Hosts,
    and in the day of his fury of exasperation.[19]

Horrific suffering

14. And it will be,
    like a hunted gazelle,
    and like sheep without anyone to gather them,
    they will, each of them, turn to his own people,
    and each to his own land they will flee.

48:3; 49:25). It is widely used in Job; only here in Isaiah. The meaning is uncertain, but the references in Genesis suggest God's almighty power to transform human helplessness. Isaiah may have been drawn to it here for the sake of assonance.

10 Heb., 'enosh used of humankind in its frailty, ordinariness, cf., v. 12; 8:1;24:6; 33:8; 51:7, 12; 56:2.

11 A 'flaming face' suggests embarrassment, in the OT sense of not only feeling shame but also reaping shame. The people and powers of earth, contrary to their hopes and boasts, find themselves helpless and at a loss.

12 9:19. See 5:25.

13 5:25.

14 'Sinners' is emphatic, stressing the moral and spiritual element in divine universal overthrow.

15 See 1:2.

16 'Pride' and 'proud airs' are two forms of the same word, 'to be high' – like the English idiom 'high and mighty'.

17 See v. 7.

18 9:19. See 5:25.

19 5:25

15. Everyone chanced upon will be pierced through,
    and everyone swept away will fall by the sword.
16. And their babies will be smashed to bits before their eyes;
    their houses will be plundered,
    and their wives – they will be raped!

Babylon doomed: The fact of divine overthrow (13:17–22)

17. Behold!
    It is I who am rousing up against them the Medes,[20]
    who think nothing of silver,
    and as for gold they find no pleasure in it.
18. And their bows will shatter the young men,
    and on the fruit of the womb they will have no compassion.[21]
    Sons, even, their eye will not pity.
19. And Babylon, the most splendid of the kingdoms,
    the beauty of the pride of the Chaldeans,
    will be like what God overturned –
    Sodom and Gomorrrah.
20. It will remain unoccupied in perpetuity
    and unlived in for generation after generation.
    The Arab will not pitch his tent there,
    nor shepherds rest their flocks there.
21. And the desert-wraiths will rest there,
    and their houses will be full of owls,
    and ostriches will reside there,
    and goat-demons will skip about there,
22. and hyenas will raise echoes in their palaces,
    and jackals in luxurious mansions.
    And soon to come is its due time,
    and its days will not be protracted.

20 A N.E. Mesopotamian people, an ally of Babylon in the demise of the Assyrian empire (Nineveh fell in 612 BC) but, a century later, an ally of Persia in the downfall of Babylon.

21 9:17.

Thought for the day: Isaiah 13:1–22

If Isaiah is foretelling the fall of Babylon why does he spend time describing the Day of Yahweh? Because that is the Bible way of looking at history and historical events: just as every next king in David's line could be the messianic King, and every next prophet could be the 'prophet like Moses' (Deut. 18:15–22; cf. John 1:21), so every next historical alarm could be the onset of Yahweh's Day – and is, at the very least, a 'trailer' of the Day that will surely come. We need to develop this perspective on the calamity-ridden world we inhabit. The nineteenth-century writers on the Second Coming saw things this way: as wars proliferated and tragedies unfolded, they saw the Return just round the corner. They were right to do so. The Lord Jesus is always near, even at the doors (Luke 21:25–28; James 5:8–9), and certainly 'nearer than when we first believed' (Rom. 13:11). So, view the unruly world, even in its most threatening, with hope and confidence. Whatever forces gather, for whatever awful purposes, it is still the Lord 'rousing up the Medes', and calling up his warriors to execute his exasperation. It could be the start of the final 'travail' (Mark 13:8); at the least it is one of the Lord's 'trailers'. He is still on the throne, still the Executive. But also take deeply into your heart the frightfulness of the judgment when it comes. Awful as it is to be alienated from God now, it will be a thousand times so when the die has been cast and the day of salvation is gone. Only in the Son of David can the world find refuge and flee from the wrath to come. From our security in the Ark of Salvation it is our duty to pray for a world sinking into wrath, to send out the lifeboat of the gospel, and throw out the life-buoys of salvation; 'by all means to save some' (1 Cor. 9:22).

Day 20   Isaiah 14:1–32

At the heart of world history: the Lord's people (14:1–2)

14:1. For Yahweh will have compassion[1] on Jacob,

    and go on choosing Israel,

    and he will give them rest in their own land,

    and the resident alien will join himself to them,

    and they will attach themselves to the house of Jacob.

2.   And peoples will take them

    and bring them to their place,

    and the house of Israel will possess them for themselves

    in Yahweh's land,

    as servants and maids:

    they will take captive their captors,

    and will dominate their taskmasters.

The end of Babylon and its king: Divine overthrow explained (14:3–23)

3.   And it will be,

    in the day Yahweh gives you rest

    from your pain and from your turmoil,

    and from the harsh servitude which was imposed on you,

4.   you will publicise this exposé[2] of the King of Babylon,

    and say:

Earth reacts to the end of persecution

    How the taskmaster has ceased!

    Insensate fury[3] has ceased!

5.   Yahweh has broken the rod of the wicked ones:

    The sceptre of rulers,

6.   striking down peoples in outbursting anger,[4]

    striking without cessation,

[1] 9:17.

[2] Lit., 'lift up (your voice) in this proverb/parable/wise insight into'. The *mashal*, originally a revealing comparison of one thing with another, came to mean anything which 'exposed' the real, 'inside story' or significance.

[3] A word of unknown meaning. All renderings are guesses.

[4] See 5:25; 9:19.

in exasperation[5] dominating nations,
persecution unsparing.

7.   All the earth is quietly at rest.
  They have burst out with loud shouting.
8.   Even the fir trees rejoice about you,
  the cedars of Lebanon:
  'Since you have lain down,
  no lumberjack[6] has come up against us!'

Sheol reacts to the anticipated arrival of the king

9.   Sheol, beneath, came trembling to you,
  to meet your coming.
  It has aroused for you the shadowy ones,[7]
  all the 'great rams'[8] of the earth!
  It has raised from their thrones
  all the kings of the nations.
10.   They answer – all of them – and say to you:
  'You too!! –
  you have been made weak like us!
  You are equal – to us!!'

The king's arrival in Sheol

11.   To Sheol your eminence has been brought down,
  the whisper of your lyres.
  Under you are spread maggots,
  worms are covering you.
12.   How you have fallen from heaven,
  Morning Star,[9] son of Dawn!
  You have been felled to the ground,
  you who prostrated nations!
13.   And you – you are the one who said in your heart,
  'To heaven itself I will go up,
  above the stars of god* I will make my throne high.
  And I will sit on the Mount of Assembly,
  the apex of Zaphon.[10]
14.   I will go up above the high places of the clouds;
  I will make myself like the Most High.'

5   See 5:25.

6   Lit., 'no cutter'.

7   The Old Testament insists that 'the dead' are 'alive', but living the half-life of those who have left, so to speak, half of themselves, their bodies, behind. This word, from *raphah*, to relax, be listless, is used of the dead in their shadowy state (26:14, 19).

8   Used of earthly rulers in the strutting pomposity.

9   An allusion to Canaanite myth in which the Morning Star, the god Ishtar, made an abortive bid for supremacy.

10   In N. Palestine, in Canaanite myth, the home of the gods.

15. To the contrary!
    To Sheol you are brought down!
    To the nadir[11] of the Pit!

The king's contrasting reputation, before and after death!

16. Those who see you – how they stare at you!
    How they see through you!
    Is this the man who was making the earth tremble,
    making kingdoms quake?

17. He made the inhabited world like a wilderness
    and its cities he tore down.
    His prisoners he did not release to go home.

18. All the kings of the nations – all of them –
    lie in state,
    each in his mausoleum,[12]

19. and you – you are thrown out from your grave,
    like a detested branch,[13]
    clothed[14] with the slain,
    those pierced with the sword,
    those going down to the rock-bottom of the pit,
    like a trampled corpse!

20. You will not be one with them in burial,[15]
    because it is your own land that you have destroyed,
    your own people you slew.[16]
    They will not be named for ever,
    The seed of evildoers.

The Lord of history[17]

21. Appoint for his sons a slaughterhouse
    in payment for the iniquity[18] of their fathers.
    They must not rise up and take possession of the earth,
    and fill the face of the world with cities.

22. I will rise up against them –
    this is the word of Yahweh of Hosts –
    and in Babylon's case, I will cut off name and remnant
    and heirs and successors[19] –
    this is the word of Yahweh of Hosts –

11 The same word as 'apex' in v. 13!
   cf., 'recesses', 37:24. It signifies
   the furthest point in whatever
   direction the context requires.

12 Lit., 'lie in glory, each
   in his house'.

13 As in 11:1, a 'branch'
   in the family tree.

14 No royal shroud but covered with
   other bodies in a common grave.

15 The kings in their
   mausoleums of v. 18.

16 Royal imperial ambitions were
   to the detriment of welfare at
   home: the king pursued conquest;
   it was his soldiers that died.

17 These verses could still be part
   of the 'exposé' of the king
   of Babylon. I have chosen
   rather to treat them as a
   reflection and comment.

18 See 1:2

19 A rarely used expression
   which clearly has a technical

23. and I will make it into a possession for hedgehogs,
    and pools of water;
    and I will brush it away with a broom of destruction –
    this is the word of Yahweh of Hosts.

Assyria: A test case, an interim assurance[20] (14:24–27)

24. Yahweh of Hosts has gone on oath, saying:
    'I swear that as I have designed so it will be,
    and as I have planned, that is what will happen:
25. the intention to break Assyria within my land,
    and that on my mountains I will trample it down.
    And its yoke will go away from upon them,
    and from every shoulder its burden will go away.'
26. This is the plan that is planned over all the earth,
    and this is the hand that is stretched out over all the nations.
27. For Yahweh of Hosts has planned –
    and who can frustrate it,
    and it is his hand that is stretched out
    and who can turn it back?

Philistia: doomed power, coming power (14:28–32)

The second power to enter Isaiah's world-review is Philistia. Since he dates this oracle by the death of Ahaz, and he addresses 'messengers' (v. 32), it looks as if Philistia had sent an official delegation to Ahaz's funeral (cf., 2 Sam. 10:2–3), and that they were crowing over another blow to the dynasty of David. Isaiah sees things differently. The world will not ultimately have ascendancy over David, rather the reverse.

28. In the year of the death of the king, Ahaz, came this oracle:
29. Do not rejoice,
    Philistia, all of you,
    that the rod which struck you has been broken.
    For from the root of the snake will emerge a viper,
    and its fruit a fiery, flying serpent.
30. And the firstborn of the poor will find pasture,

meaning and literally means 'offspring and offspring'.

20   Assyria was the current super-power, as Babylon was the rising super-power. Isaiah offers a prediction to be fulfilled within the lifetime of his hearers as an assurance that the more remote prediction of the fall of Babylon is equally certain. The destruction of Assyria 'within my land' is recorded in Isaiah 36–37.

and in safety the vulnerable will lie down.[21]
And with famine I will kill your root
and your remnant too it will slay.

31. Wail, O gate!
Shriek, O city!
Philistia – all of you – has melted,[22]
for from the north smoke[23] is coming.
None stands alone on duty.

32. And what will one reply to the messengers of the nation?
That it is Yahweh who founded Zion,
and in it the downtrodden of his people will find refuge.

---

21 The Lord's people are his flock. Drawing on this metaphor Isaiah promises provision ('pasture') and security ('lie down').The Philistines may think David's kingdom is helpless prey. The reality is far different. 'Lie down' (*rabats*) is of an animal at rest. 'Vulnerable' is *'ebyon*; from a root meaning 'to be willing' it developed a 'bad' meaning (those who can be bent to the will of stronger interests) and a 'good' meaning (those who willingly bend to the will of God); cf., 25:4; 29:19; 32:7; 41:17.

22 'Melt' as in 64:7; of the breakdown of morale; no power to resist.

23 'North', as always, signifies an attack by the great Mesopotamian powers; 'smoke', the drifting smoke of towns pillaged and fired, or (cf., Song 3:6) the dust cloud raised by marching armies.

Thought for the day: Isaiah 14:1–32

We too can take that ancient overthrow of Assyrian power (v. 25) as a 'case in point', and draw out for ourselves the assurances that Isaiah wanted his contemporaries to have. Assyria was the current super-power; its armies irresistible; its ferocity legendary. It was crushed in one night by one angel (Isa. 37:36). The threat was gone. Assyrian power was now on a steep downward curve. Before their very eyes the people of Jerusalem saw that what the Lord plans he accomplishes (v. 26) and that his hand – his ability and power of personal intervention – is mightier than all the powers of earth (v. 27). The Philistine oracle teaches the same truth. David had hammered the Philistines (2 Sam. 5:17–25), but David was lost in the mists of history and Ahaz was about to be succeeded by the untried Hezekiah (2 Kings 18:1–2). There was, however, more to Judah and Jerusalem than the memory of a former great king. It was Yahweh who founded Zion (v. 32), and it was he who would settle the destinies both of Philistia and of his own people. Downtrodden they might be, but they had present security (v. 32) and coming victory when one mightier than even David would emerge (v. 29). Surely Paul would pause to say here what he said to the Thessalonians (1 Thess. 4:18), 'Comfort one another with these words', and we have every right to do so, for look where today's passages started. The opening word, 'for' (14:1), offers an explanation of what Isaiah 13 records: the downfall of great Babylon, yes; and even more the ultimate shaking of heaven and earth in the Day of Judgment. Everything that happens in world history, past, present and ultimately, is in the interests of the divine 'mercy' (here 'compassion', heart-throbbing love) designed to implement our comfort, security and inheritance, the people he has chosen for himself.

Day 21 Isaiah 15:1–16:14

Isaiah turns to the third element in his world-review: Moab. In each of the three series of oracles (see Day 19, pages 76–82 above) the third position is reserved for the plight of the Gentile world. Moab is a case in point. How can it survive the onward march of Assyrian imperialism in all its pitiless savagery? Isaiah answers that, if only they will accept it, there is refuge for all in the House of David; the Davidic promises (14:32) are not exclusivist but universal – and (see 25:6–10) will one day be fulfilled richly for all the world (except for Moab, still gripped by its pride, 16:6; 25:10–11).

Moab

Moab: certain ruin

15:1. An oracle on Moab:

> Surely in a night it is destroyed,
> Ar in Moab is brought to silence.[1]
> Surely in a night it is destroyed;
> Kir[2] in Moab is brought to silence.

Moab's grief expressed

2. They[3] have gone up to the House – to Dibon[4] –
   to the High Places for weeping.
   On Nebo and on Medeba Moab wails.
   On their every head, baldness;
   Every beard shaved off![5]

3. In its streets they have fastened on sack-cloth.
   On its roofs
   and in its open squares everyone of them wails,
   flowing down with weeping.

4. Heshbon too and Elealeh have shrieked aloud.
   As far as Jahaz their voice has been heard.

1   See 6:5.

2   Ar is on the border of Moab (Deut. 2:18). Kir is probably Kir-Hareseth in central Moab. In this way Isaiah hints at the inward advance of the invaders.

3   Lit., 'he has gone up', Moab personified.

4   The shrine of the national god, Kemosh.

5   Baldness as a sign of mourning, 22:12.

Therefore

even the armed men of Moab themselves cry out,

their very soul shivers.

The Lord's grief over Moab

5. For Moab my heart itself shrieks out.[6]

    Its fugitives as far as Zoar![7]

    To Eglath-Shelishiyah!

    Yes, by the ascent to The Luhith with weeping they ascend!

    Yes, on the road to Horonaim they shriek at the destruction!

6. Yes, the waters of Nimrim, what a destruction they

    have become!

    Yes, the grass is withered,

    vegetation finished!

    No fresh growth!

7. Therefore,

    the profit they have made –

    their gathered store –

    over the watercourse of the willows they carry it!

8. Yes, the shrieking has circled right round the border of Moab.

    As far as Eglaim their wailing!

    And to the Well of Elim their wailing!

9. Yes, even the waters of Dimon are full of blood!

    Yes, upon Dimon I will impose added burdens –

    for the escapees of Moab, a lion –

    for the remnant in the land!

Moab's plea for shelter[8]

16:1. Send lambs to the ruler of the land,

    from Sela,[9] through the wilderness,

    to the mount of the daughter of Zion.

2. 'This is how it is:

    like fluttering birds,

    nest scattered,

    so are Moab's daughters,

    at Arnon's fords.

6   Since Yahweh must be the speaker in v. 9 it is therefore he who weeps for Moab here, the wonder of a divine lament for a Gentile and idolatrous nation.

7   The following place-names run in a general south-west direction, depicting the enemy advancing from the north. The repeated 'yes' registers the falling of blow after blow. Isaiah's short, staccato sentences and exclamations enhance the feeling of crisis.

8   Isaiah eavesdrops on a Cabinet meeting. Still writing in 'panic-stricken' style, he fancies Moab planning an appeal to Jerusalem, backed by a typical Moabite gift of sheep (2 Kings 3:4).

9   In the deep south of Moab, whither the government have taken themselves for safety.

3. Proffer advice!
   Make a decision!
   Make your shadow like night at high noon!
   Cover the fugitives!
   Do not reveal those on the run!
4. Let them find asylum with you –
   my fugitives – Moab!
   Be a covering for them from spoliation!"[10]

Security to be found in Zion[11]
   When the oppressor is no more,
   destruction over,
   crushing tyrants[12] finished from the earth,
5. in reliability[13] a throne will be secure,
   and there will sit on it in truth,[14]
   in the tent of David,
   one who judges and seeks judgment[15]
   and is swift in righteousness.[16]

Moab's grief explained
6. We have heard of Moab's pride –
   very proud!
   Its pride of this sort and its pride of that sort –
   overflowing with it!
   It is not right – its boastful talk.
7. Therefore
   Moab will wail for Moab;
   all over it, it will wail!
   For the raisin-cakes of Kir-Hareseth
   you will groan[17] – stricken indeed!
8. Because the vine-terraces of Heshbon have withered,
   the vines of Sibmah!
   The lords of the nations – they have smashed its tendrils
   which reached as far as Jazer,
   spread to the wilderness;
   its shoots luxuriated,
   crossed over the sea.[18]

10 See 13:6.

11 Was there ever an actual appeal
    from Moab for help or is Isaiah
    exercising imagination? In
    any case the reply starts here.
    The panicky speech of the
    ambassadors is replaced by a
    majestic rhythm to enunciate
    the Davidic hope. Moab
    can be as secure as Zion.

12 Lit., 'the trampler'.

13 Reliability' is *chesed,* mostly used
    of the pledged and unchanging
    devotion of the Lord to his people,
    sometimes as here 'steadfastness',
    moral reliability, in human
    relationships and responsibilities
    (40:6; 54:8, 10; 55:3; 57:1; 63:7).

14 See 10:20.

15 See 2:4.

16 See 5:7.

17 See 8:19.

18 The vine here symbolises
    prosperity, and its tendrils

The Lord's grief over Moab

9. Therefore
   I will weep in the weeping of Jazer,
   the vines of Sibmah!
   I will drench with my tears Heshbon and Elealeh,
   for on your ripe fruit and on your harvest a vintage
   shout[19] has fallen,
10. and rejoicing and exultation will be gathered away from
    the garden-land,
    and in the vineyards no shout uttered, no cheer raised.[20]
    The wine in the vats no treader will tread;
    the vintage-shout I have made to cease.
11. Therefore
    for Moab my heart-strings are plucked like a harp,[21]
    and my inner feelings for Kir-Heres.
12. And it will be
    when he shows himself,
    when he wearies himself –
    – Moab –
    on the High Places,
    and comes to his holy shrine to pray,
    he will not prevail.[22]

Moab's imminent ruin[23]

13. This is the word which Yahweh spoke then about Moab.
14. Now Yahweh has spoken, saying:
    'In three years,
    like the years of a hired man,
    Moab's glory will be degraded,
    in spite of all the huge multitude,[24]
    and what remains will be a tiny few,
    nothing much!'

---

the tentacles of Moabite influence abroad.

19 'Vintage shout' is *heydad* – the joyous cry of those treading grapes (Jer. 48:33) or the victory shout of a conqueror (Jer. 51:14).

20 Lit., 'It is not shouted aloud, not cried out', referring to the joyful shouting that greeted the vintage.

21 'My intestines murmur like a harp'. Metaphorically the 'intestines' are the seat of deep feeling.

22 Lit., 'be able', used regularly in this sense of having the ability to handle some situation, to master it. It will be too much for him.

23 Another 'case in point', an imminent fulfilment people can watch for, offering proof that the major predictions will be fulfilled too. The 'years of a hired man' (v. 14) mean years exactly measured, agreed by contract. The reference is probably to the campaign of the Assyrian Sargon in 711 BC.

24 See 5:13.

Thought for the day: Isaiah 15:1–16:14

Pride is a killer. Make no mistake. It is the very negation of the way of faith. Destructive of security now in the face of life's threats (16:5–6), and destructive too of eternal hope and joy (25:9–10). It is of no significance whether Moab, in crisis, actually made an approach to Judah or whether Isaiah is imagining a scenario. The inevitability is that when a solution by faith is offered, pride says 'no'; when a heavenly banquet is prepared, pride excludes. Shelter under the throne of David and under the promises resident there was on offer, but pride is a go-it-alone principle: why should a country with 'a huge army' (16:14) need shelter? Faith and pride cannot co-habit, and pride puts on many guises. There is denominational pride which says we have the right way to run a church; our doctrines are the essence of orthodoxy. Beware of it, for nothing will close a church faster. There is domestic pride – look at our children how they are walking with God, unlike some we could mention! And there is the dreaded personal pride, the 'I can cope' syndrome: 'I've got to work through this for myself'; 'I can handle it'. Pride is the ultimate expression of salvation by works; it is practical atheism. It shows its ugly head any day we omit Bible reading; it is leering over our shoulders when we can't find time for prayer – and, oh yes, when we neglect to gather round us the strength of fellowship or when our places are empty at the Lord's Table. Pride laughs up its sleeve when we are difficult to get on with, stubborn rather than amenable, digging our heels in instead of being open to reason. Just as there is no way we can serve both God and mammon, so there is no way we can (openly or secretly) believe in our personal omnicompetence and at the same time believe in Jesus as the Saviour of sinners.

Day 22 Isaiah 17:1–18:7

Ephraim and Damascus (17:1–18:7)
The two kingdoms of the 'seed of Abraham', 'Judah' and 'Israel', were tiny enclaves among much larger and stronger kingdoms. The question of security therefore loomed large: how could they remain safe – and sovereign – in a menacing world? This is the topic of the fourth oracle in each of the three sets (see pp. 76–78 above). Ephraim sought to secure itself by an alliance with Damascus (Aram), against advancing Assyrian imperialism. Jerusalem (22:1–25) went the way of self-sufficiency. Neither 'worked'! Only in the strong city of salvation is their security (26:1–19).

The failed alliance
17:1. An oracle on Damascus
       Behold!
       Damascus is going to be removed as a city,
       and it will become a fallen heap.[1]
2.   Forsaken will be the cities of Aroer;[2]
       just for flocks – that is what they will be –
       and they will lie down, none frightening them.
3.   And the fortress[3] will cease from Ephraim,
       and sovereignty from Damascus,
       and what is left of Aram
       will be just the same as the glory of the sons of Israel.
       This is the word of Yahweh of Hosts.

The prospect for Ephraim: Three 'in that day'[4] oracles
'In that day' (1): Ephraim reduced
4.   And it will be,
       in that day,

[1] Damascus fell to the Assyrians in 732 BC.

[2] There is no known 'Aroer' in Aram but there is an Aroer in Ephraim (Num. 32:34). Isaiah may be deliberately allowing his spotlight to play around the scene. If Damascus falls the whole alliance is finished. See v. 3.

[3] Probably referring to Aram, which Ephraim saw as its defence, but Isaiah may refer to the way in which Ephraim, bereft of Aram, had no inherent power to resist Assyrian might.

[4] The day when their mistaken policy of security

the glory of Jacob will be impoverished,
and the fatness of his flesh will be wasted.

5. And it will be
like when one gathers, in harvest, the standing grain,
and harvests the ears with his arm.
And it will be
like one gleaning ears in the valley of Rephaim.[5]

6. And there will be left in it gleanings[6]
as with the beating of an olive tree:[7]
two or three berries at the top of a branch,
four or five on its boughs, fruitful tree that it is![8]
This is the word of Yahweh, God of Israel.

'In that day' (2): spiritual awakening

7. In that day
humankind will fix their gaze on their Maker,
and it is to the Holy One of Israel their eyes will look.[9]

8. None will fix their gaze on the altars,
the work of their hands,
and to what their fingers have made they will not look –
the Asherim and the incense-altars.[10]

'In that day' (3): inevitable loss

9. In that day
their cities of fortification
will be like the abandoned areas of forest and summit
which they abandoned[11] in the face of the sons of Israel,
and it will be a desolation.

10. For you[12] have forgotten the God of your salvation,
and the Rock of your fortress you have not remembered.
Therefore
you plant pretty plants,
and you sow foreign shoots.[13]
By day you carefully protect your plants,
and in the morning bring your seed to blossom –
a heaped up harvest in the day of inheritance –
agony incurable!

through alliance with Aram
comes home to roost.

5   Just south of Jerusalem.
Scenes like Ruth 2:2 would
have been familiar.

6   Against all the odds, a
remnant survives.

7   Olives were harvested by being
beaten off with long canes.

8   This is the best that can
be made of the Hebrew
text without altering it.

9   Isaiah is describing the 'gleanings'
of v. 6, the remnant of believers.

10   Items in pagan shrines: Asherim
were wooden poles, of uncertain
significance; 'incense-altars' is no
more than a probable translation.

11   Ruins left, in the time of
Joshua, by the pre-Israelite
inhabitants of the land.

12   'You' is feminine singular. Isaiah
turns to address Ephraim as the
'mother country' of its people.

13   A reference, like 1:29–31,
to gardens cultivated for
worshipping the fertility
gods – here note the deliberate
contrast between the strength
and stability of the rock and the
frailty of the plant and shoot.

The world as a whole

Where power over the world really lies[14]

12. Oh the uproar[15] of many peoples!
    Like the roaring of the seas they are roaring!
    And the crashing of states![16]
    Like the crashing of mighty waters they are crashing!

13. States are crashing like the crashing of many waters! –
    he rebukes each,
    and it flees off into the distance,
    and is pursued like chaff on the mountains before the wind,
    and like tumbleweed before a whirlwind!

14. At evening-time,
    behold, terror;
    before morning, nothing left!
    This is the portion of those who plunder us,
    and the lot proper to those who take us as spoil.

How the world sees itself: under its own diplomacy and organisation

18:1. Ho, land of the winged cricket,
    which is in the area of the rivers of Cush,[17]

2. which is sending envoys by sea –
    in papyrus vessels over the face of the water!
    'Go, swift messengers,
    to any[18] nation long-established and equipped,[19]
    to any people to be feared,
    near and far,
    any nation of vigour and aggressiveness[20]
    whose land rivers separate off.'[21]

A different perspective on the world: the watching, Sovereign God

3. All who live in the world,
    and residents on earth,
    at the lifting up of a banner on the mountains,
    will you see it?
    And at the sounding of a trumpet,
    will you hear it?

14 From 17:12–18:7 Isaiah turns his attention to the world as a whole. In relation to 17:1–11, his purpose is to show the folly of relying on the world with its fortress cities (17:9) and forgetting the fortress-Lord (17:10). But the development of thought in 17:12–18:7 is to ask if the Lord has a purpose for the whole world, to which the prophet answers a triumphant 'yes'; a Zion-centred purpose and a world-remnant expressing devotion to the Lord.

15 See 5:13.

16 'States' gives a separate translation to a different word, *le'ummim*. The verb *la'am* (not used as such in the Old Testament) is said to mean 'to reconcile, bring together'. Commonly *leummim* is translated 'peoples'.

17 A reference to Egypt's frantic diplomacy trying to organise a united front against the rising power of Assyria. But Isaiah names no names because he wants to create a timeless impression of a busy-busy world confident that it can organise its own security.

18 Lit., simply 'a', but contextually 'any' is the obvious intention.

19 Lit., 'drawn out and stripped', i.e., with a long history and ready for action.

20 'Vigour' is a guess, see F. Brown, S. R. Driver, C A Briggs, A *Hebrew & English Lexicon of the Old Testament* (Oxford, 1906), p. 876a; 'aggression' is lit., 'treading down', possibly 'ruthlessness'.

4. For this is what Yahweh has said to me:
   'I will keep quiet and watch,
   in my dwelling,
   like the glowing heat that comes with light,
   like a dew cloud in the heat of harvest.'[22]
5. For before harvest,
   when the blossom is over,
   and the flower is becoming a ripening grape,
   he will cut off the sprigs with pruning knives,
   and the luxuriant branches he will lop and remove.
6. They will be left, all together,
   for the mountain-birds of prey,
   and for the beasts of the earth.
   And the birds of prey will pass the summer on them,
   and all the beasts of the earth will pass the winter on them.[23]

The world-remnant: universal tribute to the Lord in Zion

7. At that time,
   a homage-gift will be brought to Yahweh of Hosts
   from a people long-established and equipped;
   from a people to be feared –
   near and far;
   a nation of vigour and aggressiveness
   whose land rivers separate off,
   to the place of the name of Yahweh of Hosts,
   Mount Zion.

21 i.e., 'accessible by water', capable of being speedily reached by the envoys in their boats. Still the picture of restless urgency and busyness!

22 The unobserved Watcher, present in the very nature of things – like heat where there is light. Not, however, passive or uninvolved: as 'heat' and 'dew' he promotes the 'ripening' of the word to harvest.

23 Historically, referring to the 185,000 Assyrian dead in 37:36, but Isaiah is looking, in terms of this interim fulfilment, to the final divine judgment of the earth.

Thought for the day: Isaiah 17:1–18:7

When we read about not being 'unequally yoked with unbelievers' our minds are conditioned into thinking pretty exclusively about marriage. But in 2 Corinthians 6:14ff Paul makes no such restrictive reference. Indeed he lays down a principle covering all life: morality, influence, spiritual loyalty, a whole life without compromise. Of course, it is impossible to live as if we were out of this world or did not belong here. We can't delay boarding a bus until we find out if the driver is a believer; we have to commit our pennies to some bank or other without cross-questioning the local manager, never mind the Chief Executive Officer. Yet, on the other hand, we must constantly ask ourselves where we are looking for those more personal partnerships and associations which make for a life of well-being. What and whom are we actually relying on, putting our trust in, linking our lives, welfare, and futures with. Ephraim chose Damascus, and sank along with its chosen associate. The powers of the world offered no security, rather the reverse. Time was when 'separation from the world' was a huge, even leading, Christian concern, but, sadly, the idea of 'separation' was brought into disrepute by the points at which our elders and betters sought to make us let the difference show. Today it is a salutary exercise to ask ourselves if we are distinctive enough – the salt and shining light Jesus wants us to be. Would any candid observer see the difference? Are we careful and discriminating enough when it comes to forming relationships, taking on business partners, falling in love? Is our confidence in well-founded insurance and assurance policies, sound investments, goods laid by in store for many days? Or are we as firmly wedded to the God of our salvation and the Rock of our stronghold (17:10) as Isaiah would counsel us to be. What do our neighbours see? Much more, what does the Watcher of 18:4 see?

Day 23 Isaiah 19:1–20:6

Egypt: One world, one people, one God

The fifth place in Isaiah's world panorama (pp. 76–78) is devoted to showing that the God of Israel has something glorious in mind for the whole earth. We saw a hint of this in the world-remnant of 18:7, but now, pondering Egypt, the first enslaver of the Lord's people, the prophet opens up a truly magnificent vista which includes thinking of Egypt as 'my people' (19:25).

The smiting of Egypt

19:1. An oracle on Egypt:
    Behold,
    Yahweh riding on a swift cloud,
    and coming to Egypt!

Religious and social collapse
    And the no-gods[1] of Egypt tremble before him
    and Egypt's heart melts within it.
2.   And I will incite Egypt against Egypt;
    and each will go to war against his brother –
    each against his contemporary –
    city against city,
    kingdom against kingdom.[2]
3.   And the spirit of Egypt will be demoralised[3] within it,
    and its plans I will swallow up.[4]
    And they will seek after the no-gods and the ghosts[5]
    and the mediums and the 'knowing ones'.[6]
4.   And I will consign Egypt into the hand of a harsh overlord,
    and a strong king will rule over them.
    This is the word of the Sovereign, Yahweh of Hosts.

1   See 2:8.

2   The revival of the ancient divisions of Egypt into 'upper' and 'lower' kingdoms.

3   Lit., 'emptied out'.

4   See 3:12.

5   A word only found here, meaning the spirits of the dead.

Economic collapse

5. And the waters will be dried up from the sea,[7]
   and the River itself will become arid and dry,

6. and the rivers will stink:
   Egypt's irrigation canals[8] will run low and become arid.
   Reed and rush wither.

7. The bulrushes by the Nile,
   by the brink of the Nile,
   and all the arable land along the Nile
   will become dry, eroded and be no more.

8. And the fishermen will weep and wail,
   all who cast a hook into the Nile,
   and spread out nets on the face of the water fade away.

9. And those who work at carding flax will reap shame[9]
   and those who weave cotton.

10. And its foundations will be crushed;
    all wage-earners grieved to the heart.[10]

Political collapse

11. What fools the princes of Zoan!
    Pharaoh's wisest advisors!
    Their advice is senseless.
    How can you[11] say to Pharaoh:
    'A son of the wise am I;
    a son of kings of former time!'?[12]

12. Where are they, then, your[13] wise men?
    And, if you please, let them tell you,
    and let them know
    what Yahweh of Hosts has counseled about Egypt.

13. The princes of Zoan prove themselves fools;
    the princes of Noph are deceived;
    they have led Egypt astray –
    the cornerstones of its tribes.

Divine action

14. Yahweh himself has concocted within it a topsy-turvy spirit,
    and they lead Egypt astray in all its works,
    like a drunkard lets himself stray into his own vomit!

6   See 8:19.

7   The proverbial fertility of Egypt's land – and therefore national prosperity – depended totally on the Nile.

8   Lit., '(Little) Niles', plural of the word translated 'Nile' in vv. 7–8, referring to the irrigation channels which carried the Nile-waters over the land.

9   The verb 'to be ashamed' includes the feeling of embarrassment but much more the failure of hopes, the dashing of expectations, hence 'to reap shame'. See 1:29.

10 Since this is the climax of a section dealing with economic collapse, it is not difficult to understand 'foundations' as those on whom the economy is founded – employers, entrepreneurs, wealth-creators. This meaning suits the following and contrasting line's reference to employees.

11 'You' plural, addressing the 'wise men'.

12 Or 'kings of the east'.

13 'You' singular, referring to Pharaoh.

15. And there is nothing Egypt can do,
    such as head or tail, frond or rush,[14] might do.

The healing of Egypt[15]

In that day (1): The fear of the Lord

16. In that day,
    Egypt will become like women,
    and will tremble,
    and become apprehensive of the waving of the hand[16] of
    Yahweh of Hosts
    which he is going to wave over it.

17. And the land of Judah will become to Egypt a cause
    of instability.
    Everyone who has cause to remember it will be apprehensive
    because of the counsel of Yahweh of Hosts
    which he is counselling about it.

In that day (2): One language, one Lord

18. In that day,
    there will be five cities in the land of Egypt,
    speaking the language[17] of Canaan,
    and swearing allegiance to Yahweh of Hosts.
    'City of Destruction' shall be said respecting one.[18]

In that day (3): True religion

19. In that day,
    there will be an altar to Yahweh in the middle of the land
    of Egypt,
    and a pillar by its border to Yahweh.

20. And it will be a sign and a witness to Yahweh of Hosts
    in the land of Egypt:
    when they shriek out to Yahweh because of oppressors,
    he will send to them a saviour, indeed a great one,
    and he will deliver them.

21. And Yahweh will make himself known to Egypt,
    and Egypt will know Yahweh in that day,
    and they will serve with sacrifice and offering,

14 See 9:14.

15 Alongside the world's problems (vs 1–15), Isaiah now sets the Lord's solution (vs 16–25) in a series of five 'in that day' oracles, difficult sometimes to understand and to apply historically to Egypt, but each containing its own message of restoration.

16 Is Isaiah thinking of the consummate ease with which Yahweh disposed of the Assyrian threat in 701 BC (Is 37:36–38)? This could have evoked awe in all who saw it, but to Isaiah it was also a foreshadowing of that reverential regard for Yahweh which would some day bring the Gentile world to him.

17 'lip'.

18 There is no agreement but plenty of guesses what the details of v. 18 mean. What were the five cities and why is one called City of Destruction? But the sequence of thought is plain: following on the spiritual reverence of vv. 16–17, there comes identification with Yahweh and unity with his people in one language.

and they will vow a vow to Yahweh,
and they will fulfil it.
22. And Yahweh will smite Egypt,
smiting[19] and healing,
and they will turn back to Yahweh,
and he will let himself be entreated for them,
and he will heal them.

In that day (4): The world in the harmony of worship
23. In that day,
there will be a causeway
from Egypt to Assyria,
and Assyria will go into Egypt,
and Egypt into Assyria,
and Egypt together with Assyria will serve.[20]

In that day (5): One world, one people, one Lord
24. In that day,
Israel will be a third, in addition to Egypt and to Assyria,
a blessing in the middle of the earth,
25. in that Yahweh of Hosts has blessed each, saying:
'Blessed be my people, Egypt,
and the work of my hands, Assyria,
and my possession, Israel.'

Egypt: A test case, an interim assurance (20:1–6)
As in 14:24–27 Isaiah offers an 'interim fulfilment' –
a prediction relating to events which happen 'before the very
eyes' of his hearers. This is intended to act as an assurance
that the greater and more distant predictions also will be
fulfilled. From 715 BC what is called the 'Ethiopian Dynasty'
ruled Egypt and constantly tried to stir up and co-ordinate
the Palestinian states against Assyria. With this backing
there was a rebellion centred on Ashdod in 713 BC, and in
711 BC the Assyrian official, the Tartan, came to deal with
the rebels. At some time in all this Isaiah had mimed the

[19] The verb 'to smite' as in Exod. 12:23, 27. Then there was only smiting for Egypt, but now Isaiah foresees healing.

[20] The verb 'to serve' is used in the sense of 'to worship' – largely like we speak of holding a 'service'.

fate of those taken captive by Assyria, and thus exposed the weakness of Egypt and the folly of trusting its promises. When his contemporaries saw this acted word of the Lord fulfilled, they could be certain that the promises of 19:24–25 were equally reliable.

20:1 In the year that Tartan came to Ashdod,
      when Sargon, king of Assyria, sent him,
2.   he fought against Ashdod and took it.
      At that time Yahweh spoke by[21] Isaiah, son of Amoz, saying:
      'Go, and undo the sackcloth from your waist,
      and take off your sandals from your feet.'
      And he did so,
      going round stripped and barefoot.[22]
3.   And Yahweh said:
      'Just as my servant, Isaiah, has gone round
      stripped and barefoot,
      for three years –
      a sign and portent about Egypt and about Cush –
4.   so the king of Assyria will lead away
      the captives of Egypt and the exiles of Cush
      young and old,
      stripped and barefoot and bare-buttocked,
      the nakedness of Egypt.'
5.   And they[23] will be shattered and reap shame[24]
      because of Cush, the ground of their confidence,
      and because of Egypt, the object of their admiration.
6.   And the inhabitants of this coastal strip[25] will say,
      in that day:
      'Behold,
      thus it is with our ground of confidence,
      where we fled for help,
      to be delivered from the king of Assyria,
      and, we ourselves, how will we be rescued?'

21   'By the hand of', i.e., 'through the agency of'.

22   When the prophets embodied their message in acts, it was more than a visual aid. It doubled the expression of the potent word of God – verbally and visually – and therefore offered a double guarantee that it must happen.

23   Any in Judah who were inclined to trust Egypt's promises, rely on its supposed strength, and who might be thus seduced into rebellion against Assyria.

24   See 19:9.

25   i.e., all Palestine. On 'iyyim see 41:1.

Thought for the day: Isaiah 19:1–20:6

It is remarkable that even when the Bible seems at its most obscure, there is always something to learn, some thought to cherish and practise. The 'five cities' passage (19:19–22) baffles our poor minds! Whatever is all this about five cities? Yes indeed, very puzzling, but look how it reveals five marks of true religion: (1) First comes the 'altar' (v. 19), the place of substitutionary sacrifice, the blood of reconciliation, where the holy God accepts sinners into his very presence (Heb. 10:19–22). Everything starts at Calvary. (2) Then there is prayer (v. 20), a speaking relationship with the Lord. We cry out in helplessness; he sends a saviour and delivers us. Next, (3) and (4) belong together: revelation and response (v. 21). The Lord makes himself known as we open his holy Word, and, responsively, we take up Samuel's place: Speak, Lord, for your servant hears (1 Sam. 3:9–10). Every revelation of himself that the Lord may make to us brings us yet again to the Cross. That is the proof of hearing a genuine truth of God, always near the Cross, always back to the Cross – 'Dear dying Lamb, thy precious blood will never lose its power' – and not least its power to draw us out in fuller consecration. (5) There is quiet, assured trustfulness under the providential hand of God. It is he who determines life's experiences and plans the twists and turns of our earthly pathway (1 Cor. 10:13). So, says Isaiah, when 'smiting' is needed (v. 22) it is his hand, but always with the intention of 'healing', of bringing us to a new wholeness and fullness of life. Just as the Cross remains central to our intimate life with the Lord, opening and hearing his Word (v. 21), so prayer is the continuing element in our daily experience of his providences. In his chastening his ear is open to our cry; he lets himself be entreated, and sends healing (Ps. 107:19–20).

Day 24 Isaiah 21:1–17

Here Isaiah begins his second series of five oracles. This time they are marked off by cryptic titles (21;1, 11, 13; 22:1) except in the last (23:1), but even there Tyre is plainly used as symbolic of an idea. The sequence is the same as in the first series: the downfall of human attempts to bring order to the world by super-power domination (21:1–10); the long-drawn-out course of history, with no end in sight but the assurance of a coming day (21:11, 12); the Gentile world in travail, trying now the solution of collective security and finding it to fail (21:13–17); the Lord's professing people turning to self-sufficiency – and committing the unpardonable sin (22:1–25); but ultimately even the most 'worldly' nation becoming 'holiness to the Lord' (23:1–18).

The desert by the sea: The Babylon principle; imperialism a false trail (21:1–10)

21:1. An oracle on the Wilderness of the Sea.[1]

The vision received
>   As whirlwinds in the Negeb[2] come one after another,
>   from the wilderness it comes!
>   From a land to be feared!
> 2.   It is a harsh vision that has been declared to me:
>   The deceiver goes on deceiving;[3]
>   and the destroyer goes on destroying.
>   'Up, Elam!
>   Besiege, Media!'

The end envisaged
>   All sighing I have determined to bring to an end.

1   This may refer to the area round the Persian Gulf – the general location of Babylon – but maybe it is better to find the location of what Isaiah sees as sweeping calamities nearer home: storms sweeping through the wilderness of the Dead Sea. In any case, behind the cryptic title the fall of Babylon is the topic of the oracle.

2   The wilderness of South Judah.

3   Almost any interpretation of such allusive material is hazardous, but the verse makes sense if we see it as referring to three protagonists: Assyria, the arch-deceiver, pursues

Reaction (1): horror

3. Therefore
   my stomach is full of nausea;
   pangs have gripped me like the pangs of a woman in labour.
   I am racked by what I hear,
   terrified by what I see;
4. my heart palpitates;[4]
   shuddering alarms me.
   The twilight of my longing[5]
   he has made into trembling for me.[6]

Reaction (2): pleasure

5. The laying of tables,[7]
   the spreading of rugs,
   the eating,
   the drinking!
   'Up, princes!
   Anoint the shield!'[8]

The end accomplished

6. For[9] this is what the Sovereign has said to me:
   'Go, set a lookout
   who will tell what he sees.
7. And when he sees a mounted[10] troop,
   with paired horses,
   a mounted troop on donkeys,
   a mounted troop on camels,
   let him pay close attention,
   great attention!'
8–9. And – lion[11] that he is! – he cried out:
   'On the lookout, Sovereign, I stand,
   constantly, daily,
   and on my duty-watch I post myself
   night after night,
   and – behold now! – it comes,
   a mounted troop of men,
   with paired horses.'

its iniquitous way; Merodach-Baladan of Babylon encourages Elam and Media to join him in an anti-Assyrian coalition; Yahweh has determined to bring all the suffering caused by the wars of the 'great' powers to an end.

4 Lit., 'wanders', the reference may not be to the beating heart but to a mind flitting from one thought to another, unable to concentrate.

5 i.e, 'which I longed for'. Noun *chesheq*, from *chashaq*, cf., on 38:17.

6 'Twilight' (Jer. 13:16), the gathering gloom of divine judgment. Isaiah longed to see the Lord's just judgment on the foes of his people but now its sheer awfulness overwhelms him. Compare the Lord's reactions, 15:9; 16:9.

7 The confident rebels against Assyria celebrate before the event, and anoint their shields as for a holy crusade. How little they know (vv. 6–9)!

8 Is this a high-ranking politician making an after-dinner speech, blithely sending others to war?

9 'For' looks back to Isaiah's terror (v. 4) and explains it.

10 Riding one horse and leading a spare mount. This is the sign the lookout is to watch for.

11 Animal names used to describe human characteristics (Gen. 16:12; 49:21) – here a man of lion-like courage and voice.

And one answered[12] and said:
'Fallen, fallen is Babylon,
  and all the images of its gods
  he has shattered to the ground.'

The message reported
10. Oh you, my crushed one,
    consigned to my threshing floor,[13]
  what I have heard
    directly from Yahweh of Hosts, the God of Israel,
    I have told you.

Silence:[14] Prolonged darkness; hope deferred (21:11–12)

Like the second oracle in each set, the topic is the prospect for the Gentile world. In 14:28–32, Gentiles (contrary to present appearances) are to come under the dominion of the restored and enhanced power of the House of David. In 21:11–12 there is the long-drawn-out period when nothing seems to change. And in 24:21–23, 'after many days', the glorious reign of Yahweh begins in Zion over the kings of the earth.

11. An oracle on Silence.
    To me someone is calling from Seir:
    'O Keeper, what remains of the night?
    O Keeper, what remains of the night?'
12. The Keeper said:
    'Morning is sure to come,
    and also night.
    If you will enquire, enquire.
    Come back again!'

Desert-evening: Gentile needs unsolved by collective security (21:13–17)

In the third oracle of the first set, Moab, under dire threat, could have sheltered under the umbrella of the throne of David but was held back by pride (15:1–16:14; N.B. 16:6–7).

---

12 We are to understand that the watchman did his duty and challenged the newcomers.

13 Lit., 'my crushing and son of my threshing floor'. 'Son of' in its idiomatic use to describe the condition someone is in. Isaiah turns to report to crushed Jerusalem the downfall of Babylon. But it is the Lord who has crushed them, though with the purposeful crushing that produces the final crop.

14 'Silence' (*dumah*) is also a place name in Edom. In this cryptic way Isaiah prepares us for a query coming from Seir, another name for Edom. This more than mysterious oracle (about which we know nothing except what these verses say) records an approach to the prophet from Edom asking about the future. The enquirer is told that a protracted sequence of night and day lies ahead, but the door is left open for further enquiry, plainly hinting that at some point a message of hope will be given.

Would threatened Gentile lands do any better by mutual support? Isaiah thinks not. The historical background is probably still the period of unrest caused by abortive rebellion against Assyria (c. 703 BC), with consequent Assyrian reprisal. The Dedanites are in flight; the Temanites are urged to offer sustenance (vv. 13–15), but the imminent fate of Kedar (vv. 16–17) invites us to conclude it is all in vain.

13. An oracle on Arabian-Eventide.[15]
   In Arabian-Eventide,
   you must lodge in the thickets,
   O caravans of Dedanites.[16]

14. To meet the thirsty bring water,
   you who live in the land of Tema.[17]
   With bread for each they anticipate the wanderer.

15. For from the swords they have wandered off,
   from the unsheathed sword,
   and from the drawn bow,
   and from the heaviness of war.

16. For this is what the Sovereign has said to me:[18]
   Within a year,
   like the years of a hired man,[19]
   all the glory of Kedar[20] will be over,

17. and what is left, a few bowmen,
   warriors of the sons of Kedar,
   will be small,
   for it is Yahweh, the God of Israel, who has spoken.

15 Isaiah, continuing in cryptic mode, contrives a word which forces the reader to hover between the meanings 'Arabia' and 'Evening'. The former announces a subject in line with chs 15–16 and ch. 25 – how will things fare with the Gentile world? The latter continues the 'darkness' theme of vv. 11–12.

16 A southern Sinai Arabian tribe.

17 An oasis city deep in Sinai.

18 Another interim fulfilment. When they see this being fulfilled they will be assured of the truth of Isaiah's oracles about Gentile needs and how they will or will not be met.

19 See 16:14.

20 Nomads of the Syro-Arabian desert.

Thought for the day: Isaiah 21:1–17

When we look at the more frightful aspects of the world around we are rightly horrified and appalled, but, Bible in hand, we should always add, 'But not as frightful as it might be.' And when we see shining good deeds done by people who have no thought of God, then, Bible in hand, we should say, 'How lovely, but how very unnatural.' We live in a world held together by the undeserved kindness and patience of God who is not willing that any should perish, and whose patience makes room for repentance. It is called the 'common grace' of God, the light of Christ still glimmering in the fallen and desperately wicked human heart (John 1:9). But, some day, common grace will be withdrawn, and wickedness will be unfettered. Death will reign – including the death of every kindly thought and helpful deed; self-concern will be rampant, hateful and hating. Even with the utmost stretch of our imaginations we cannot sound the depths of sin in a world finally become the unrestrained victim of its own choices, left to itself, without God, without common grace. Isaiah caught a glimpse of this in the overthrow of Babylon. It was a thing he wanted, because he desired freedom from overlordship for his people: Oh yes, Lord, please deliver your dear people; end the enslavement, the cruelty, the suffering. Don't we rightly raise the same cry for oppressed brothers and sisters? But suddenly Isaiah saw the reverse side of the coin; suddenly he saw what it would be like when the judgment of God came in all its justness and exactitude, when holiness at last stepped out of the shadows and was displayed in the full reality of a sin-hating God. He was left racked, terrified, palpitating, shuddering. He discovered what Hebrews would later put into words, that 'it is a fearful thing to fall into the hands of the living God' (Hebrews 10:31).

Day 25   Isaiah 22:1–25

The Valley of Vision: Jerusalem – the unforgiveable sin (22:1–25)

The fourth place in each series of oracles is given to the Lord's people (see pp. 76–78). Ephraim chose security by alliance (17:1–18:7) and fell with its chosen guardian; Jerusalem now chooses the way of self-sufficiency – cannibalising its houses to strengthen its walls, boring its water-tunnel – only to find that this is the sin that cannot be forgiven. Verses 15–25 offer an illustration of the same sin on an individual scale, with the same outcome. Isaiah 26:1–19 is the fourth oracle in the final series: security exists only in the strong city of salvation.

Questionable joy

22:1. An oracle on the Valley of Vision.[1]

> What has got into you, then, that you have gone up, everyone of you,
> to the housetops.[2]

2.   Full of hub-bub,
>   noisy city,
>   exultant town!

Coming calamity

> Your slain, not slain by the sword,[3]
> and not dead in battle.

3.   All your chiefs have scattered together,
>   caught without a shot being fired.[4]
>   All yours who could be found were caught together,
>   fled into the distance!

4.   Therefore
>   I said:

[1]   The oracle turns out to be about Jerusalem. Typically of this second series, Isaiah uses a cryptic title but adds no explanation.

[2]   Housetops were also a place of communal lament (15:3); here of city-wide joy.

[3]   With the sort of leap that dramatic poetry can make, Isaiah suddenly imposes on the mood of popular hilarity what he sees as the reality, a doomed city. 'Slain but not by the sword' points to siege conditions, with death through starvation and disease.

[4]   Lit., 'without a bow', taken without a fight; or 'unarmed', with no intention of putting up a fight, concerned only to run.

'Stop staring at me.
I must indulge bitter weeping.
Do not be in a hurry to comfort me
regarding the spoliation[5] of the daughter of my people.'

5   See 13:6.

Explanation: a day the Lord has instigated

5. For it is a day of unrest and trampling and uncertainty
   belonging to the Sovereign, Yahweh of Hosts
   in the Valley of Vision:
   they bring walls crashing down;
   and the uproar reaches to the mountains.

6. Elam has taken up the quiver,
   with cavalry – men – horses –
   and Kir has bared the shield,

7. and the choicest of your valleys are full of cavalry,
   and they have positioned the horses carefully at the gate.

Past choices

8. When he removed Judah's protective cover,[6]
   you looked,
   in that day,
   to the arsenal of the House of the Forest[7]

9. and the gaps in the city of David –
   you saw that they were numerous;
   and you collected water in the lower pool,

10. and you counted the houses of Jerusalem,
    and you demolished the houses to fortify the wall.

11. And you made a reservoir between the double-walls
    for the waters of the old pool.[8]
    And you did not look to him who had made it,
    and him who had fashioned it long since
    you did not see.

Culpable joy; the unforgiveable sin

12. And the Sovereign, Yahweh of Hosts, called,
    in that day,

6   During the Assyrian Invasions, c. 701 BC, Judah was supposedly 'covered' by a covenant with Egypt (see 28:14–15). Sennacherib defeated the Egyptian Army, removing any hope of 'covering' from that quarter. 'He' (v. 8) could refer to Sennacherib, but more probably to Yahweh who would not tolerate that his people be protected by any other than himself.

7   See 1 Kings 7:2 ff. We do not know its function in Solomon's day, but by Isaiah's time it had evidently become an arsenal.

8   Jerusalem's water-supply was its vulnerable feature – otherwise it was virtually impregnable. Water came from the spring of Gihon, outside the city (1 Kings 1:33; 2 Chron. 32:30) along an overground conduit (Isa. 7:3) into

for weeping and for mourning,
and for baldness and for wearing sackcloth,

13. and behold
happiness and rejoicing,
killing oxen and slaughtering sheep,
eating flesh and drinking wine –
eating and drinking for tomorrow we die!

14. And in my hearing Yahweh of Hosts has revealed himself:
'I swear
this iniquity[9] will not be atoned[10] for you until you die!'
the Sovereign, Yahweh of Hosts, has said.

Illustration: A case study; an interim fulfilment; a tale of two men[11]

The Lord's opposition to Shebna

15. This is what the Sovereign, Yahweh of Hosts, has said:
Go quickly to this lackey,[12] Shebna, who is over the house:[13]
'What have you here,[14]
and whom have you here,
that you have carved out for yourself here a grave?'
Carving out his grave on high!
Cutting in the rock a dwelling for himself!

17. Behold,
Yahweh is about to hurl you right away, big man –
wrapping you right up –

18. parcelling you up like a parcel,
like a ball, into a wide-reaching land.
There you will die,
and there the chariots of your glory will be,
you blot on your master's house!

19. And I will oust you from your post,
and from your status he[15] will tear you down.

The Lord's plan for Eliakim

20. And it will be, in that day,
I will call my servant, Eliakim, son of Hilkiah,[16]

the 'old pool'. Hezekiah cut a tunnel from Gihon to the 'lower pool' inside the city walls.

9 See 1:2.

10 See 6:7.

11 Isaiah sees in the king's chief minister, Shebna, the essentially self-sufficient man – making his own way, looking after number one, needing no outside assistance – the spirit of Jerusalem incarnate in one man. His predicted downfall will be a foretaste of the downfall of self-sufficient Jerusalem. And if Shebna's replacement, Eliakim, fall into the same error, he too will fall.

12 The feminine form of this word is used of David's nursemaid (1 Kings 1:2, 4). Here it catches the yes-man, fawning, attitude by which Shebna feathered his own nest.

13 cf., 1 Kings 4:6; 18:3, etc.; a position of 'prime minister'.

14 Identical words used in v. 1, but not as easy to pin down in meaning. Is Isaiah saying 'What right have you to your position and how many in fact support your claim?' Or is he saying – you have neither personal claim to your position nor family right?

15 We use the indefinite 'they' where for some reason the subject cannot or may not be

21. and I will dress him in your robe,
    and with your girdle I will make him strong,
    and your dominion I will put into his hand,
    and he will become a father
    to those living in Jerusalem and to the house of Judah.
22. And I will put the key of the House of David on his shoulder:
    he will open and none can shut,
    and shut and none can open.
23. And I will fasten him like a peg in a secure place.[17]

Warning
    Should, however, he become a throne of glory for his
    father's house,
24. and they hang on him all the glory of his father's house,[18]
    offspring and issue[19] –
    all the smallest vessels,
    vessels like bowls and all sorts of vessels like flagons[20] –
25. in that day
    (this is the word of Yahweh of Hosts)
    the peg fastened in a sure place will give way,
    and be chopped down and fall,
    and the burden which was on it will be cut down.
    For it is Yahweh who has spoken.

16 given, Hebrew uses a third
    person singular indefinite, 'he',
    equivalent in effect to a passive
    verb, 'you will be torn down'.

16 36:3; 37:2.

17 A fine picture of a strong,
    reliable ruler giving stability
    to the whole fabric of society
    like a firmly planted tent-
    peg holds a tent in place.

18 The corruption of power: the
    tent-peg of stability changes
    into a peg for hanging things
    on – the exercise of nepotism.
    This is the same sin of human self-
    sufficiency on an individual scale.

19 i.e., present prosperity (offspring)
    and future development (issue).

20 Isaiah lets his imagination run
    on in the development of his
    illustration – everything in the
    household coming to hang on
    the one peg! What a picture of
    'hangers-on' and of nepotism!

Thought for the day: Isaiah 22:1–25

How extraordinary to say Hezekiah's Tunnel is the unforgiveable sin! Was it not rather one of the engineering marvels of the day? It was 330 metres in a direct line from the Gihon Spring to the city, but the tunnel was much longer since it twisted and turned to avoid difficulties or follow fissures. Gangs of workmen started at opposite ends and (amazingly) met in the middle – and by this one dazzling achievement Jerusalem's single vulnerable point (its overland water supply) was rectified and, perched on its hill, surrounded by fortified walls, the city was at last secure. But thereby hangs the real tale. Jerusalem was the city the Lord chose for his people and for himself (Deut. 12:11; 1 Kings 8:29; Ps. 132:13). Did he not know all about its water-supply when he chose it? Did he make a mistake? Was he culpable of exposing his people to a deadly risk? Since the answers to these questions is 'No', then put the matter the other way round: Did he not knowingly choose a city with a vulnerable water supply so that living in his city actually required an attitude and commitment of faith that what he thus chose he would also himself safeguard? It is no sin to improve our amenities, nor is it wrong to allow human (God-given) ingenuity to devise better technological marvels, but it is a sin to depart from a position of simple, uncomplicated, trustful faith, and to replace it with man-made devices and securities. Where the Lord has made promises our calling is to trust that he will keep his word, and to pray, and look to him that he will do so. The greatest of sins is to abandon the way of faith, because to do so dislocates our relationship of trust in our God, and cuts us off from the saving benefits – including the blessing of forgiveness of sins – which are only ours by faith.

Day 26 Isaiah 23:1–18

For this fifth oracle in the second series (pp. 76–78) Isaiah suddenly abandons his cryptic titles and openly addresses the great commercial empire of Tyre. The change is deliberate: the Lord's rule of the world touches on real and known people, places and practices. It is in this world he works his marvels of sovereign government and direction, and from this world that he will be glorified in the final outcome of things. Commerce brought Tyre into the life of the Lord's people (1 Kings 5:6), and it stayed to corrupt (1 Kings 11:5), but even Tyre will one day enter the realm of holiness!

Tyre: Holiness to the Lord (23:1–18)

Lament for Tyre

23:1. An oracle on Tyre:
> Wail, ships of Tarshish,[1]
> for it has been devastated –
> no haven, no harbour.[2]
> From the land of Kittim[3] it has been revealed to them.

2. Be silent,
> dwellers on the Isle,[4]
> which the merchant community of Sidon,
> traversing the sea, replenished.

3. In many waters –
> the seed of Shichor, the harvest of the Nile[5] –
> was its profit,
> and it was the source of revenue of the nations.

4. Reap shame,[6] Sidon,
> for the sea has spoken, the fortress of the sea,[7] saying:
> 'I have not travailed; and I have not given birth;

1 Usually understood as ships capable of the long voyage to 'Tarshish' in Spain, the largest and strongest ships in the fleet.

2 Lit., 'no house, no entrance'.

3 Isaiah never hesitated to give free rein to his imagination. The great ships making for Tyre are met by a message from Cyprus (Kittim) that their intended land-fall no longer exists. It is a vivid pictorial way of sketching the wide-ranging results of the fall of the commercial empire.

4 Tyre was an island-fortress as well as a mainland city. On *'iyyim*, 41:1.

and I have not nurtured young men,
reared young women.'

5. When the news reaches Egypt they will writhe in pain
   as when the news reached Tyre.[8]
6. Cross to Tarshish.[9]
   Wail, you who live in the Isle.
7. Is this your exulting one[10]
   whose antiquity is from the days of antiquity,
   whose feet used to carry her far off to live as
   an immigrant?[11]
8. Who planned this against Tyre, the king-maker,[12]
   whose merchants were princes,
   her traders earth's honoured ones?
9. It is Yahweh of Hosts who planned it,
   to defile the pride of all beauty,
   to belittle all earth's honoured ones.
10. Traverse your land like the Nile, daughter of Tarshish.[13]
    There is no restraint[14] any more.
11. His hand he has stretched out over the sea.
    He made kingdoms tremble.
    It is Yahweh who has commanded regarding Canaan,
    to destroy its strong points.
12. And he has said:
    'You will never exult again,
    crushed one, daughter of Sidon.
    To Kittim get up and cross.
    Even there you will have no rest.'
13. Behold the land of the Chaldeans –
    this non-existent people;
    Assyria has made it over[15] to the desert beasts.
    They raised up, each his siege-towers;[16]
    they stripped its palaces;
    he made it a fallen ruin.
14. Wail, ships of Tarshish,
    for your fortress has been devastated.

5   'Shichor' was a general name for Egyptian waterways. The unfailing Nile-waters made Egypt proverbially fertile, the granary of the world. Tyrian/Sidonian merchants were involved in Egyptian export trade.

6   See 19:9.

7   As a seafaring nation, the sea was Tyre's strength and source of security. If the sea spoke against it, all was lost. Isaiah's imaginative way of saying Tyre is doomed.

8   Isaiah can be so crisply allusive that it is not easy to expand his words into a plain meaning: here 'According as to Egypt they will writhe in pain like news to Tyre'. The sea is still the speaker. Egypt will be as distraught over the sea's verdict as was Tyre itself.

9   Isaiah's imagination is still working full-blast as he pictures Tyre's refugees heading for Tarshish – the route pioneered by commerce becomes the route for flight!

10 'Your' is feminine, referring to the city, Tyre.

11 Tyre was not interested in conquest, only in setting up trading posts, hence 'living as an immigrant'.

12 The Tyrians remained immigrants but sought to put their nominees into places of power.

13 Ezek. 29:3, 9 uses the Nile as a symbol of independence and self-sufficiency. This is probably the idea here: now Tyre is gone, Tarshish can enjoy independence.

The future for Tyre[17]

15. And it will be,
    in that day,
    Tyre will remain forgotten for seventy years,
    like the days of one king.[18]
    At the end of the seventy years
    it will be for Tyre like the song of the prostitute:
16. 'Take a harp.
    Tour the city, forgotten prostitute.
    Play good music.
    Sing a great deal so as to be remembered.'
17. And it will be,
    at the end of the seventy years,
    Yahweh will visit Tyre,
    and she will return to her money-making,[19]
    and she will work as a prostitute with the kingdoms of the
    earth.
18. And her trade and her money-making will be
    'Holiness to Yahweh' –
    not stored or hoarded away,
    but for those who live in Yahweh's presence will her trade be
    for eating sufficiently and for choice clothing.[20]

---

14 In Job 12:21; Ps. 109:19 this word (*metsach*) means 'belt', here used metaphorically of the confining influence and power of Tyre.

15 Lit., 'founded it for'. The devastation wrought by Assyria in southern Mesopotamia was notorious in the ancient world. 'Chaldea' is a frightening example of what Assyria is capable of.

16 A speculative translation.

17 Another 'interim fulfilment', something in the near future to be watched for. Sennacherib laid mainland Tyre waste in 701 BC but by 630 BC the steep decline of Assyrian power made way for commercial Tyre to revive.

18 Ancient kings kept daily journals of events. The Lord, likewise, itemises the days and notes when his appointed time comes.

19 The word used in Deut. 23:18 for earnings by prostitution.

20 Tyre was trading with the returned exiles (Ezra 3:7) but Isaiah sees this – as, later, he sees the Return itself – as a symbol of the fulfilment of the promise of the riches of all the 'Tyres' of the world coming as a dedicated offering to Yahweh (60:5).

Thought for the day: Isaiah 23:1–18

'Holiness to the Lord' is one of the most honoured descriptions in the whole Bible. It was inscribed on the pure gold medallion which adorned the High Priest's brow. In the case of the rather pathetic Aaron (Exod. 28:36) it constituted a stark contrast between his status and his state, but pointed forward to the total purity, dedication and holiness which was actually true of the Lord Jesus and fitted him to be the High Priest we need (Heb. 7:26–27): the Lamb of God and our sin-bearing Saviour – as Exodus 12:5 requires, 'your lamb must be perfect'. And, since we are priests – indeed High Priests (Heb. 10:19–20) – in Christ, are we not to wear garments 'for glory and beauty' (Exod. 28:40) – the most glorious garments of all, as we 'put on the Lord Jesus Christ' (Rom. 13:14)? Isaiah would have been fully aware of all this when he wrote the sacred words 'Holiness to the Lord', but how different, and how serious the new direction in which he sent them on their way! Tyre stands for what has since been called 'the unacceptable face of capitalism': the covetousness which never can have enough money; the exploitative use of wealth to secure influence and manipulate people and affairs; the not too scrupulous ways in which the money supply was kept flowing (cf., Amos 1:9–10). And now it is *that* – that money which is to be 'Holiness to the Lord'. In a word, holiness – the holiness the Lord seeks – is (of course) everything that makes us like Jesus, but it includes (says Isaiah) our money. Whatever, in our life without Jesus, has been tainted by the world, corrupted and misused – or gained – by our sinfulness, everything that characterised the old life, must now be rescued, re-orientated, dedicated. It must wear as its banner and declaration of intent the gold medallion, 'Holiness to the Lord', just like our forebears at Sinai poured the gold of Egypt (Exod. 12:35–36) into the treasury of the Tabernacle (Exod. 25:2–8; 35:4–9).

Day 27   Isaiah 24:1–20

With chapter 24 we come to the third set of five visions of the future, see pages 76–78 above. In the first set Isaiah looked at the world around him; in the second, using cryptic titles, he probed forward but found the same features dominating the future as he had seen in the present. Now he is looking right to the End. There are no divisions (everything is merging into a single vision), but the same five aspects emerge: the collapse of the 'world-city', the human attempt to organise the world into one 'global village' (24:1–20); at long last, the Lord's reign over the kings of the earth in Zion (24:21–23); Gentile problems at last solved in the great messianic feast (25:1–12); the Lord's people secure in the strong city of salvation (26:1–21); and the joy of the world-vineyard (27:1–13).

The end of the world-city (24:1–20)

Earth devastated: divine action

24:1. Behold

    Yahweh is going to devastate the earth and lay it waste.

    And he will distort its surface,

    and scatter its inhabitants.

2.   And it will be

    like people like priest,[1]

    like servant like his master,

    like maid like her mistress,

    like buyer like seller,

    like lender like borrower,

    like creditor just as the one he gives credit to.

3.   The earth will be utterly devastated and utterly despoiled,

    for it is Yahweh who has spoken this word.

[1] Precisely as we say 'like father like son', here a doom embraces all alike, on the religious, domestic, and commercial scenes.

The Earth withered: explanation

4.   The earth has mourned, wilted;
      the world has grown feeble, wilted.[2]
      The top people of the earth have grown feeble,

5.   and the earth itself has become polluted under its inhabitants,
      for they have transgressed laws,
      changed statutes,
      annulled the eternal covenant.[3]

6.   Therefore
      a very curse has eaten the earth
      and those living in it are guilty.
      Therefore
      those living on earth have diminished,[4]
      and but few of mortal mankind[5] is left.

The song stilled: the fall of the city

7.   The new wine mourns,
      the vine has grown feeble;
      all those rejoicing in heart groan.

8.   The delight of the timbrils has ceased;
      the noise of those exulting has ceased;
      the delight of the harp has ceased.

9.   They do not drink wine with song;
      intoxicants are sour to those drinking them.

10. The City of Meaninglessness[6] has been broken up;
      every house is locked against entrance.

11. Outside, screaming over the wine;
      all rejoicing has reached evening;
      the delight of the earth has gone into captivity.

12. In the City desolation remains,
      and to destruction the gate has been crushed.

The song overheard: the Lord's gleanings

13. For this is how it will be,
      in the midst of the earth,
      among the peoples:
      like the beating off of olives,[7]

2   Where Hebrew uses two verbs side by side, without a conjunction, the second carries the main thought and the first an adverbial qualification. It does not seem possible always to reflect this usage in English and most simply put an 'and' between the verbs.

3   We could translate 'the laws … the statute'. The absence of the definite article may be intended to signify 'every law' or 'law as such'. 'Statute' translates *choq*, something carved in the rock so as to be permanent, unchangeable. On 'covenant' cf., Gen. 9:16.

4   'Diminished' is an uncertain translation. The more obvious 'burn (with anger)' does not seem suitable. Should we find here a form of *chawar*, 'to grow pale', used in 29:22? This meaning is suitable but it would require an adjustment of the Hebrew text.

5   See 8:1; 13:7.

6   'Meaninglessness' translates *tohu*, which Gen. 1:2 uses to describe the material substrata of creation before the Creator gave it shape, order, light, life, and meaning. Jeremiah (4:23–26) uses the same word when he foresees creation under judgment, bereft of light, stability, living creatures, ordered growth and organised society. Isaiah sees the world as a city (man's greatest effort at organised society) where 'nothing adds up' and where, under judgment, everything comes crashing down – like Babel, humankind's first city,

like gleanings as soon as the vintage is finished.

14. These are the ones who raise their voice;
    they shout aloud over the majesty of Yahweh;
    they scream with excitement[8] from the west.
15. Therefore,
    in eastern light,[9]
    glorify Yahweh;
    in the coastlands[10] of the sea,
    the name of Yahweh, the God of Israel.
16. From the wings of the earth songs we have heard,
    'Beauty belongs to the Righteous One.'[11]

Personal wasting away: grief over the ultimate consequence of sin[12]

And I said:
    'I shrivel away, I shrivel away!
    Woe is me!
    Deceivers are determined to deceive;
    With deception deceivers determine to deceive.
17. Apprehension and pit and trap are upon you,
    you who live on earth.
18. And it will be,
    the fugitive from the voice of apprehension
    will fall into the pit;
    and whoever gets up out of the pit
    will be caught in the trap.'

Earth devastated: moral/spiritual causation

For the very windows on high will be opened[13]
    and the foundations of the earth will shake.
19. The earth will be utterly broken in pieces.
    The earth will be utterly split apart.
    The earth will slip in all directions.
20. The earth will stagger this way and that like a drunk,
    and sway about like a shed:
    its rebellion will lie heavily on it
    and it will fall and never rise again.

7   See 17:6.

8   The verb which provided the
     noun 'screaming' in v. 11.
     There giving vent to anguish;
     here to exhilaration. The
     words 'with excitement' are
     inserted to secure this sense.

9   Lit., 'the lights'; 'the sea'
     (a Palestinian orientation,
     referring to the Mediterranean,
     signifies westward).

10   See 41:1.

11   Or simply 'to the righteous'; the
     beauty Yahweh gives to the people
     he 'gleans' from the whole earth,
     the believing remnant on whom
     he bestows his righteousness.

12   Exactly as 21:3–4 where also
     Isaiah expresses his revulsion
     at the outworking judgment.

13   cf., Gen. 7:11.

with its meaningless gabble and
its unfinished tower (Gen. 11:1–9).

Thought for the day: Isaiah 24:1–20

To say the world we live in 'doesn't add up' is a pretty accurate description. Hardly a day passes but we ask why this or that has happened, why it has happened to him/her/them/me/us, why now, why so prolonged – and so on. This is what Ecclesiastes meant by saying 'all is vanity' (1:2; etc). Trying to explain the world and what happens in it is like trying to grab a handful of wind! Bible in hand, we know that this is because a higher wisdom than ours rules all, a more complete justice than we can bring to bear. An almighty power is having its way, and a total love, quite beyond our understanding, is directing everything, parcelling out experiences, determining times and seasons. But as regards the sort of logical descriptions of things that the unbelieving mind seeks, the world around us simply 'does not add up'. From the Tower of Babel in Genesis 11 to the United Nations mankind has been striving after a world that is safe, organised, neat, unified, fortified against threat. This is a correct aim, and we should constantly feel obliged to obey the apostolic command to pray for 'kings and all in authority that we may lead a quiet and peaceable life' (1 Tim. 2:2). At the same time, we know that sin is ever divisive, Satan is ever sowing weeds in the best soil and seed, and humankind's best endeavours for peace can suddenly become literally explosive. Our security is not in human organisation nor national strength nor personal insurance policies and sound banking, nor in our ability to 'explain', but only in the hand of Jesus, enfolded in the hand of the Father (John 10:28). Within that security, while the changes and chances of the world may touch us (but only by his will, 1 Cor. 10:13), they can never dislodge us, and one day we will be there – we, the Lord's gleanings from the wide earth – when the kingdoms of the world have become the kingdom of our Lord and of his Messiah (Rev. 11:15).

Day 28 Isaiah 24:21–25:12

In the first set of oracles (see pp. 76–78), Isaiah provided titles drawn from the map of the world around him; in the second set he provided titles again, most of them cryptic, implying that, as he probed forward, the world was in principle the same and, through what he saw around him, he could sketch the unnamed future. Now, in the third set of oracles, there are no headings, but, following changes of topic we find the same five sections and the same principles at work in the world right up to the End. In this section we have Isaiah's second and third topics: the future glorious reign of the Lord in Zion (24:21–23); the fulfilment of the Davidic promise of 14:28–32, and, coming as it does, 'after many days' the termination of the prolonged day and night sequence of 21:11–12. In 25:1–12, Gentile needs are at last met in Mount Zion at the great messianic banquet. This is the shelter that Moab, in pride, refused (15:1–16:13), and a go-it-alone spirit of pride still shuts Moab out (25:10b–12); likewise Zion provides the blessed solution for the Gentile world that self-help and mutual reliance failed to do (21:13–17).

Ultimately … the King (24:21–23)

24:21. And it will be,
    in that day,
    Yahweh will attend to the hosts of the height in the height,
    and to the kings of the earth on the earth.
22.   And they will be fully collected together,
    each one bound, into a dungeon,[1]
    and they will be detained under detention:
    after many days they will be attended to!
23.   And the white (moon) will be disgraced,

1   Lit., 'pit' (*bor*), but here, as, e.g., Jer 37:16, of a 'dungeon'.

and the (sun's) heat[2] will reap shame,
    for Yahweh of Hosts will certainly be king
    in Mount Zion and in Jerusalem,
    and in the presence of his elders,
    in glory.

Salvation; the world gathered on Mount Zion (25:1–12)

Individual testimony to deliverance[3]

25:1. Yahweh,
    You are my God.
    I will exalt you,
    give thanks for your name,
    for you have accomplished wonderful plans,[4]
    from long before,
    in total faithfulness.
2. For you have made it, from being a city,[5] into a heap,
    a fortified town into a fallen ruin.
    An aliens' castle no longer a city;
    for ever it will remain unbuilt.
3. Therefore
    strong people will give you glory;
    even the town of terrifying nations itself will fear you,
4. for you have proved to be a fortress for the poor,[6]
    a fortress for the vulnerable[7] in his every adversity,
    refuge from inundation,
    shade from heat,
    when the wind of the terrifying
    was like an inundation against a wall.
5. Like heat in an arid land,
    the clamour of the aliens you subdue –
    heat by the shade of a cloud.
    The music-making of the terrifying ones falls low.

The banquet: The Lord providing, excluding

6. And Yahweh of Hosts will make
    for all the peoples,

2 'The white (one)', poetical synonym for the moon; 'the heat', synonym for the sun. 'Disgraced…reap shame' – as if their claim to be the brightest things by night and by day are exposed as a sham in the greater light of the divine glory.

3 The worldwide singing of 24:14–16a is now heard more clearly. The pilgrimage of the 'gleanings' of the world has reached its goal in Zion; the King is in his city (24:23), the table is spread (25:6).

4 Lit., 'you have done a wonder, plans/counsels'. The two nouns that gave us 'Wonderful Counsellor' in 9:6 are here.

5 i.e., 'the city of meaningless' – the 'world-city' – of 24:10.

6 See 10:2. Both 'poor' and 'vulnerable' are in the singular, and, while this can be seen as a collective use, it nevertheless points to the individuality of the Lord's protective care.

7 See 14:30.

on this mountain,
a banquet of rich food,
a banquet of matured wines,
rich food, full of nourishment,
matured wines fully clarified.

7. And on this mountain
   he will swallow up[8]
   the expansive covering that covers all the peoples,
   and the web woven over all the nations.
8. He will swallow up death in perpetuity,
   and the Sovereign, Yahweh, will wipe the tears from
   upon all faces,
   and his people's reproach[9] he will remove from upon
   all the earth.
   For it is Yahweh who has spoken.

Communal testimony

9. And each will say,
   in that day,
   'Behold,
   this is our God!
   We have waited confidently for him to save us.
   This is Yahweh for whom we have waited confidently.
   We will exult and rejoice in his salvation'.
10. For Yahweh's hand will rest on this mountain.

The midden: the other side of the coin

    And Moab will be trampled down in its place,
    like straw is trampled down into a manure heap.
11. And he will spread out his hands in the middle of it
    just as a swimmer[10] spreads them out to swim.
    And he will demean his pride along with the cunning
    of his hands.
12. And the fortification of the top-security of your walls
    he has determined to bring down, lay low,
    bring to the ground, right to the dust.

8   See 3:12.

9   All those ways in which, on earth, the experience of the Lord's people falls below what might have been expected and for which they receive the taunts of the world; e.g., Ps. 42:3.

10 Even in this extremity Moab still remains self-reliant. Could there be a better illustration of 'do-it-yourself' salvation than swimming? 'He will demean' could refer to Yahweh who will not permit any to be his own saviour, but can also be Moab: self-salvation is its own destruction.

Thought for the day: Isaiah 24:21–25:12

The Lord Jesus pre-viewed the messianic banquet in the feeding miracles (Mark 6:30–44; 8:1–9), and even more particularly in the Parable of the Ten Bridesmaids (Matt. 25:1–13), where the wedding feast, with the welcomed guests securely shut in with the Bridegroom (Matt. 25:10), anticipates the marriage feast of the Lamb (Rev. 19:1–9). Reading and re-reading Isaiah 25:6–9 it is impressed on us that this is one of the Bible's high spots: ultimate, eternal reality is a banquet, with no expense spared, every provision made and, lest there should be anything to mar our enjoyment of it, every tear dried (cf., Rev. 7:17). And this is no mere flight of prophetic fancy or some 'wouldn't it be nice' pie in the sky. It is confirmed by Jesus and reiterated by one who was, so to speak, allowed to be there, the seer John caught up to heaven and shown its delights. Isaiah gives us three aspects of the heavenly banquet to ponder: first, it is characteristic of our God to have such an end in view, to bring us to the enjoyment of it, and to spread all his heavenly riches out for our participation – 'This is our God' (v. 9a). Secondly, this is what salvation is. Eternal bounty, the pure hilarious joy of the Lamb's wedding breakfast, 'the shout of them that triumph, the song of them that feast.' 'We exult in his salvation' (v. 9). Thirdly, it is a matter of confident and patient expectancy, a call to the upward and onward gaze, the eye trained on the skies for the appearing of the Son of Man, patient to wait, imminent and urgent in expectancy, sure in outcome. Twice Isaiah has felt it necessary to assure us of the divine authenticity of what he says: first regarding the winding up of this present sorry order of things (24:3), and then again regarding the utter bliss of the envisaged eternity (25:8), lest we fail to take seriously either aspect of the 'terminus', 'This is what Yahweh has said.'

Day 29   Isaiah 26:1–21

The fourth section in each series is devoted to the people of God and their security. Israel (17:1ff) sought safety in an alliance; Jerusalem (22:1ff) tried to make itself safe by fortifying its walls (at the expense of its houses) and securing its water-supply. But neither the way of worldly reliance nor of self-reliance succeeded. The Lord's people are only safe in his strong city of salvation. Within its walls they are preserved and can wait expectantly and confidently.

Secure in peace

26:1. In that day,

> this song will be sung in the land of Judah:
> A city of strength we have.
> Salvation he will set up:
> walls and surrounding rampart.

2.   Open the gates
> so that a righteous nation may come in,
> one preserving fidelity.[1]

3.   The one of sustained frame of mind
> you will preserve in true, unbroken peace,[2]
> because in you trust is reposed.

4.   Trust[3] in Yahweh for ever,
> for in himself Yah[4] Yahweh is a truly eternal rock.

Down to the dust: the lofty city trampled[5]

5.   For he has brought down the inhabitants of the height,[6]
> the city with top-security!
> He lays it low, totally and utterly,[7] on the ground,
> brings it right to the dust.

1   'Open' is a plural imperative, a call to the gatekeepers/ watchmen to admit those who are imagined as approaching. The ground of admission is their status of righteousness, of being right with God, and the evidence of that status is fidelity.

2   Lit., 'peace, peace'. Hebrew uses repetition to affirm that the subject in question is the 'real thing', and that it is the total truth about the matter in hand.

3   Another plural imperative. Those who enter the city

6.   The foot tramples on it,
     the feet of the downtrodden,[8]
     the steps of the poor.

The divinely smoothed pathway

7.   The path each righteous one has is perfectly level;
     you, O Upright One, level the track for each righteous one.[9]
8.   Why, yes, it is in the path of your judgments,[10]
     Yahweh, we have awaited you –
     for your name and your memorial[11]
     with longing of soul.
9.   With my soul I have longed for you in the night,
     indeed, in my inmost spirit I look for your dawning,
     for when your judgments touch the earth
     those who live in the world learn righteousness.

Impenetrable blindness[12]

10. Let the wicked be shown favour –
     he never learns righteousness!
     In straightforward circumstances[13] he goes wrong,
     and never does he see the majesty of Yahweh.
11. Yahweh, when your hand is uplifted
     never do they perceive it.
     Your jealous zeal for your people
     they will perceive – and reap shame.
     Yes indeed, the fire your adversaries deserve will eat
     them up.[14]

Divinely ordained peace[15]

12. It is you, Yahweh, who appoint peace for us,
     for indeed all things that have been done for us
     you have accomplished for us.
13. Yahweh our God,
     sovereigns other than you have lorded it over us,
     through you alone have we kept your name in remembrance.
14. Dead! They will not live!

4   See 12:2.

5   This could, of course, continue the song announced in v. 1. On the other hand vv. 5ff can be seen as offering comment on the situation the song sketches.

6   See 24:4 (where the same word appears as 'topmost'), and 24:21 as background to this reference to the fall of the high city. Part of the security of salvation is the defeat of every opposition. Isaiah 26:21 shows that this overthrow, here seen as past, is in fact yet to come. The past tense teaches the Lord's people to live in the present certainty of an achieved victory which is yet to be consummated. The lofty city symbolises the world organised by human wisdom and without God.

7   The verb 'lays it low' is used twice (with slight variation of form), an instance of the idiom of repetition used to express a perfect example of its kind and the total truth of the matter. See v. 3 above; also 3:1.

8   See 3:14.

9   In each case 'righteous' is singular, treated here as individualising. It refers, as often, to being 'right with God'.

10   'Judgment' (*mishpat*) arises from *shaphat*, 'to make authoritative decisions'. 'Judgment' is, therefore, both what is authoritatively right and just, and also the correct decision in any given case.

Shadowy ones![16] They will not rise up!
Therefore you have visited and destroyed them,
and made every memory of them perish.

15. You have added to the nation, Yahweh;
you have added to the nation;
you have brought glory to yourself;
you have extended all the limits of the land.

Out of the dust[17]

16. Yahweh, in distress they visited you,
poured out a whisper
when they experienced your chastening.

17. Like a pregnant woman
who is near to giving birth,
writhes, shrieks in her pains,
so have we been in your presence, Yahweh.

18. We have writhed in child-birth –
as it were we have given birth to wind:
salvation we have in no way accomplished on earth,
nor have those living on earth at all come to birth.[18]

19. 'Your dead will live;
my corpses will rise up.'[19]
Awake and shout aloud, residents in the dust,
for your dew is the dew of light itself,[20]
and the earth will itself give birth[21] to the shadowy ones.

Secure from wrath[22]

20. Come, my people,
enter your inner rooms,
and lock your doors behind you.
Hide for just a brief moment
until the indignation[23] passes over.

21. For behold, Yahweh is about to go out from his place,
to visit on each the iniquity[24] of those living on earth,
and the earth will lay bare its blood-guiltiness,
and will no longer cover its slain ones.

11. How the Lord wishes to be remembered, his self-revelation, his name (Exod. 3:15).

12. Following the references to divine judgments abroad in the world, Isaiah ponders the absence of general response to Yahweh. Neither acts of grace (10a) nor ordinary life (10b), nor special acts of divine intervention (11a) prompt a response, but a different day is coming (11b).

13. Lit., 'in a land of straightforward things'.

14. Much of the translation of this last sentence is inevitably interpretative. Isaiah sticks to a blunt allusiveness: ' … jealous zeal of the people … the fire of your adversaries …'

15. Matching the 'divinely ordained peace' of vv. 7–9, Isaiah returned here to the lot of the Lord's people: everything they have ever enjoyed or experienced has been due to him. It has to be so seeing that humanity as such (vv. 10–11a) is of such impenetrable blindness.

16. See 14:9.

17. Contrasting with 'down into the dust', vv. 5–6, the fate of the oppressive city, the Lord's people, for all the distresses and pains they have experienced, can look forward to rising out of the dust into a new morning.

18. Lit., 'fallen'. The verb 'to fall' has many shades of meaning. 'Falling', as before an opponent would be suitable here, but since the verb gives rise to a noun meaning 'an abortion or miscarriage' (e.g.,

Job 3:16) it could itself signify 'come to birth', which suits the child–birth imagery of the context. In relation to 'salvation', 'birth' is what the New Testament will call 'the birth from above', being 'born again', regeneration.

19   Contrast the unaltered death, absence of resurrection of the erstwhile 'lords' (v. 14). Here the voice of the church's failure (v. 18) is answered by the voice of Yahweh affirming the resurrection of the body. Yahweh affirms that even the corpses of his people are his and will rise.

20   'Dew', a metaphor for God's blessing; 'light' a metaphor for life. The sense, therefore, is, 'The blessing coming from Yahweh is the blessing of life itself'.

21   As in v. 18.

22   Matching the opening verses, 'Secure in peace,' the poem ends by assuring the Lord's people of their abiding security: a 'passover' picture of the door shut behind them and their safety inside the house (Exod. 12:13, 22–23). Divine wrath is coming but they are safe and sheltered.

23   See 5:25.

24   See 1:2.

Thought for the day: Isaiah 26:1–21

Inheriting as we do the classification of the Bible into two 'testaments', people still ask – and quite a few people at that – why we need to bother with the Old Testament. It is one of the greatest, most important and most thrilling discoveries to find that the Bible is not two testaments but one book – one Jesus people, one divine purpose in Christ, one consistent revelation of God, one world, and (oh what joy!) one way of salvation. Isaiah 26 is a good place to start in order to feel the truth of all this. The citizens of the City of Salvation are those who are 'right with God', a relationship which shows itself in a reliable life-style (v. 2). Those who are right with God enjoy his peace, because they have put their trust in him (v. 3), and this faith gives them eternal security (v. 4). The people of faith are, in themselves, without resources (poor) and without strength (downtrodden) but because their God has cast down the strong city of the enemy they can enter into his victory and trample down their foes (vv. 5–6). Their life in this world is one of changes and chances – they have security, not immunity (vv. 8a, 16–17) – but they know that their life is not 'chance' but ruled by divine decision ('judgment' v. 8), and through thick and thin their deepest longing is to know God (v. 8). They live in a hostile, unresponsive world (v. 10), but their eternal expectation is sure. By contrast with unbelievers (v. 14), the people of the city, the people of peace and faith, look forward to a resurrection that is resurrection indeed, not the shadowy life of the soul dislocated from the body, but the whole person resurrected (v. 19). And until that day comes, they are the Passover people, safe under the blood of the lamb (v. 20).

Day 30 Isaiah 27:1–13

Matching 19:1–25 and 23:1–18, this fifth section foresees the world gathered to the Lord. There are four 'in that day' pronouncements: two to start with and two at the end. In the first (v. 1) the Lord deals with his supernatural foes, and in the last (v. 13) the 'great trumpet' heralds the Jubilee for the whole world. In the second pronouncement (vv. 2–6) his vineyard people are destined to fill the world, and in the third (v. 12) he harvests his worldwide people.

The final gathering: The universal Israel (Isaiah 27:1–13)

Victory in the heavenlies: The great sword

27:1. In that day,
Yahweh will visit,
with his sword, fierce and great and strong,
Leviathan, the swift serpent,
and Leviathan, the wriggling serpent,
and he will kill the Monster which is in the sea.

The Lord's vineyard people, destined to fill the world

2. In that day,
a vineyard of sparkling wine!¹
Sing of it!
3. I, Yahweh, keep it safe;
moment by moment I water it,
lest anyone intrude² upon it.
Night and day I keep it safe.
4. Rage³ – I have none!
Oh that I had thorns and briers!⁴
In battle I would stride out against each,
set them alight all together.

1   Or 'a vineyard of delight'!

2   Lit., 'visit it'. 'To visit' (*paqad*) means 'to pay (close) attention to'. Here 'to pay unwanted attention'.

3   See 5:25.

4   Like a lover itching to do battle on behalf of his beloved, the Lord is represented as even wishing something would invade the vineyard so that he could demonstrate his commitment!

5.   Or let him grasp at my protection,
     make peace with me;
     yes, let him make peace with me!⁵
6.   As for the future,⁶
     Jacob will take root,
     Israel will blossom and bloom,
     and they will fill the face of the world
     with fruitfulness.

The Lord's dealings with his people

1. Past forbearance

7.   As with the smiting of those who smote him
     did he smite him?
     Or as with the killing of those killed by him
     was he killed?⁷
8.   By shooing away,
     by sending it away,
     you pursued your case against it:
     he expelled by his rough wind in a day of east wind.⁸

Future atonement

9.   Therefore,
     in this way will the atonement-price⁹ of Jacob's
     iniquity¹⁰ be paid,¹¹
     and the whole fruit¹² of the removing of his sin is this –
     when he makes all the stones of the altar like
     pulverised limestone;
     Asherim and incense-altars will not rise up.

Ultimate Conquest

10.   For the fortified city is utterly isolated,¹³
     a habitation dismissed and forsaken,
     like a wilderness;
     there the calf will pasture,
     and there lie down,
     and finish its branches.

5   Isaiah, the master of the mixed metaphor, combines here the ideas of weeds in the vineyard and enemies against whom the Lord marches out.

6   Lit., 'the coming ones'. Not found elsewhere as a simple description of 'the future', but most probably an ellipsis for 'the coming (days)'.

7   To whom do all these pronouns refer? Enemies smote Israel and the Lord smote them in recompense, but he never smote Israel to that extent; the Lord killed off Israel's would-be murderers but Israel himself was not thus killed.

8   The change of pronoun to feminine probably indicates that this saying originally referred to either nation or city considered as the 'mother' of its people. The Lord's way with Israel was not destruction but exile.

9   See 6:7.

10   See 1:2.

11   'Therefore' looks back to the forbearance evident in past history. 'In this way' means a like forbearance will be evident in the work of price-paying.

12   The 'fruit' (result) of the great atonement is the end of altar-religion, the offering of

11. When its shoots have withered they will be broken up,
    women coming, setting it alight,
    for it is not a people of true discernment,
    therefore he who made it will not have compassion on it,
    and he who shaped it will not give it grace.

The Lord's harvested people
Gathered from the world
12. And it will be,
    in that day,
    Yahweh will reap his harvest[14]
    from the River's stream to Egypt's watercourse,[15]
    and you – you will be gleaned one by one, sons of Israel.

The Lord's Jubilee on earth
The great trumpet[16]
13. And it will be,
    in that day,
    a call will be sounded on a great trumpet,
    and those who were perishing in the land of Assyria
    will come,
    and those who were banished in the land of Egypt,
    and they will bow in worship to Yahweh
    on the mountain of holiness, Jerusalem.

---

required sacrifices, and the end of illegal, false worship (Asherim and incense altars).

13 Lit., 'is an isolation', i.e., has come to be the very quintessence of what 'isolation' means.

14 Here *chabat*, to beat, beat off; either 'to thresh' (Judg. 6:11) or to beat off olives (Deut. 24:20).

15 Isaiah speaks of the world as he knew it. His implication is that wherever the Lord's elect are, worldwide, they will be gathered. Euphrates to Nile also represent the 'ideal' bounds of the Promised Land (Gen. 15:18; Exod. 23:31; Ps. 72:8).

16 The trumpet heralded the Day of Atonement in the Year of Jubilee.

Thought for the day: Isaiah 27:1–13

The Lord will have his own way: what he wants will happen; his promises will be kept; his will achieved; his future brought to pass. This is the message of Isaiah 27. It is the third time Isaiah has spoken of the Lord's vineyard: in 3:13–15, the vineyard was savaged by bad rulers and the vineyard people crushed; in 5:1–7, the vineyard was the subject of every possible divine care and attention but its people failed to produce the justice and righteousness the Lord wished, yielding only rotten fruit. But the Lord never abandons any project he has undertaken, not only against human mismanagement (3:14), but also against what is to us the insurmountable obstacle of our own sinfulness – and, in 27:1, additionally against all that Satan can hurl at him. For our extreme encouragement it is written in his book that the vineyard is weed free, the divine Gardener is in full command, every need is supplied, and those who were once the 'stink-fruit' people are now filling the whole earth with fruitfulness. Imagine it! Just think what it is to experience the security and stability of a rooted existence (v. 6a) with all the changes and chances and fluctuations of the present world things of the past; to be at last the Lord's fruitful people, bringing forth, eternally and universally, to his glory. And all of this is because (as the centrepiece of the chapter indicates) the price of our iniquity has been paid, sin has been removed (v. 9), and the presence and hostile strength of our soul's enemy has been crushed for ever (v. 10). If the trumpet is the trumpet of Jubilee, it announces our freedom from everything in the past that would bind and blight us; if it is the trumpet of Exodus 19:13, it calls us to come near to God; but for sure it is the trumpet that announces the longed-for return of Jesus (1 Thess. 4:16).

Day 31 Isaiah 28:1–29

Isaiah 28–37

We have seen how Isaiah intersperses his vision of the ultimate future with 'interim fulfilments' which act as assurances that the greater predictions also can be trusted. Chapters 28–36 are the longest of his 'interim fulfilments'. His vision of the End made use of Israel, Egypt and Assyria as symbolic components (e.g., 19:14, 25; 27:12–13). In order that we may be fully assured that what the Lord plans he is able to do, Isaiah now turns to a period of history in which exactly those three powers were involved. Assyria was making imperialistic inroads into West Palestine and Judah was under threat; Egypt was making its typical anti-Assyrian noises and promising military aid. Isaiah reveals how the Lord was sovereign over all: protecting Judah, marginalising Egypt, and destroying Assyria. Chapters 36–37 are then added to set the capstone of actual historical events on the prophetic meditation of chapters 28–35.

Chapters 28–35 contain six sections, each opening with the word 'ho' or 'woe' (28:1–29; 29:1–14; 29:15–24; 30:1–33; 31:1–32:20; 33:1–35:10). These 'summons' match each other in pairs (the first with the fourth; second with the fifth; third with the sixth). The first three contain no names of nations, dealing with the situation in principle; the second three come to grips with names and events.

The first summons: The Word of God and the ways of God (28:1–22)

Samaria: a sinister parallel and a surprising hope

28:1. Ho there![1]

> Crown of pride of the drunkards of Ephraim,
> and fading blossom of the adornment of its beauty,

[1] The word *hoy* means 'ho there!' or 'woe to' according to context. The present case could be 'woe to' since it brings Samaria

which is on the head of boundlessly fertile valley.[2]
Shattered with wine!

2. Behold,
   the Sovereign has one resolute[3] and strong.
   Like an inundation of hail,
   a storm-wind of pestilential destruction;
   like an inundation of abundant, overflowing waters,
   he will for sure bring it down to the ground,
   by hand.
3. By foot,
   the crown of pride of the drunkards of Ephraim
   will be trampled
4. and the fading blossom of the adornment of its beauty,
   which is on the head of the boundlessly fertile valley,[4]
   will be like its own first-ripe figs before harvest
   which someone sees:
   no sooner is it in his hand[5] than he swallows it!
5. In that day[6]
   Yahweh of Hosts will become
   a crown of adornment,
   and a diadem of beauty,
   for the remnant of his people,
6. and a spirit of judgment for the one who sits in judgment,[7]
   and warrior strength for those who bring back the
   battle to the gate.[8]

Application: Jerusalem, giving itself to dissolute joy
7. And through wine these too are astray,
   and through intoxication have lost their way.
   Priest, even, and prophet, too, are astray through intoxication.
   They have been swallowed by wine!
   They have lost their way through intoxication;
   they are astray in vision;
   they stagger about in decision-making.
8. For all the tables are full of spew, of vomit,
   without exception.

under condemnation, but the word of summons, 'Ho', offers a better understanding of all six occurrences.

2 Lit., 'valley of fatnesses', plural of abundance, every sort of fatness. The 'crown' of pride is Samaria itself, a hill-top town, capital of the northern kingdom (1 Kings 16:23–24).

3 Both these words mean strong, but the first (*'amets*) in usage leans towards the firmness, stoutness, and resoluteness that strength gives.

4 See v. 1.

5 See 1:15.

6 In Isaiah the note of hope usually 'intrudes' in this abrupt, unannounced fashion. The day will yet come when Yahweh's people will find that, after all, he is their glory. It shows how strong was Isaiah's message of hope that he risks blunting the edge of his illustration (the fate of Samaria is coming to Jerusalem) by suddenly sketching in a glorious future.

7 'Sits' i.e., enthroned, the promised Davidic King. 'Judgment', as so often, the right, authoritative decision, royal authority.

8 Either to drive back to the gate those who have broken into the city, or to drive enemies back to their own gate and besiege them there. Two pictures of victory.

The inescapable Word[9]

9. Whom will he teach knowledge?
   And whom will he make to discern the message? –
   those weaned off milk,
   removed from the breasts!
10. For it is
   'Do and do, do and do;
   don't and don't, don't and don't.
   There, little one; there, little one."[10]
11. Exactly! – with a stammering lips and with a
   different tongue
   he will speak to this people,
12. to whom he said:
   'This is the place of rest.
   Give rest to the weary.
   And this is the place of repose.'
   And none was willing to hear.
13. And Yahweh's word to them will be:
   'Do and do, do and do;
   don't and don't, don't and don't.
   There, little one; there, little one.'
   In order that they may go on and stumble backwards,
   and be broken and ensnared and captured.

True and false security[11]

14. Therefore,
   hear Yahweh's word, men of cynicism,[12]
   ruling this people who are in Jerusalem,
15. because you have said:
   'We have inaugurated a covenant with Death,[13]
   and with Sheol we have made common cause.[14]
   Even a flooding scourge when it passes by
   will not come against us,
   for we have made untruth our refuge
   and in falsehood we have taken cover."[15]
16. Therefore,
   this is what the Sovereign Yahweh has said:

9 In vv. 9–13 the simplicity of Isaiah's message is mocked as fit only for a creche (9–10); Isaiah warns that if the simple Word of God is rejected it will be replaced by the unintelligible (vs 11–12), but the Word in all its simplicity cannot be escaped (v. 13).

10 These are the words in which Isaiah was mocked. If 'do' and 'don't' are in any way accurate, he is scorned as offering simplistic directions and prohibitions inapplicable to the 'real' world in which the politicians live. But they may be meant to represent the meaningless sounds adults make to infants, clucking and 'oo-ing'.

11 The reference here is to an alliance with Egypt by which Judah's political elite fancied they had made themselves safe against Assyria. To Isaiah it was signing their own death warrant, for in doing so they had abandoned the way of faith.

12 'Cynicism' (*latson*), often translated 'scorn'. 'Scorning' is the ultimate in cynical rejection of God and morality. Here it is the practical atheism of politicians who do not take the Lord and his promises into account in their policies.

'Behold,
I have laid in Zion a foundation stone,[16]
a stone of testing,[17]
a cornerstone most precious,
a foundation stone well founded.
Whoever trusts will not panic.

17. And I will make judgment the line
and righteousness the plumbline,[18]
and hail will sweep away the refuge of untruth,
and the waters will flood the covering.'

18. And your covenant with Death will be annulled,
and your common cause with Sheol will not stand.
As for the flooding scourge when it passes by,
you will be for it to trample on.

19. As often as it passes by it will catch you,
for morning by morning it will pass by,
by day and by night,
and it will be nothing but trepidation to discern the message.

20. For the bed is too short to stretch oneself out,
and the blanket too narrow when one curls up.

21. For as at Mount Perazim Yahweh will rise up;[19]
as in the valley of Gibeon be agitated,[20]
in order to do his work –
strange is his work –
and in order to perform his service –
alien is his service.[21]

Appeal

22. Now then, do not show yourselves to be scorners,[22]
lest your bonds become strong,
for a complete end – and one determined upon –
I have heard straight from the Sovereign, Yahweh of Hosts,
concerning the whole earth.

13 Of course they said no such thing! They said 'Pharaoh… Egypt' but Isaiah put into words the implications of what they had done.

14 Lit., 'made a vision'.

15 'Untruth … falsehood'; again they would have said 'Pharaoh…Egypt', but Isaiah sees through the false promises.

16 Lit., 'founded in Zion a stone'.

17 Either meaning 'a tested stone' or a stone which tests people (cf.8:14). Is the stone the city itself (the dwelling of Yahweh and the locus of his promises) or the throne of David about which divine promises have been made?

18 On 'judgment … righteousness', see 2:4; 26:8. The meaning here is that the Lord will remain true to his word in principle (righteousness) and practice (judgment).

19 2 Sam 5:17ff.

20 Josh. 10:11; 2 Sam. 5:22ff; 1 Chr. 14:16.

21 'Strange … alien' because what Yahweh once did for his people he proposes to do against them.

22 See v. 14.

A meditation: Divine discrimination in sowing and reaping[23]

23. Listen and hear my voice.
    Pay attention and hear my speech.

24. Throughout the whole day does the ploughman plough
    in order to sow,
    does he keep breaking open and harrowing the ground?

25. Is it not so that when he has levelled its surface
    he scatters black cummin and sprinkles cummin,
    and sets wheat in rows,
    and barley in its appointed place,
    and spelt in its own area?

26. For he trains him regarding the right decision[24] –
    it is his God who teaches him.

27. For not with a threshing-sledge is black cummin crushed,
    nor is a cartwheel turned on cummin,
    for it is with a stick that black cummin is beaten out,
    and cummin with a rod.

28. Regarding bread, there has to be a grinding,
    yet not endlessly does one keep on crushing it
    and keep his cartwheel on the move;
    nor with his horses does he keep grinding it.

29. Straight from Yahweh of Hosts this too has issued.
    He works wonders in counselling,
    great things by his efficiency.

23 Isaiah looks back to the parallel he drew between Samaria and Jerusalem (28:1–6). How far can such parallels be taken? Does it have to be for Jerusalem *exactly* as for Samaria? The meditation on the ways of the farmer says, not necessarily. Each seed is in its own appropriate place (v. 25), and each crop must be harvested in its own proper way (vv. 27–28). Such discrimination comes from the Lord (vv. 26, 29), and so it will be with Samaria and Jerusalem. This prepares for the contents of the second Summons, 29:1–24, with its indication that the road ahead for Jerusalem is significantly different from that of Samaria.

24 Lit., 'judgment', an excellent example of the word in its basic meaning of authoritative decision.

Thought for the day: Isaiah 28:1–29

The ways of God are past understanding, but that does not mean they lack planning, point and purpose. It just means that not only are his ways not our ways but neither are our thoughts his thoughts. What he chooses for us – and for our family, and friends, for Christians across the world – are a major source of bewilderment! And our old friend 'Why?' reappears to be our companion. Isaiah must have found life just the same – otherwise why write the meditation on life's changes and chances that is preserved in verses 23–29? He shares deep and precious observations with us by putting aside for a moment his gifts as a prophet and becoming a Wise Man. Isaiah 28:23–29 could well be in the book of Proverbs. The farmer, says Isaiah, knows how to prepare the ground (v. 24), where exactly to plant each type of seed (v. 25). He knows also how to harvest each crop so as to conserve its precious fruit. If we could give a voice to the elements in this process, would not the ground cry out under the plough, and the cummin when it feels the rod? Would not bread marvel at the harsh treatment which cannot be avoided if it is to be prepared for the master's enjoyment (v. 28)? So when we ask why am I in this place and circumstance? Why is life so hard? Why these blows, at this moment, with this severity? – think of the farmer. The seed is where he put it, harvested as he knows how. Fruitfulness is achieved by the treatment which he knows is the only way to bring the crop to harvest. And, beyond all else, Isaiah says, ask where the farmer acquired this knowledge and skill – why, he learned it from the Lord who is to be marvelled at for his effective working (vv. 26,29). We are where we are by his design; the roughnesses of life are the only ways which lead to the harvest he desires.

Day 32   Isaiah 29:1–14

The second summons: A problem solved, a problem raised
The first summons left a question hanging in the air: Jerusalem
deserves to be treated as Samaria, but will the divine Farmer,
who deals knowledgeably with each different crop, simply
follow one pattern for both cities? 29:1–8 says, 'No, it will be
different for Jerusalem', but that leaves a different problem
as yet unsolved – Jerusalem's spiritual blindness and spiritual
need. Has the Lord an answer for this?

Chastening and deliverance

29:1. Ho there,
    Ariel, Ariel, city where David camped.[1]
    Add year to year,
    let the festivals circle round,
2.   and I will bring distress to Ariel,
    and there will be groaning and moaning,
    and it will become to me a veritable Ariel!
3.   And I will camp all round against you,
    and I will besiege you with military outposts,
    and I will raise up siege-works against you,
4.   and you will be abased;
    out of the ground you will speak,
    and out of the dust your speech will squeal.
5.   And the throng[2] of your adversaries will be like fine dust,
    and like chaff passing away the throng of the terrifying ones.
    And it will happen with instantaneous suddenness.[3]
6.   From the very presence of Yahweh of Hosts
    there will be a visitation,
    with thunder and with earthquake and with great noise,
    whirlwind and tempest and flame of devouring fire.

[1] 'Ariel' means 'altar-hearth'. Isaiah uses it as a symbolic name for Zion – with the double meaning of the place where Yahweh has set his altar and the place where his holy fire burns. The latter reappears in v. 2 and the former in vv. 6–7. Zion is both privileged and endangered by the presence of the holy God. Therefore both liable to judgment and to protection.

[2] See 5:13, also for 'throng' in v. 7.

[3] See chapter 37 for the fulfilment of this message: Jerusalem brought to the ground by the Assyrian threat, squealing

7. And like a dream, a night vision,
   will be the throng of all the nations crowding against Ariel –
   all crowding against it and its stronghold,
   and putting pressure on it.
8. And it will be
   as when a hungry person dreams, and, behold, he is eating,
   and he wakes up and his soul[4] is empty,
   and as when a thirsty one dreams, and, behold,
   he is drinking,
   and he wakes up, and, behold, he is faint,
   and his soul is parched:[5]
   so will be the throng of all the nations crowding
   against Mount Zion.

The deeper problem: spiritual blindness, its cause and its cure[6]

9. Hesitate, and remain perplexed!
   Blind yourselves, and be blind!
   They are intoxicated, but it is not wine!
   Unsteady, but it is not intoxication!
10. For Yahweh has poured on them a spirit of torpor –
    he has shut their eyes (the prophets),
    and their heads (the seers) he has covered over.
11. And the vision of the whole[7] has become to them
    like the words of a closed book,
    which they give to one who knows how to read,[8]
    saying, 'Please read this,'
    and he says, 'I cannot, for it is closed'.
12. And the book is given to one who does not know
    how to read,
    saying, 'Please read this,'
    and he says, 'I do not know how to read'.
13. And the Sovereign said:
    'Because this people has approached with their mouth,
    and with their lips have honoured me,
    and their heart they have distanced from me,
    and their fear of me is a human commandment,
    something taught,

---

for help, and totally and instantaneously delivered, the threat utterly dismissed.

4 'Soul' (*nephesh*) here in the sense of 'appetite' or 'desire'.

5 Or, possibly, 'agitated'.

6 Spiritual blindness is a deliberate decision (v. 9) and also a divine judgment on that decision (v. 10). It is refusal of the truth (vv. 11–12) and can only be cured by divine action (vv. 13–14).

7 This is a literal translation. The reference may be to the ability to see the whole picture, but possibly the intention is 'any and every vision'; they totally lack spiritual perception.

8 Lit., 'knows the book', possesses book-learning, is educated.

14. therefore, behold,
    I will once again perform a marvel among this people,
    perform a marvel, a marvel indeed,[9]
    and the wisdom of their wise ones will perish,
    and the discernment of their discerning ones will hide
    itself away!'

9 'Once again' looks back to the divine marvel of the sudden deliverance of Jerusalem from the Assyrian threat (vs 5–8; 37:36–37). The new, unspecified, marvel will be in the spiritual realm.

Thought for the day: Isaiah 29:1–14.

Isaiah paints a very vivid picture. Here is a closed book and the person who is able to read can't be bothered; it's too much trouble to open it. And the person who can't read is content to leave it like that; it's of no importance to try to find out what the book is about. But the book in question is God's book, his Word of truth: it brings the knowledge of God; without it all is at best surmise, at worst idle fancy and error. How swiftly Isaiah's picture leaps over the 2,700 years since he put it on paper! He might well be living today and describing how things are all round. Here is a life-long churchgoer, a devout, serious man (I could tell you his name), but he says, 'Never at any time in my life have I read the Bible for myself.' He can read, but can't be bothered, and – tragedy of tragedies – the church he attends encourages religion and ritual but not personal Bible-reading. And here is a man talking confidently of life after death, sure that 'Gran' is there, 'watching over us like she always did', himself unafraid in the face of death. He might as well not be able to read because the Bible does not matter. And here is a converted, committed Christian with a datable experience of accepting the Lord Jesus as Saviour, and for the sake of thirty extra minutes in bed, or because life's busyness comes crowding in, or because at the day's end tiredness makes its claim, it's suddenly too much trouble to open the closed book, not important enough to read, receive, welcome and expose mind, heart and soul to the precious Word of God. And here is a Christian worker – believe me: I'm not inventing but quoting – 'I'm occupied with the Bible all day so when I get to bed it's a relief to read a novel'. Thus we join those who honour Jesus with our lips but we have distanced our hearts from him. No Bible, no spirituality; God at arm's length.

Day 33 Isaiah 29:15–24

The third summons: Spiritual transformation
The second summons dwelt on the fact that no matter how great and impressive are the Lord's earthly interventions and deliverances they leave the deeper question of spiritual blindness still to be solved. The third summons insists that this deeper need is within the Lord's competence. It does not say how he will act but what he will achieve.

The folly of merely human wisdom: the mind without God

29:15. Ho, there!
> You who go to great depths
> to conceal plans from Yahweh –
> those whose works are in the dark,
> and who have said:
> 'Who sees us?'
> and 'Who knows us?'

16. How you get things upside-down!¹
> Or is the potter reckoned to be like the clay?
> Indeed, can the thing made say to its maker,
> 'He did not make me'?
> And has the pot said of a potter,
> 'He has no discernment'?

The coming transformation

17. Is it not yet a very little while
> that Lebanon will turn back into garden-land,
> and garden-land be reckoned a forest?²
18. And in that day the deaf will hear the word of the book,
> and out of mist and out of darkness
> the eyes of the blind will see.

1 The noun used here as an exclamation is *hephek* (only elsewhere, Ezek. 16:34, 'the opposite'). Here Isaiah exclaims, 'Oh your upside-downness!'

2 Lebanon is regularly symbolic of uncultivated growth that has always been there, independent of the ordering hand of man. The coming transformation will

19. And the downtrodden[3] will find new joy in Yahweh,
    and in the Holy One of Israel
    the vulnerable[4] among mankind will exult.
20. For he who strikes terror will cease to be,
    and the cynic[5] will end,
    and all those alert to make trouble[6] will be cut off –
21. who put a person in the wrong by a word
    and keep laying snares for one who reproves in the gate,
    and turn away the innocent party[7] for no good reason.[8]

Promises kept; the Lord's people renewed
22. Therefore,
    this is what Yahweh has said to the house of Jacob –
    he who ransomed Abraham:[9]
    'Not now will Jacob reap shame;[10]
    and not now will his face grow pale.
23. For when he sees his children,
    the work of my hands,
    in his midst,
    they will acknowledge the holiness of my name,
    and they will acknowledge the holiness of the Holy
    One of Jacob,
    and the God of Israel they will hold in terror.
24. And the wayward in spirit will know discernment,
    and the grumblers will learn certitude.'[11]

---

be like that: wildness tamed and ordered, and what is now thought to be an ordered garden will then by comparison seem wild!

3 See 11:4.

4 See 14:20.

5 See 28:14.

6 See 1:13.

7 'Righteous' in its forensic use, 'the innocent party' in a court case.

8 The word is *tohu*, see 24:10.

9 cf., Gen. 48:16 where the parallel verb 'to redeem' is used of the Lord's guardian care of Jacob in all the trials of life. cf., our use of 'to bail out' of helping someone in one of life's scrapes.

10 Jacob is depicted here as the distressed observer of the fortunes of his descendants, and, finally, feeling delight at the ultimate outcome.

11 *Leqach* is generally translated as 'doctrine' or something like that. But its derivation from *laqach* 'to take, receive, accept, seize' etc., suggests a basic meaning of 'grasp (of truth)'. cf., Prov. 1:5; 9:9. Those of unsettled mind will at last 'get a grip'.

Thought for the day: Isaiah 29:15–24

The first – and major – sign that the Lord is working a spiritual transformation in people is their new awareness of the truth (v. 18), a new ability to understand and appropriate, and a growth in discernment and grasp (v. 24). After their walk to Emmaus in company with the unrecognised Jesus, they testified that their heart burned while he opened the Scriptures. The instructed mind led to the burning heart; the mind was opened to and by the truth and the emotions followed. That, incidentally, is the biblical order of things: mind first, emotions to follow.

When Isaiah dealt with the same topic he reverts to his 'book' illustration of 29:11–12. Now, as the Lord works his miracle of renewal, the book becomes precious and the blocked ear becomes able and avid to hear – a transformation as dramatic and as humanly impossible as turning Lebanon into a garden. The unconverted mind, Paul teaches, 'is not subject to the law of God, nor indeed can be' (Rom. 8:7); the converted mind cries out, 'O how I love thy law' (Ps. 119:97). A one-time atheist, so dogmatically committed that he insisted his wife-to-be renounce her non-practising Christianity and join him in atheism, was astounded when a voice, in an empty sitting room, said, 'But I do exist, you know.' So convinced was he that the non-existent God had spoken that he went straight out and bought a Bible. That's real!

The first and major indication of a transforming work of God is a new need for the truth, a conviction where the truth is to be found, a zeal for the Word of Truth, an appetite for God's Book. And not just the first sign, but also God's recipe for progress to maturity. As Peter put it: 'Grow in the grace and knowledge of our Lord' (2 Pet. 3:18); as Paul instructed Timothy, 'Abide in the things you have learned … the sacred writings … all Holy Scripture …' (2 Tim. 3:14–16). To love and constantly ponder Scripture is our hall-mark.

Day 34   Isaiah 30:1–33

The fourth summons: Faithless people, faithful God (30:1–33)

The first summons (28:1–29) insisted that there is only one sure foundation for life in this uncertain world: Yahweh, his promises, and the monarchy and city of David in which those promises are set. There is no security – only certain death – in worldly securities and human wisdom. The fourth summons matches this by 'earthing' it in the actual situation in Isaiah's day. Assyria was on the march, threatening to sweep little Judah into its empire. Egypt was promising protection. Jerusalem's politicians were negotiating an Egyptian alliance. Isaiah knew this to be a fatal choice, a way of death, but he never lost his grip on the glorious ultimate future.

Contemporary events: Egypt no help

30:1. Ho, there,

    stubborn sons –
    this is the Word of Yahweh –
    bent on making plans, but not from me;
    bent on covering with a covering,[1] but not my Spirit!
    Purposing to add sin to sin.

2.   They are travelling to go down to Egypt,
    and my mouth[2] they have not asked!
    Bent on finding strength in the stronghold of Pharaoh,
    and on taking refuge in Egypt's shadow.

3.   And Pharaoh's stronghold will become your shame,
    and refuge in Egypt's shadow ignominy.

4.   For though their princes are in Zoan,
    and their messengers reach even to Hanes,[3]

5.   everyone will for sure reap shame

1   cf., 28:20.

2   i.e., 'opinion', cf., Josh. 9:14.

3   Zoan in the North Delta, and Hanes, well south of the tip of the delta, are leading cities of

over a people that cannot bring them profit –
not for help and not for profit,
but for shame and also for reproach.

A poem on the folly of relying on Egypt

6. An oracle on the beasts in the Negeb:[4]
    In a land of affliction and pressure,
    whence lioness and lion,
    cobra and flying snake,
    they are carrying on donkeys' backs their resources,
    and on camels' humps their treasures,
    to a people that cannot profit.
7. Egypt!
    Insubstantial and empty is their help!
    Therefore I have called that one
    'Boaster-Do-Nothing'.[5]

The refusal of the Word, the way of death

8. Go, then,
    write it on a tablet where they are,[6]
    and inscribe it in a book,[7]
    so that it may exist till a future day,[8]
    for ever, unto eternity:
9. that this is a mutinous people,
    mendacious sons,
    sons unwilling ever to hear Yahweh's teaching;
10. who have said to the seers, 'Stop seeing',
    and to the visionaries,
    'Do not bring us visions of what is right.
    Speak to us agreeable things.
    Have visions of illusions.
11. Depart from the way.
    Lead us off the path.
    Let us have no more of the Holy One of Israel!'[9]
12. Therefore,
    this is what the Holy One of Israel has said:

Egypt to which Isaiah pictures Judah's envoys trailing off.

4   The Negeb is the wilderness, in the south of Judah, which was chosen as the route to Egypt, avoiding for some reason the ordinary route through Philistia. The beasts are the wretched pack animals which have to endure the journey in order to bring gifts, hopefully to secure Egypt's aid.

5   Or 'Rahab (are) they, sitting down.' Rahab was in currency as a nickname for Egypt – cf. 51:9; Ps. 87:4. As a word it means 'turbulence, arrogance'. Isaiah saw Egypt as an 'armchair big-mouth'.

6   Lit., 'with them'.

7   The 'tablet' would be a public record (cf., 8:1), as on a hoarding; the book a private account, cf., 8:16.

8   'A day (coming) after'.

9   It is unlikely Isaiah is quoting their actual words, but is reading back to them the implications of what they were saying.

'Because you have scorned this word,
     and have put your trust in oppression and cunning
     and relied on them,
13.   therefore
     this iniquity will become for you
     like a crack, running down, bulging out, in a high wall,
     when, with instant suddenness, comes its shattering.'
14.   And he will shatter it,
     like the shattering of a potter's vessel,
     pulverised without sparing,
     and in its bits there will not be found
     a sherd to snatch up fire from the hearth,
     and to skim water from a tank.
15.   For this is what the Sovereign, Yahweh, the Holy One of
     Israel, said:
     'By coming back and resting you will be saved;
     in keeping quiet, and in trust will be your warrior strength.
     And you were not willing.'
16.   And you said:
     'Indeed not!
     For on horses we will flee.'
     Therefore you will indeed flee.
     And:
     'On swift beasts we will ride.'
     Therefore your pursuers will be swift.
17.   One thousand at the threat of one!
     At the threat of five you will flee
     until what remains of you will be
     like a pole on a mountain top,
     and like a flagstaff on a hill.'

The waiting God: sure glory
18.   Therefore
     Yahweh waits in order to be gracious to you,
     and therefore
     he will be exalted in order to show you compassion,[10]

10   See 9:17. 'Grace' is the Lord's
     sovereign determination

for Yahweh is a God of judgment;[11]
blessedly happy[12] are all who wait expectantly[13] for him.

19. For the people in Zion,
living in Jerusalem,
will surely not weep.
He will be truly gracious to you
at the voice of your shrieking.
As soon as he hears he has determined to answer you.

20. Though* the Sovereign give you
bread of adversity and water of oppression,
your Teacher will not any more hide himself away —
your eyes will themselves see your Teacher,[14]

21. and your ears will themselves hear a word behind you, saying,
'This is the way;
walk in it' —
when you must turn right and when you must turn left.

22. And you will defile your silver-plated idols,
and your gold-covered molten images:
you will fling them off like a soiled cloth.
'Out,' you will say to each.

23. And he will give rain for your seed with which you sow
the ground,
and bread, the product of the ground,
and it will be succulent and nutritious.[15]
Your livestock will feed, in that day,
in an enlarged pasture,

24. and the cattle and the donkeys, working the ground,
will eat well-flavoured fodder, winnowed with both
fork and sieve.[16]

25. And there will be,
on every high mountain, and on every upraised hill,
channels, streams of water,
in a day of great slaughter,
when towers fall.[17]

26. And the light of the white one will be like the light of the
hot one,[18]

to bless the undeserving;
'compassion' is his overflowing
passionate love for his people.

11 *mishpat*, see 2:4; 26:8. Here, the
God who knows how to make the
right decision at the right time.

12 *'ashrey* merits the translations
'blessed' (under the blessing
of God), 'happy' in what one
is doing, and 'right' (doing
the right thing in a given
circumstance). Context decides.

13 See 8:17.

14 'Teacher' is plural, understood
here as a plural of majesty,
referring to the Lord as the
Great Teacher of his people. This
corresponds to v. 9 where Yahweh's
teaching has been spurned.

15 Synonyms, both meaning 'fat',
both used of nourishing food.

16 Lit., 'which one winnows ...'; an
indefinite subject, used as equivalent
to a passive and sometimes, as here,
inevitably treated as such. 'Fork
... sieve', a time so prosperous
that even animal feed is twice
purified before being served out.

17 According to v. 18, the day of
mercy must delay until the
appointed judgment has been
executed. The wording of
v. 25 recalls the overthrow of
the 'world-city' in ch. 24.

and the light of the hot one will be multiplied by seven,
like seven days' light,
in the day Yahweh bandages the fractures of his people,
and heals the wounds caused by his blows.

Contemporary events: the failure of the Assyrian invasion[19]

27. Behold,
the name of Yahweh is going to come from afar,[20]
burning with his exasperation,[21]
and dense with billowing smoke.[22]
Full are his lips of indignation,
and his tongue is like devouring fire.

28. And his Spirit[23] is like a watercourse in spate,
sundering at the neck,
purposing to sieve nations in a sieve of falsehood,[24]
with* a bridle leading them astray in the jaws of the peoples.

29. Your part will be the song,
like in the night you sanctify yourselves for the feast,
and rejoicing of heart as when one goes with the flute
to come to the Mount of Yahweh,
to the Rock of Israel.

30. And Yahweh will make them hear the splendour
of his voice,
and make them see the coming down of his arm,
with a storm of exasperation[25] and flame of devouring fire,
cloudburst and downpour and hailstones.

31. For by the voice of Yahweh Assyria will be shattered –
the one who, like a rod, was smiting![26]

32. And every sweep of the destined staff,
which Yahweh will lay on him,
will be to the accompaniment of drums and of harps,
and with battles of shaking[27] he is sure to battle against them.

33. For arranged from earlier on is Topheth[28] –
indeed, for the king it has been set up,
deep, broad,
its pyre ablaze with wood in plenty,
Yahweh's breath like a watercourse of sulphur igniting it!

18 cf., 24:23.

19 Isaiah's prediction of the events recorded in chapter 37.

20 i.e., Yahweh himself is coming in the fullness of the revelation his name expresses – that is, as the God of the Exodus who saves his people and overthrows his foes.

21 See 5:25, also for 'indignation'.

22 Lit., 'with heaviness of an uprising'.

23 Or 'and his breath', continuing the personal metaphors of lips and tongue, but 'Spirit' is theologically correct. It is typical of Isaiah to turn from figurative expressions to the truth they express.

24 i.e., a sieve designed to separate the false from the true.

25 See 5:25.

26 See 10:5.

27 cf., the 'sieve' metaphor in v. 28. It is the Hebrew equivalent of our expression 'he will sort them out'.

28 This name is not found elsewhere, but is presumably a reference to the place of burning elsewhere called Topheth. (cf., Jer. 7:31; 19:6, 11, 13. The Assyrian king marched on Jerusalem little knowing that he was on his way to his own funeral pyre.

Thought for the day: Isaiah 30:1–33

Look back quickly over the chapter you have just read, for here, as very often in the Bible, there is a message in the 'shape' of a passage as well as in the individual verses. Isaiah 30 belongs right in the thick of the huge political decisions and national emergencies of 705–701 BC. It starts with the folly of the politicians of the day who sought security in worldly alliance (Egypt) rather than in Yahweh; it ends with the dreaded onrush of the Assyrians. Each passage punches home its message: to start with, the folly of leaving God – his wisdom, his Spirit, and his holy Word – out of the equation; at the end, the almighty power of Yahweh which guarantees that everyone who attacks his people is on the way to an already prepared grave. Ponder it! Here is a world-view for today. Everywhere all sorts of powers are ranged against the people of Jesus, inflicting sore hurt. Listen with Isaiah's ears and you will hear the funeral pyre already crackling in readiness. Here too is a clarion call to the Lord's people: to set aside the Word of God is to guarantee disaster – where nothing remains but a flagpole to show that there were once people here (v. 17)!

The centre of the chapter depicts the waiting God (v. 18): grace is in reserve, glory lies ahead. Where the Lord's people are concerned the voice of judgment, however deserved, never has the last word. There are wonders in store outshining anything ever experienced or imagined (vv. 23–26), and the waiting God knows exactly when to withhold and when to bestow, when to tarry and when to hurry. He is a 'God of judgment', always making the right decision at exactly the right time, never panicking, never at a loss what to do, calmly in charge, perfect in wisdom, precise in action. Ponder this too. It also is a clarion call for today, a call to the quiet trustfulness and expectancy (v. 15) that first brought us our salvation and is still, in every situation, the way of strength.

Day 35 Isaiah 31:1–32:20

This is the fifth summons, parallel to the second (29:1–14). There the principle was asserted that there is still hope in Yahweh when all earthly hope has gone – the hope of circumstantial and spiritual transformation. Isaiah now applies this to the actual situation in 701 BC when the politicians were trusting Egypt and the aggressive Assyrians were triumphing on all fronts. He wants to show that the Lord's principles of action and his promises really hold for life in the actualities of this world.

Prologue: disaster and deliverance

31:1. Ho, there!
    You who are going down to Egypt for help!
    It is on horses that they are relying,
    and they have put their trust in chariotry because
    it is plentiful,
    and in horsemen because they are so very mighty,
    and they have not fixed their gaze on the Holy One of Israel,
    and Yahweh they have not sought.[1]

2.   And he too is wise!
    and is bound to bring calamity,
    and not to retract his words.
    And he will rise against the house of evildoers,
    and against the help proffered by trouble-makers.[2]

3.   The Egyptians are humans, and not God*,
    and their horses are flesh and not Spirit.
    And Yahweh will himself stretch out his hand
    and the helper will stumble,
    and the helped will fall,
    and together all of them will come to an end.

1   See 8:19.

2   See 1:13.

4. For this is what Yahweh has said to me:
    As when a lion growls[3] –
    a mature lion, over his prey –
    when shepherds in full and plenty are summoned against
him
    he is not shattered by their voice,
    nor downtrodden by their commotion,[4]
    so Yahweh of Hosts will come down to wage war,
    upon mount Zion and upon its hill.
5. Like little birds flying,
    so Yahweh of Hosts will shield Jerusalem[5] –
    shielding and delivering,
    passing over[6] –
    and he will rescue.

Call to repent in the light of the future
6. Come back to him from whom
    the sons of Israel have deeply revolted.
7. For in that day
    they will scorn – everyone –
    his silver no-gods and his gold no-gods[7]
    which your hands have made for you –
    sin!
8. And Assyria will fall by a sword – not a man's,
    and a sword – not human – will devour him.
    And they each will take their flight from the sword,[8]
    and their young men will become slave-labour.
    And their Rock,[9] through terror, will pass away,[10]
    and their princes, because of the banner,[11] will be shattered.
    This is the word of Yahweh
    who has a fire in Zion,
    and a furnace in Jerusalem.[12]

Righteous king,[13] new society[14]

The king
32:1. Behold,
    a king of righteousness will reign,

3   See 8:19.

4   See 5:13.

5   The 'lion' is Assyria, the 'prey' Jerusalem, the would-be helper Egypt. The illustration is of the complete mastery of Yahweh over the whole situation and everyone involved. Jerusalem he rescues, Egypt he marginalises, Assyria he destroys – and not by any superlative exercise of divine power, but (so to speak) as imperceptibly as 'little birds flying'.

6   The same verb as Exod. 12:13, 23, 27.

7   See 2:8.

8   37:36–37.

9   Not the word used for Yahweh as Israel's Rock (30:29), but a word meaning 'cliff, crag', referring to the king of Assyria who is passing out of history, in contrast with the true King (32:1) coming into view.

10 Yahweh's verb, to pass over, v. 5, used here in ironic contrast.

11 Yahweh's upraised banner is sufficient to make his enemies collapse.

12 An allusion to 'Ariel', see 29:1.

and regarding princes,[15] they will be princes of judgment.[16]

2. And a man[17] will be like a hiding place from the wind
    and a covering from the downpour,
    like streams of water in dryness,
    like the shadow of an impressive rock in an exhausting land.

New people, new society

3. And the eyes of those who see will not be blurred,
    and the ears of those who hear will pay attention,

4. and the heart of the impetuous will discern so as to know,
    and the stammerers' tongue will be quick to speak
    with clarity.

5. No more will the morally obtuse[18] be called noble,
    nor the unprincipled[19] said to be generous.

6. For –
    the morally obtuse speaks what is amoral,
    and his heart makes mischief,[20]
    to practice apostasy,
    and to speak what is misleading about Yahweh,
    to leave the soul of the hungry empty,
    and to deprive the thirsty of drink.

7. And the unprincipled – his methods are evil.
    He is just the one to devise schemes,
    to ruin the downtrodden with words of untruth,
    and by speaking, the vulnerable, at law.[21]

8. And as for the noble person, the truly noble[22] is what he plans,
    and for what is truly noble he rises up.[23]

Call to listen in the light of the future[24]

9. O women[25] of unconcerned ease,
    get up,
    hear my voice.
    O daughters complacently confident,
    listen to my speech.

10. In days over a year
    you will tremble, complacently confident ones,

13 The messianic king of chapters 9 and 11.

14 The first of two references in this summons to the light that shines beyond the coming darkness. See 32:15–18. Isaiah would suddenly move from Assyrian darkness to messianic light, as here, in the same way that we allow the light of the Lord's coming to shine behind every darkness in our experience.

15 See 1:23.

16 See 2:4; 26:8.

17 The messianic Man, the royal son of David.

18 See 9:17.

19 The person who works for his own advantage without scruple. In a time of true perception, his donations would be seen for what they are, yet more attempts to further his own interests and feather his nest.

20 See 1:13.

21 *mishpat*, 'judgment'; see 2:4; 26:8. Here, of the judicial decision from the bench.

22 Plural expressing what is always true and of the essence of the matter.

23 Equivalent to our expression 'to stand up and be counted'.

24 Matching the 'call' in 31:6–9.

25 As at 3:16–23 Isaiah uses the womenfolk as typifying the nation.

for the vintage is doomed to fail,
   the ingathering will come to nothing.

11. Shudder, unconcerned ones;
   tremble, complacently confident ones;
   strip off and go bare,
   and gird the loins,[26]

12. as you beat your breasts in mourning
   over the delightful fields, over the fruitful vines,

13. over the land of my people where thorns and briars
   come up;
   indeed over all the houses of delight,
   the exultant city.

14. For the palace is deserted,
   the bustle[27] of the city abandoned.
   Ophel and Bahan have become but wastelands for ever,[28]
   donkeys' delight, pasturage for flocks,

Outpoured Spirit, new society[29]

15. until the Spirit is poured out on us from on high,
   and the wilderness becomes garden-land,
   and garden-land is reckoned a forest.[30]

16. And in the wilderness judgment will reside,
   and righteousness[31] will live in the garden-land.

17. And the effect of righteousness will be peace,
   and the achievement of righteousness
   quietness and trustfulness for ever.

18. And my people will live in dwellings of peace,
   and in habitations of total trustfulness[32]
   and in homes of restful ease.

Epilogue: humiliation and blessedness[33]

19. And hail will fall when the forest comes down,
   and in humiliation the city will be humbled.

20. Blessed[34] you will be who sow beside all waters,
   letting the foot of oxen and donkey range free!

26   'Strip … go bare' are not used of mourning. They are here the evidences of captivity and enslavement. The loins are girded for slave-labour. cf., 47:2.

27   See 5:13.

28   Ophel and Bahan could be translated 'hill and tower' but were probably identifiable districts in Jerusalem in Isaiah's day.

29   In the structure of the summons, this section matches 32:1–8.

30   See 29:17.

31   See 5:7.

32   'Total' is inserted because 'trustfulness' is a plural of amplitude, every sort of trustfulness.

33   Matching the prologue, 31:1–5 where imminent disaster is transformed into sudden deliverance.

34   See 30:18.

Thought for the day: Isaiah 31:1–32:20

Where are you going and what are you looking at? In principle these are the questions Isaiah asked his people and now asks us. They were going to Egypt for military resource in a day of military threat; they were looking to Pharaoh for shelter in a day of national emergency (31:1–3). Where are we going? What are we looking at? Every day brings its threats and needs, great and small, and Isaiah's questions remain vital. What direction are we moving in? Where are our eyes fixed? Are we ever and always getting closer to Jesus, ever and always 'seeing him more clearly, loving him more dearly', turning our eyes on Jesus, looking full in his wonderful face? Imagine – we might well say – going to *Egypt,* the would-be genocidal enslaver (Exod. 1:11, 14, 22), for *deliverance*! Imagine looking to *Pharaoh*, the instigator of the death-threat, for *protection*! Sheer madness! But whenever we move in any direction other than holiness, whenever we allow our eyes to wander to any solution other than Jesus, are we not copying the Galatians, who, to Paul's consternation, were deserting God for those who by nature are not gods, and leaving the way of salvation in favour of 'weak and beggarly elements' which could only bring them back into bondage (Gal. 4:8–9). Now this can be said in Judah's favour in Isaiah's day: they were in a serious, life and death, national crisis. The Assyrian invasion spelled the end of all they had and hoped. But it is not always (or usually) the 'big' occasions that defeat us. Very often they send us fleeing to Jesus in a more determined way. It is the small daily decisions. There is the silly-sounding decision whether to get out of bed to read our Bibles and seek our Saviour or to have another twenty minutes under the blankets. Silly-sounding, but actually deadly serious. Do we fill our eyes with him before the world clamours for our attention? Do we sit in his presence and commit ourselves to holiness for the day ahead, winning the battle before we reach the battlefield? Where are we going? What are we gazing at?

Day 36 Isaiah 33:1–24

The sixth is the longest summons, extending from 33:1–35:10. Like its partner, the third summons (29:15–24), it is wholly visionary and eschatological. We can 'read' historical events between the lines, but our eyes are held throughout on the undated future.

Ultimate realities

1. Salvation for Zion

33:1. Ho, there,

    Destroyer, yourself undestroyed!

    Treacherous one with whom others were not treacherous!

    When you have finished, Destroyer, you will be destroyed;

    when you have ceased to deal treacherously

    they will deal treacherously with you.[1]

2.   Yahweh, be gracious[2] to us:

    for you we have waited confidently.[3]

    Be their arm morning by morning;

    yes, indeed, our salvation in the time of adversity.[4]

3.   At the voice of the hub-bub[5] the peoples must flee away;

    at your exaltedness the nations must scatter.[6]

4.   And your[7] spoil will be gathered like young locusts gather,

    like the swarming of locusts they swarm upon it!

5.   Raised high aloft is Yahweh,

    for he resides on high.

    He has determined to fill Zion with judgment

    and righteousness,[8]

6.   and he will be the stability of your times,[9]

    a wealth of salvation in full and plenty,[10]

    wisdom and knowledge.

    The fear of Yahweh is his treasure.[11]

1   The background is the Assyrian advance. 'Destroyer' reflects the ruthlessness of the Assyrian assault; treachery was its hallmark, cf., 2 Kings 18:13–17 where Hezekiah bought off Sennacherib's threat, and Sennacherib accepted the treasure but attacked anyway!

2   See 30:18.

3   See 8:17.

4   Instead of saying that in trouble the Lord's people resort to prayer, Isaiah inserts a little cameo of prayer actually taking place, with one voice saying 'us' and 'our' and another responding with 'their'.

5   See 5:13.

2. Judgment for the peoples[12]

7. Behold,
   even their military men[13] who shriek outside,
   their messengers of peace keep weeping bitterly.[14]
8. Highways have become deserted,
   the traveller by road has stopped.
   He has annulled the covenant,
   scorned cities,
   set no value on humans.
9. Earth has become sadly withered;
   Lebanon is ashamed of itself, disease-ridden;
   Sharon has become like a bare plain;
   and Bashan and Carmel are losing their foliage.[15]
10. Now I will arise,
    Yahweh keeps saying,
    now I will exalt myself.
    Now I will lift myself up.
11. You conceive chaff, give birth to stubble,
    Your own spirit is the fire which devours you.
12. And the peoples will become conflagrations for lime:
    thornbushes, chopped down, set ablaze with fire.[16]

Universal proclamations

Proclamation 1: Zion's citizens and Zion's king

13. You who are far off, hear what I have done;
    and you who are near, know my warrior strength!
14. In Zion the sinners are apprehensive,
    trembling has gripped the degenerate:[17]
    'Who of us can tarry in the devouring fire?
    Who of us can tarry in the everlasting inferno?'
15. Whoever walks in complete righteousness,
    and speaks what is straight;
    whoever scorns any sort of extortionate gain;
    whoever shakes his grip[18] free from taking hold of a bribe;
    whoever seals his ear from hearing of blood-guiltiness,
    and shuts his eyes from seeing evil –

6   The 'hub-bub' could be the fear of an Egyptian intervention, 2 Kings 19:9. If human intervention causes flight, what will be the result when Yahweh rises up? The verbs 'flee ... scatter' are perfect tenses expresses certainty of outcome. Hence 'must'.

7   'You' plural, referring to the spoil left by the nations when they flee. cf. 37:36 and cf., 2 Chron. 20:25 for gathering spoil.

8   See 5:7.

9   Either 'he is the one who provides stability at all times', or 'in every conceivable situation he remains his reliable self'.

10 Lit., 'of salvations', plural of amplitude, every sort of.

11 i.e., Yahweh has treasured up the fear of himself to bestow on his people, this being the beginning of wisdom and the foundation of every other blessing.

12 As history nears its end, no one knows the answer to problems (v. 7). The world has become a dangerous place(v. 8a), because its ruler ('he', v. 8b) has annulled moral values (covenant), destroyed past achievements (cities) and human rights are violated (humankind). And just as the first sin produced 'thorns and thistles' (Gen. 3:18) so at the end there will be total environmental collapse (v. 9).

13 Another form of the word found only at 2 Sam. 23:20; 1 Chron. 11:22 ('lion-like'). No meaning is beyond doubt.

14 Men of war, men of peace – totality expressed by contrast; all alike at their wits' end.

16. he it is who will reside in the heights,
    with the strong points of the crags as his high security,
    his bread given,
    his water reliable.

17. Of the king in his beauty your eyes will catch the vision;
    they will see the land of far horizons.

18. Your heart will muse[19] on the horror:
    'Where is the one who noted things down?
    Where is the one who weighed things out?
    Where is the one who noted down the towers?'[20]

19. Arrogant[21] people you will not see,
    people of speech too guttural to understand,[22]
    a staccato tongue beyond discerning.

20. See this vision:
    Zion, the city of our assemblies!
    Your very eyes will see Jerusalem,
    a habitation at restful ease,
    a tent not to be packed up,
    whose pegs will not ever be moved,
    nor any of its ropes snapped.

21. On the contrary!
    There, Yahweh, that majestic One, is on our side,
    a place of rivers, streams widely extending.[23]
    There will not go in it a galley,
    nor will a majestic ship pass through it,[24]

22. for Yahweh is our Judge,[25]
    Yahweh is our Law-giver,
    Yahweh is our King:
    He it is who will save us.

23. Your rigging hung loose;[26]
    they did not secure the foot of their mast;
    they did not spread the sail.
    Then an even abundant spoil will certainly be
    apportioned out.
    The lame took the prey!

24. And the resident will not say,

15 Lit., 'are shaking (off their leaves)'.

16 The reference to lime-burning is a picture of intensity of fire; the burning thorns a picture of helplessness in the fire.

17 See 9:17.

18 See. 1:15.

19 See 8:19.

20 In context, the references are to a victorious conqueror appointing his officials to keep records, to record the names of those marked down for captivity (or execution), to list the weight of valuables taken as spoil, to select towers for demolition. cf. 2 Kings 24–25.

21 Or 'foreign, alien'. The context requires a word describing the insolence of a foreign conqueror.

22 Lit., 'lip too deep to hear'.

23 Lit., 'wide on both hands', in both directions.

24 Well-watered but without threat of warship or need of commercial shipping; secure and self-sufficient. The words used of shipping here are non-specific but this is the likely meaning.

25 See 2:4.

26 A concluding contrast (cf., 32:19–20). The old helpless Zion seen as a 'ship of state', 'ill-found', unprepared, yet in the end it is Zion that takes the prey!

'I am sick.'
The people who live in it will have their iniquity
carried away.[27]

27 The final line defines the 'sickness'
as moral and spiritual, cf., 53:4.

Thought for the day: Isaiah 33:1–24

Even the least nautical of us find ourselves warming to Isaiah's beautiful word-picture of the Zion that is yet to be, with its far-horizons, and its calm vista of rivers and streams wherever the eye may roam, no sea-going vessels but (possibly?) some 'messing around in boats'. The reality and certainty of it is secured solely by the Lord and his salvation. Once sin is forgiven the heavenly City lies open, fully furnished in all its security, loveliness and peace, and we, once lame and sick in our sin, now enter its gates without restriction – and without contribution on our part. The Zion that was – the 'Old Testament' Zion – is our pre-history, we who belong to Jesus; the true Zion to which we have come in Christ – the Jerusalem that is above – is our present home and citizenship (Gal. 4:26; Heb. 12:22–24), and our eternal expectation is the holy city, Jerusalem, coming down from God out of heaven (Rev. 21:10). Not only, however, does forgiveness of sins bring us into these wonderful and eternal blessings. At the deepest of all levels, God, in the fullness of the divine nature, is satisfied; he asks no more. It is as 'judge, lawgiver, and king' that he saves us (v. 22) : the Judge who would otherwise condemn acquits, the claims of the law of God have been met, the king throws his city open so that we may enter by the gates (Rev. 22:14)! Was there ever such a 'package deal'? But now take forgiveness of sins one step further. Faith is its immediate cause, bringing forgiveness to the individual believer; God is its ultimate cause, as the one who determined upon our salvation and planned its accomplishment; but its effective cause – how and why it actually 'works' – is that one bore and carried away our sins for us. This is what Isaiah chooses to affirm: we are (literally) 'the people carried away in respect of our sins' (v. 24). We have a sin-bearing Saviour, and the sins he carried away into the awful desert place of Calvary (Mark 15:34) are never to be seen again (Lev. 16:21–22).

Day 37   Isaiah 34:1–17

Continuing the sixth and final summons of the series, chapter 34 is a second universal proclamation. The theme of the first was Zion's citizens and Zion's king (33:13). This is matched by the theme of the final overthrow of the world in all its hostility to God's rule.

Proclamation 2: The final overthrow

Final divine judgment

34:1. Come near, nations, to hear,
    and, peoples, to pay attention.
    The earth must hear, and all that fills it,
    the world, and all its products.

2.   For Yahweh has lost patience[1] with all the nations;
    his rage is hot against all their host.
    He has appointed them to utter destruction,
    consigned them to slaughter,
    and, as for their slain, they will be thrown out,
    and as for their corpses, their stench will rise up,
    and mountains will be dissolved by their blood,

4.   and all the host of heaven will rot,
    and like a scroll the heavens will be rolled up,
    and all their host will wither,
    as a leaf withers from the vine,
    and like what withers from the fig tree.

5.   When my sword has been saturated in the heavens, behold,
    upon Edom it will come down,[2]
    and, for judgment,
    upon a people I have appointed to destruction:

6.   Yahweh has a sword,

1   See 5:25, also for 'rage'.

2   The prophets came to use Edom as a symbol of hostility to the Lord and his people.

full of blood,
nourished with fat,
with the blood of lambs and he-goats,
with the fat of the kidneys of rams,
for Yahweh has a sacrifice in Bozrah,[3]
and great slaughter in the land of Edom.

7. And wild oxen will come down along with them –
young bulls and great bulls alike –
and their land will be saturated with blood,
and with fat their dust will be nourished.

8. Yahweh has a day of vengeance,
a year for the full settlement of Zion's case.

9. And its[4] watercourses will be turned into pitch,
and its dust into sulphur,
and its land will become burning pitch.

10. Night and day it will not be quenched;
for ever its smoke will rise up;
from generation to generation it will lie waste.
To the perpetuity of perpetuities no one will traverse it.

11. And the owl and the hedgehog will possess it
and the long-eared owl and the raven will reside in it,
and he will stretch out over it a measuring
line of meaninglessness,
and a plumbline of emptiness.[5]

12. As for its nobles, there is nothing there they could
call a kingdom;
and all its princes will come to nothing

13. and their palaces will grow high with thorns –
weeds and nettles in their fortifications.
And it will be a habitat for jackals;
a settlement for ostriches.

14. And desert creatures will meet with hyenas,
and the goat-demon will call out to its mate.
Yes, the night-hag will stretch out there, and find a
home for herself.[6]

15. There the tree-snake will nest, and produce,
and hatch, and gather its young into its shadow.

What happened historically (Gen. 33:4–16; Num. 20:14–21; Amos 1:11) became a useful and obvious eschatological motif. Only David had conquered Edom (2 Sam. 8:14) and the end-time conquest of 'Edom' becomes a feature of the return of 'David' (Amos 9:11–12; Ezek. 34:23 and 35:1–15).

3   Capital of Edom.

4   Edom's.

5   'Meaninglessness' (see 24:10) and 'emptiness' are 'without form' and 'void' in Gen. 1:2: i.e., the condition of the physical substrate of earth before the Lord imposed meaning and order, and introduced light and life (cf., Jer. 4:23). The 'measuring line' and 'plumbline' are surveyor's instruments exposing the real condition of land and building.

6   Doubt surrounds the translations offered for the animals, here, and the translations 'hatch' and 'produce' in the next verse.

The Lord's Sure Plan: a Final Summons

16. Search out of Yahweh's book, and read.
   Not one of these can ever be missing;
   not one will ever seek its mate in vain.
   For it is my mouth which has commanded,
   and it is his Spirit which is sure to gather them.

17. And it is he who has cast lots for them,
   and it is his hand which has allocated their portion by line.[7]
   For ever they will possess it;
   to generation after generation they will reside in it.

7   cf., Josh 14:1ff for the idea of allocation by lot. The Lord has decided the future of 'Edom' in just the same precise way.

Thought for the day: Isaiah 34:1–17

Serious passages about divine wrath and judgment are hard to take, and this is one of them. Isaiah does not try to spare our feelings, and we, for the most part, do not feel, as he did (21:4), that our hearts are broken for the lost who feel the blow of the divine hand. But it will come. The wages of sin is death, and death it will be, the outpouring of divine exasperation when once divine patience has reached its terminus. Isaiah's picture of mountains eroded by the colossal flood of the blood of the slain is, as we say, 'only' a picture, but it will be matched by the reality when the day comes. Praise God, the company of the saved will be innumerable, but that does not take away from the multitudes who will stand unready, unfit, hopeless, in the valley of that eternal decision. Jesus did not hide his face, or ours, from it (Matt. 25:46), nor did John make any attempt to camouflage the grim procession to the lake of fire (Rev. 20:12–15). And these are people we know, sometimes people we love, always people for whom we have a responsibility in the gospel. Today is the day to ponder these things, but it is the day also, in the light of God's Word, to look to ourselves and to determine to flee from sin, for, though in Christ 'the wrath of a sin-hating God with me can have nothing to do', and our eternity is as secure as if we were already before the Throne (which, in reality, we are, Eph. 2:4–6), yet, as long as he leaves us tarrying on earth, sin still brings death. Like our ancestors in Deuteronomy 30:15–16 we face daily the choice of life or death – to choose the good and not the evil, to refuse disobedience and cultivate obedience, for it is the Lord's Word, his commands, which bring life ('that you may live'), and progress ('and multiply'), blessing and inheritance ('possess'). God, Peter taught, gives his Holy Spirit to those who obey him (Acts 5:32).

Day 38 Isaiah 35:1–10

The sixth summons ends with this glorious picture of the final 'Exodus' pilgrimage of the Lord's people to their eternal and blissful destination in Zion. The summons began with the message of salvation in Zion (33:1–6). It set up a contrast between the eternal destiny of the saved and the unsaved (33:7–34:17), and now it ends where it began, a pilgrim people, only referred to as 'them' (vv. 1, 8) and 'they' (vv. 2, 10), and defined as the Lord's redeemed and ransomed (vv. 9–10). We met them before in 24:14–25:9. They are the worldwide Israel of the saved. The matching third summons (29:15–24) contained an understated reference to redemption (29:22). We now read the full story – a protected path, assured arrival, safe home-coming and unbroken happiness.

A transformed world, a promise to 'them'
35:1. The wilderness and the parched land will be glad
  of them[1]
  and oh may the arid plain exult and bloom like an asphodel,
2. burst into bloom,
  and exult, yes, with exultation and loud shouting!
  The very glory of Lebanon has been appointed for it,
  the splendour of Carmel and Sharon.[2]
  They[3] will themselves see the glory of Yahweh,
  the splendour of our God.

Fortitude: the Lord is coming
3. Strengthen the listless hands,
  and make firm the unsteady knees.
4. Say to those whose hearts are racing,
  'Be strong,

[1] Many (cf., NIV) omit any reference to 'them' – because the pronoun is attached as a direct object to a verb which, in English, could only govern an indirect object, 'to be glad'. Hebrew is, however, more flexible than English over such verbs, and usually the (to us, unexpected) occurrence of a direct object is intended to achieve a greater emphasis. The imagery of this verse is drawn from the Exodus where the menacing wilderness became habitable and even supportive of the pilgrims (Deut. 8:2–3, 15–16).

[2] Lebanon stands for natural abundant fertility, Carmel for order, and Sharon for beauty.

do not be afraid.
Behold! Your God!
With vengeance he will come,
with divine retribution.
He will himself come and save you.'

Salvation and renewal

5. Then[4] the eyes of the blind will be opened,
   and the ears of the deaf will be unlocked.[5]
6. Then like a deer, the lame will leap about,
   and the tongue of the dumb will shout aloud.
   For[6] in the wilderness water will break out,
   and watercourses in the arid plain.
7. And the parched ground will become a pool,
   and the thirsty ground a place bubbling with water.
   In the habitat of jackals, each in its den,
   grass as well as reeds and rushes.

The highway and the homecoming

8. And a highway will be there – a way:
   the way of holiness it will be called.
   An unclean person will not traverse it –
   it is for them!
   Whoever walks the way –
   even simpletons could not go astray!
9. Not even the most ferocious beast[7] will go up[8] on it.
   It will not be found there.
   And the redeemed[9] will walk;
10. and Yahweh's ransomed[10] ones will return
    and they will come to Zion with loud shouting.
    And eternal rejoicing will be upon their heads:
    and they will overtake[11] happiness and rejoicing,
    and sorrow and sighing will flee away.

3 The still anonymous 'them' of v. 1.

4 Emphatic 'then' of time, here and at the beginning of v. 6.

5 Except for 42:20, the first verb (*paqach*) is only used of opening eyes. The second verb (*pathach*) is a general verb of opening (gates, doors, bottles, wombs). 'Unlocked' is offered for variation.

6 In the context of wilderness imagery water is the transforming agent. It is in that sense that Isaiah introduces it here.

7 Lit., 'the ferocious one of a beast', i.e., such as might, by innate strength and a capacity to strike terror, force its way on to the way.

8 A 'highway' means what it says, a road built up above the surrounding land.

9 The verb *ga'al* is frequently used in Isaiah from now on. Its participle, *go'el*, is used of the next of kin whose right it is to intervene on behalf of a mistreated or helpless relative,

and to take upon himself his relative's need, burden or debt as if it were his own. cf., Ruth 3:13. Isaiah emphasises Yahweh as 'Redeemer', his people's next-of-kin: 43:1, 14; 44:6, 22–24; 48:20; 52:3; 59:20; 60:16; 63:9, 16.

10   See 1:27. This verb stresses the price paid; the other verb, *ga'al*, stresses the person who does the paying.

11   What always eluded them before, they finally catch up with. Now it is sorrow that gets away!

Thought for the day: Isaiah 35:1–10

Sometimes even Isaiah excels himself! He was a master wordsmith and poet; in chapter 35 he is at his highest and best. But if the beauty of Isaiah's words and thoughts thrills us, how great is our excitement when we realise that he is writing about us! We are the enigmatic 'them' and 'they' (vv. 1, 2, 8), the anonymous ones around whom the poem moves, because we are the redeemed and ransomed (vv. 9–10) with whom it ends. The 'ransomed' (v. 10) are those for whom the price has been paid; the 'redeemed' (v. 9) are those with whom the Lord, the divine next-of-kin, has identified himself, saying to us: 'What is your problem? Give it to me. What is your need? I will meet it. What is your burden? Lay it on my shoulders.' That is the way with the *Goel*, the kinsman-redeemer. He bears it all, pays it all, does it all. He the doer, we the recipients. But now that we know who the 'them' and 'they' are, follow through what Isaiah says about them, about us. First, whatever our circumstances appear to be (the desert, the parched land, v. 1), we may confidently expect to be provided for. No other eye but ours, the eye of faith, will see the blossoming, but the blossom will be there. Secondly, we endure as seeing him who is invisible (Heb. 11:27). In every situation, in every place, the glory of the Lord is present – and, remember, his glory is not an abstract 'something', the Lord's glory is the Lord in all his glory, with us, recognised by faith, all along the way. Thirdly, to the outward eye, the road may seem full of twists and turns, but it is a protected pathway from which no hazard can dislodge the pilgrim (v. 9). It is a 'highway' (v. 8), running in a straight line from conversion to glory. And, finally, the end is guaranteed: emphasise the verb, 'the redeemed *shall* come'. Everything that made the journey a sad experience will take to its legs; every unalloyed delight that slipped like soap out of the pilgrim's grasp will be finally possessed. Zion admits no disappointment.

Day 39   Isaiah 36:1–22

36:1–37:38. The rock of history

Isaiah ends this first section of his book with two chapters of history – the record of what happened in 701 BC when Sennacherib the King of Assyria advanced against Judah and Jerusalem. In many ways it would have helped if he had placed this account before chapter 28, because, in fact, it outlines the historical background to Isaiah's ministry in chapters 28–37: the Assyrian advance, culminating in Hezekiah's belated adoption of a position of faith and the consequent demolition of Assyria's forces by the Angel of the Lord. It was this threat which drove Jerusalem's politicians into the arms of Egypt and the Egyptian alliance, which Isaiah saw as their death warrant (28:14–19). Isaiah rather chose to use the historical narrative as a rock of certainty, confirming all he had said, and therefore proving how trustworthy is the Word of the Lord.

The first Assyrian embassy to Jerusalem: The helpless king (36:1–37:7)

No salvation in faith

36:1. And this is what happened: in the fourteenth year of King Hezekiah,[1] Sennacherib King of Assyria[2] came up against all the fortified cities of Judah and took them.

2. And the king of Assyria sent the Rab-Shakeh[3] from Lachish[4] to Jerusalem to king Hezekiah with an impressive force. And he took his stand at the aqueduct of the top pool on the highway to the Launderer's Field.

3. And Eliakim son of Hilkiah who was over the House, and Shebna the Scribe, and Joah the son of Asaph, the Recorder, went out to him.

4. And the Rab-Shakeh said to them:

1   701 BC.

2   Acceded 705 BC. And until 703 BC he was occupied with the rebellion of Merodach Baladan of Babylon. Then he turned to deal with rebels in western Palestine. He crushed the Philistines and Tyre submitted. He defeated the Egyptian army at its one and only attempt to intervene. By 701 Hezekiah was bereft of all human help.

'Please say to Hezekiah, This is what the great king, the king of Assyria, has said: What is this confidence on which you are relying?

5. I have said, Nothing but a word of the lips[5] is the plan and the strength for war. Now then, on whom have you trusted that you have revolted against me?

6. Behold – you have put your trust on the support of this crushed reed, Egypt, which, when anyone leans on it, it goes into his hand[6] and pierces it! Such is Pharaoh king of Egypt to all who put trust in him!

7. And should you say to me, It is in Yahweh our God that we have put our trust, is it not he whose High Places and altars Hezekiah has removed, and has said to Judah and to Jerusalem, Before this altar you must bow in worship?

8. Now then, do make a bargain, if you please, with my master, the king, the king of Assyria, and let me give you a thousand horses, on condition that you are able, on your part, to put riders on them

9. – so however could you turn back the face of a single commander of the very least of my master's servants? – and you have put your trust in Egypt for chariotry and for horsemen!

10. Now then, is it wholly apart from Yahweh that I have come up against this land to destroy it? It was Yahweh who said to me, Go up against this land and destroy it!'

A popular appeal for surrender

11. And Eliakim and Shebna and Joah said to Rab-Shakeh, 'Please speak to your servants in Aramaic,[7] for we understand it. And do not speak to us in Judaean in the hearing of the people who are on the wall.'

12. And Rab-Shakeh said, 'Is it to your master and to you that my master sent me to speak these words? Is it not to the inhabitants, on the wall, destined with you to eat their excrement and to drink their urine?'[8]

3   The title of some high functionary, hence 'the'. After v. 4, Rab-Shakeh is used as if a personal name.

4   About thirty miles south-west of Jerusalem.

5   A mere word without substance.

6   See 1:15.

7   Aramaic was the language of international diplomacy. 'Understand', lit., 'hear', a regular use of the verb.

8   The revolting conditions within a besieged city.

13. And Rab-shakeh stood and called out in a great voice in Judaean, and said: 'Hear the words of the great king, the king of Assyria.

14. This is what the king has said: Do not let Hezekiah deceive you, for he will not be able to deliver you.

15. And do not let Hezekiah make you trust in Yahweh, saying: 'Yahweh will without doubt deliver us. This city will not be given into the hand of the king of Assyria.'

16. Do not listen to Hezekiah, for this is what the king of Assyria has said: Secure a blessing with my help[9] and come out to me, and eat[10] each one his vine and each his fig tree and each drink water from his well,[11]

17. until I come and take you to a land like your land, a land of grain and new wine, a land of bread and vineyards

18. – lest Hezekiah dupe you, saying: Yahweh himself will deliver us. Have the gods of the nations delivered, any one of them, his land from the king of Assyria's hand?

19. Where is the god of Hamath and Arpad? Where is the god of Sepharvaim? And is it so that they delivered Samaria from my hand?[12]

20. Who, among all the gods of these lands, are there who delivered their land from my hand, that Yahweh should deliver Jerusalem from my hand?'

21. And they were silent, and did not answer him a word, for this was the king's command, saying, You are not to answer him.

22. And Eliakim son of Hilkiah, who was over the house, and Shebna the Scribe, and Joah the son of Asaph, the recorder, came to Hezekiah, with their clothes torn, and told him the words of Rab-Shakeh.

9   Lit., 'Make a blessing with me', a unique phrase of uncertain sense.

10 A second imperative like this is intended to express certainty – 'and you will for certain eat ...' It is the Hebrew idiom, the imperative of assured outcome.

11 'Vine ... fig ... well' symbolise individual prosperity.

12 Possibly, ironically, 'Oh sure! – they delivered Samaria! ...'

Thought for the day: Isaiah 36:1–22

We must neither be enticed from the way of faith, nor fall for the promises and delights of the world. But the way of faith is not a soft option, nor is it always easy to see through the world's attractions. The Lord's power, of course, is such that he could have put paid to Assyria in any of a thousand ways, but he chose to allow that power to bring his people right into the jaws of terror and death. Part of the explanation (see Isaiah 10:5–15) was that this course suited the Lord's holy and moral government of the world; another part is that the Lord is serious about requiring his people to live by faith. Had Assyria been cut off on its home ground it would have called for rejoicing, but not for faith. Judah had to feel its total helplessness in the face of power, its terror in the face of the threat of deportation if it was to hear and respond to the call for faith and to cast itself utterly into the arms of the divine promises. It is a truth for us. When the trial comes that prompts the unbelieving 'Why?' we must rather drill our minds to hear the call for faith, to recall the Lord's promises, and cast ourselves utterly onto the reliable rock of his Word. And that clever man, the Rab-Shakeh, had enough truth on his side to make his enticements seem a live option. Hezekiah had in fact pulled down Yahweh's altars, and obviously the Rab-Shakeh knew something of what Isaiah had said, for example, at 10:5–6, to enable him to claim divine authorisation for his attack. But no, even should we have failed the Lord, and proved faithless, he abides faithful (2 Tim. 2:13). He is still the trustworthy God and still calls and recalls us to trust. Likewise, the example of Jesus is our sure guide. Let Satan skew the Word of God for his own purposes; the Word remains sure and the Lord will always be as good as his Word.

Day 40 Isaiah 37:1–38

The king's reaction: Faith at last!

Hezekiah is depicted throughout as a good man, but, as always in the Bible, there is no whitewash. He was easily swayed when his *amour propre* as a king was involved. Hence his (to us) colossal stupidity in involving himself in rebellion against the world's then super-power. But by 37:1 he has reached the end of his tether and, at last, finds his way back to faith and prayer.

37:1. And when king Hezekiah heard, he tore his clothes and covered himself with sack-cloth, and went into Yahweh's house.

2. And he sent Eliakim who was over the house, and Shebna the Scribe, and the elders of the priests, covered with sack-cloth, to Isaiah, son of Amoz, the prophet,

3. and they said to him, This is what Hezekiah has said: This day is a day of affliction and rebuke and scorn, for sons have come to the point of being born[1] and there is no strength at all to give birth.

4. Perhaps Yahweh your God will hear the words of Rab-Shakeh whom the king of Assyria, his master, sent to revile a living God, and will rebuke the word which Yahweh your God has heard, and perhaps you will lift up a prayer on behalf of the remnant that happens to be left.

5. And the servants of king Hezekiah came to Isaiah,

6. and Isaiah said to them, This is what you are to say to your master: This is what Yahweh has said: 'Do not be afraid of the words which you have heard, with which the flunkeys[2] of the king of Assyria have defamed me.

1   Lit., 'to the place of breaking/breach'.

2   'Young men', in the general sense of underlings: here, deliberately

7. Behold, I am going to put a spirit in him, and he will hear news, and will return to his land, and I will make him fall by the sword in his land.'

The second Assyrian embassy: The godly king

8. And Rab-Shakeh went back, and he found the king of Assyria making war against Libnah, for he had heard that he had moved on from Lachish.³

9. He had heard regarding Tirhakah, king of Cush,⁴ saying, He has come out to go to war with you. He heard, and he sent messengers to Hezekiah, saying,

10. This is what you are to say to Hezekiah, king of Judah: Do not let your God in whom you are trusting deceive you, saying, Jerusalem will not be given into the hand of the king of Assyria.

11. Behold, you yourself have heard what the kings of Assyria have done to all the lands, consigning them to destruction, and you — will you be delivered?

12. Did the gods of the nations deliver them when my fathers destroyed Gozan and Haran and Rezeph and the sons of Eden who were in Talassar?

13. Where is the king of Hamath and the king of Arpad and the king belonging to the city of Sepharvaim, Hena and Ivvah?

14. And Hezekiah took the letter from the hand of the messengers, and read it, and went up to Yahweh's house, and Hezekiah spread it out before Yahweh.

15. And Hezekiah prayed to Yahweh, saying:

16. 'Yahweh of Hosts, God of Israel, enthroned on the cherubim, you are the real God, you alone, for all the kingdoms of the earth. It was you who made the heavens and the earth.

17. Turn your ear, Yahweh, and hear. Open your eyes, Yahweh, and see. And hear all the words of Sennacherib who has sent to revile a living God.

18. In truth, Yahweh, the kings of Assyria have devastated

pricking the pomposity of such a high official as the Rab-Shakeh. 'The king of Assyria's lads'.

3 Lachish was thirty miles south-west of Jerusalem; Libnah is thought to be some miles north of Lachish, the Assyrian army moving away from the supposed Egyptian threat.

4 Tirhakah belonged to the 'Ethiopian' dynasty of Pharaohs – kings of Ethiopia (Cush) who by 712 BC had conquered Egypt. Tirhakah did not actually become Pharaoh of Egypt till 690 BC, eleven years later than the present event, but he was in his twenties, possibly with the courtesy title of 'King of Cush', and acting under his Pharaoh brother, Shebitku. Or, of course, he could here be called 'King of Cush' proleptically, just as we say 'the queen was born in 1926', meaning a child was born who would later be queen.

all the lands – and their own land!⁵ –

19. and have put their gods into the fire, for they were not
Gods but only the work of human hands, wood and
stone, and they destroyed them.

20. Now then, Yahweh
our God, save us from his hand, so that all the kingdoms
of the earth may know that you, Yahweh, are unique.'

21. And Isaiah the son of Amoz sent to Hezekiah, saying:
This is what Yahweh, the God of Israel, has said:
Regarding the fact that you have prayed to me
about Sennacherib, king of Assyria,

22. this is the word which Yahweh has spoken about him:
She has despised you;
she has mocked you,
the virgin, daughter of Zion.⁶
As you retreated,⁷
she has tossed her head,
the daughter of Jerusalem.

23. Whom have you reviled and defamed?
And against whom have you raised your voice,
and lifted your eyes on high?
Against the Holy One of Israel!

24. By the hand of your servants you have reviled the Sovereign!
And you said:
By the abundance of my chariotry
I have myself gone up to the heights of the mountains,
into the recesses of Lebanon,
that I might cut down its loftiest cedars,
its choicest firs;
and that I might come to its utmost height,
its densest forest!

25. I have myself bored wells and drunk waters,
and, with the sole of my foot,
dried up all the irrigation canals of Egypt.

26. Have you not heard?
In time long ago, this is what I prepared;

5 Most alter the Hebrew text here to match 2 Kings 19:17, 'all the nations and their land'. But the Hebrew as it stands could be an awry allusion to the fact that each Assyrian king in turn was greeted by rebellion at home and only secured his throne by making war in the homelands.

6 'Daughter' follows the convention of thinking of cities as feminine, but also indicates an inherited authority, prompting the question who is the power behind the throne. cf., v. 23. 'Virgin' signifies, unviolated, in spite of the Assyrian threat.

7 Lit., 'after you', here, not 'behind your back', but 'as you retreated'.

in days of old I fashioned it.
Now I have brought it about –
namely, that you should be the one
to make fortified cities crash into ruined heaps,

27. and that their inhabitants, rendered ineffective,[8]
should be shattered and reap shame.
They have become green plants of the field and tender shoots,
roof-top grass,
and terraced fields devoid of growth.[9]

28. And each stop you make,
and your going and your coming,
I know –
and how you excite yourself against me!

29. Because your exciting yourself against me,
and your complacency,
have come up into my ears,
I will put my hook in your nose,
and my bridle in your lips,
and I will turn you back by the road by which you came.

30. And this is the sign for you:[10]
Eating this year what grows of itself,[11]
and next year what springs from that,
and in the third year, sow and reap,
and plant vineyards and eat their fruit.[12]

31. And again the escapees of the house of Jacob who are left
(will send their) root downward and produce fruit upward.[13]

32. For from Jerusalem will come forth a remnant,
and an escaped company from Mount Zion.
The zeal of Yahweh of Hosts will achieve this.

33. Therefore
this is what Yahweh has said about the king of Assyria:
He will not come into this city,
nor will he shoot an arrow there,
nor will he confront it with a shield,
nor will he heap up a siege mound against it.

34. By the road by which he came he will go back,

8   Lit., 'short of hand'. The hand
is the symbol of personal
intervention and agency.
The hand that cannot reach
its target is ineffective.

9   The agricultural metaphors
underline how Assyria sees all the
earth as a harvest to be reaped
for its advantage. 'Tender shoots'
points to helplessness; 'house-top
grass', weak growth, transient,
unresisting; 'terraced fields'
etc., is a piece of Hebrew that
defies translation – the Assyrian
intention to sweep the world bare.

10   'You' is masculine singular.
Without warning Isaiah's
message turns from
Sennacherib to Hezekiah.

11   In case people thought Assyrian
withdrawal was just coincidental
or by chance, the Lord offers a
sign so that they may know he
has been at work. A year's sowing
had been lost while the land was
under enemy occupation, but self-
set crops would prove sufficient
'this year'. Likewise since the
Assyrian presence had made
sowing for next year impossible,
again chance growth would
be enough. Then sowing and
reaping could recommence, and
settled conditions would permit
agriculture to resume operation.

and into this city he will not come.
This is Yahweh's Word.

35. And I will shield this city so as to save it,
    for my own sake and for my servant David's sake.

36. And the Angel of Yahweh went out, and struck down
    in the camp of Assyria a hundred and eighty-five
    thousand. And when they got up early in the morning,
    behold, all of them were corpses – dead!

37. And Sennacherib king of Assyria moved on and went
    and returned, and lived in Nineveh.

38. And it came about that, while he was bowing in
    worship in the house of Nisroch his god, Adrammelech
    and Sharezer his sons struck him down with the sword,
    and they, for their part, made their escape to the land of
    Ararat, and Esar-haddon his son became king in his place.

---

12 These last four imperatives
    are plural, referring to
    the whole people.

13 The Hebrew text in the first
    part of this line is simply 'a root
    downward', lacking verb. The
    meaning, however, is plain.

Thought for the day: Isaiah 37:1–38

It's an odd thing, but if you are with a group of Christian people and raise the topic of prayer, in a short time someone will say, 'But there are all sorts of things we must do as well as pray'. Quite right too! There are! But when Jesus said that we should 'always pray and not lose heart' (Luke 18:1) he meant that there is something that comes first, keeps company with everything else, and goes on after they have stopped – prayer. If Hezekiah had turned to prayer first instead of last, what a lot of bother and worry he would have saved himself! Prayer is the foremost evidence of faith. Even Sennacherib somehow knew that Hezekiah was adopting a position of faith – verse 10, 'your God in whom you are trusting' – but the evidence given to us is that when he received the letter he no longer sent to Isaiah to pray (v. 4) but himself spread the whole matter out before the Lord (v. 14). He 'took it to the Lord in prayer'. Just that; nothing else! It's a great thing, of course, to associate others with us in prayer, and Hezekiah did nothing wrong in seeking Isaiah's prayer – for prayer-ministry was one aspect of a prophet's office (Genesis 20:7), but it was in direct response to Hezekiah's own prayer that the answer came in all its abundance. And remember, Hezekiah was in trouble hugely and mostly by his own fault, seeking alliances against his Assyrian overlord. But the power of prayer does not reside in the place where it starts but in the place it reaches. The kneeling king may be wholly unworthy, but the King on the Throne is full of power, grace and sufficiency (Hebrews 4:14–16). Consequently, the answer to prayer – the belated prayer of the man in trouble through his own folly – undertook the whole need, dealt with the whole problem (vv. 36–38). Sadly Jesus wondered if, at his return, he would find faith like this on earth – the faith that flees to prayer and leaves it to the prayer-answering God (Luke 18:7–8).

PART THREE

THE BOOK OF THE SERVANT
(Isaiah 38–55)

Day 41   Isaiah 38:1–20

**Historical prologue: Hezekiah's fatal choice
(Isaiah 38–39)**
When Isaiah had set the scene for his ministry in chapters 1–5,
he immediately foresaw a coming King, a second David, as
the solution to his people's needs (chs. 6–37), but developing
circumstances exposed another, and deeper need. This is
developed in chapters 38–39: Hezekiah's great sin and its
aftermath. He fell for the enticements of Babylon to rebel
against Assyria (39:1–8) and by doing so turned from the
promises of God made to him in his illness (38:5–6): the
promise of healing and of delivering him and his city from
Assyria. In effect Isaiah responded: If, instead of relying on the
promises, you choose Babylon, then you shall have Babylon –
as a captive, exiled people and a defunct monarchy. By saying
this Isaiah seemed, of course, to call in question the glorious
promises he had made of a coming King. Therefore he was
now in the position where he must either repudiate what he
had previously predicted or he must go further and show how
the Lord's glorious promises will be worked out in this new
context. The Lord's answer, through Isaiah, is the prediction
of the Servant of the Lord who by bearing his people's sins
will bring them back to the Lord, and in whom the Davidic
promises will be fulfilled. This is the theme of Isaiah 38–55.

Hezekiah's Illness (Isaiah 38:1–20)
One prayer, two answers

38:1. In those days, Hezekiah became sick, to death,[1] and
Isaiah, the son of Amoz, the prophet, came to him and
said to him: This is what Yahweh has said: 'Command
your house,[2] for you are about to die: you will not live.'

[1] We would say 'fell terminally ill'.

[2] The idiom for, 'Set your
affairs in order.'

2. And Hezekiah turned his face to the wall, and he prayed
   to Yahweh,

3. and he said: 'Ah, please, Yahweh, do remember that I
   have walked[3] before you truly and whole-heartedly and
   that which is good in your eyes I have done.' And
   Hezekiah wept copiously.[4]

4. And Yahweh's word came to Isaiah, saying:

5. Go and say to Hezekiah: 'This is what Yahweh, the
   God of your father David, has said: I have heard your prayer;
   I have seen your tears. Behold I am going to add to your
   days fifteen years.

6. And from the grip[5] of the king of Assyria I will deliver
   you, and this city: I will shield this city.

7. And this is the sign for you, straight from Yahweh, that
   Yahweh will perform this word which he has spoken:

8. Behold, I am going to bring back the shadow on the
   steps – where the sun has gone down on the steps of Ahaz –
   ten steps backwards.[6] And the sun did go back ten steps
   on the steps where it had gone down.

Hezekiah's record of his experience

9. The writing by Hezekiah, king of Judah, when he was sick,
   and recovered from his sickness:

*An unwelcome exchange: The land of the living for the land of the
departed*

10. I myself said:
    At the mid-point of my days
    I must go through the gates of Sheol.
    I have been sentenced to lose[7]
    the remainder of my years.

11. I said,
    I will not see Yah – Yah![8] – in the land of the living.
    No more will I behold humankind,
    being in the company of those
    who inhabit cessation.[9]

3 'Walked up and down/
   about', cf., Gen. 13:17.

4 'With great weeping'.

5 See 1:15.

6 This translation simplifies what
   may be a dislocated piece of
   Hebrew: 'Behold I am going
   to bring back the shadow
   (masculine) on the steps, which
   it (feminine) has gone down on
   the steps of Ahaz by the sun ...'
   Presumably Ahaz (2 Kings 16:1),
   Hezekiah's father, had built these
   steps which – whether by accident
   or design – acted as a sundial.

7 Lit., 'I have been visited in respect
   of'. The verb 'to visit' is used of
   Yahweh's oversight of our lives,
   whether to bless or to punish.

8 The affectionate diminutive of the
   divine name, see 12:2. In effect,
   as if to say 'my dear Yahweh'. The
   repeated 'Yah' underlines the loss
   involved – 'Imagine not seeing him!'

Divine hostility: images of despair

12. My life-span has been plucked up
    and removed from me,
    like a shepherd's tent![10]
    Like a weaver, I have rolled up my life,
    from the loom-threads – how he has snipped me off.
    From day to night[11] you finish me off!

13. Did I but compose myself until morning,[12]
    like a lion
    so would he shatter all my bones.
    From day to night you finish me off!

14. I moan[13] like a dove.
    Weakly my eyes gaze up:[14]
    O Sovereign One,
    I am under oppression.
    Undertake for me.[15]

Divine Restoration:commitment

15. What am I to say, and one say to me,
    since he is himself sure to act?
    I will watch my step all my years,
    on account of my bitter experience.[16]

16. Sovereign One,
    it is in respect of these things people should live,
    and regarding everything in them shall be the life
    of my spirit.[17]
    And you will make me strong, and certainly keep me alive.[18]

17. Behold,
    it was for well-being that I had such bitter experience,[19]
    and you yourself in love kept my soul from the terminal pit,[20]
    for you have thrown behind your back all my sins.
    A welcome exchange: the land of the departed for the land
    of the living

18. For it is not Sheol that will give you thanks,
    death that will praise you.
    Those who descend to the pit do not await[21]
    your faithfulness.[22]

9   i.e., 'who have come to the
    end' of this life and live on
    when life here has ceased.

10 As easily and resistlessly
    as dismantling a tent.

11 Probably meaning 'before a day
    is out', an idiom for imminent,
    speedy action. cf., Job 4:20.

12 i.e., there is no way to evade
    what the Lord wills. Even
    if I managed to survive one
    more night, morning would
    bring his shattering.

13 See 8:19

14 Lit., 'My eyes languish
    to the height'.

15 Lit., 'Become my guarantor/
    Go bail for me'.

16 Lit., 'my bitterness of soul'.

17 i.e., all should live with awareness
    of the uncertainties, calamities,
    and such like, of life, and with the
    assurance that the Lord hears and
    answers prayer. Hezekiah himself
    professes that life's sad experiences
    have quickened his spirit.

18 Regarding the translation of v. 16
    no one can say more than that
    the Hebrew probably intends
    something like this. The final verb
    is an imperative, treated here as
    an imperative of certain outcome.

19. It is the living one, the living one who gives you thanks,
as I do today.
Father to sons imparts knowledge of your faithfulness.
20. Yahweh was committed to saving me,
and with my music we will sing
all the days of our life
at the house of Yahweh.

19 Lit., 'the bitterness I
had was bitter'.

20 Lit., 'loved my soul from
…': *chashaq* occurs here for
the only time in Isaiah. It
expresses the yearning of love
in both passion and tenderness.
cf., Deut. 7:7; 10:15.

21 See 8:17.

22 Not that the dead go to a
praiseless existence but that
they can no longer offer the
praise due to the Lord's earthly
faithfulnesses such as Hezekiah
has just experienced.

Thought for the day: Isaiah 38:1–20

We would probably hesitate to come to the Lord pleading our past godliness ('I have walked before you') and obedience ('what is good in your eyes I have done'), but Hezekiah did not hesitate, and neither would the Bible as a whole. No, he is not turning at this point from salvation by faith to salvation by works; he is putting into words the Bible truth that 'God is a rewarder of those who seek him' (Heb. 11:6). Hebrews teaches also that 'God is not unjust to forget your work' (6:10). The danger we need to guard against, of course, is any thought that, by walking with the Lord in faithfulness and truth, we are creating a sort of bargaining counter for use in some future crisis. Not so do the Lord's children live within his family, where grace is the unvarying ruling principle. It is by grace that we have been saved (Eph. 2:6); it is under grace that we live (Heb. 4:14–16); and we are called to grow in grace (2 Pet. 3:18). John Newton put it well that it is 'grace hath brought us safe thus far, and grace will lead us home', and even in heaven our expectation is an ever richer display of grace (Eph. 2:7). If therefore we make any progress in Christ, produce any fruits of Christ-likeness, and then find that heaven-sent enrichments now attend our way, both the work of obedience and its rewards are all of grace. Grace has prompted and enabled the achievement, and grace has given the reward. On our side we are ever and in all things the undeserving; on his side, he is ever the God of all grace (1 Pet. 5:10). Nevertheless – and it is a huge 'nevertheless' – our calling is to live worthy of the gospel (Phil. 1:27), 'to live a life worthy of the Lord, fully pleasing, fruitful in every good work' (Col. 1:10). In a race, Paul notes, only one receives the prize; therefore, he adds, 'Run in such a way that you may obtain it' (1 Cor. 9:24).

Day 42 Isaiah 38:21–39:8

Hezekiah's weakness was that he was easily seduced into rebellion. In chapter 39 we see him fall for an invitation (contained by inference in the letter of 39:1) from Merodach Baladan. Merodach was a Babylon freedom fighter, passionate to deliver Babylon from Assyrian rule. He largely succeeded in this, reigning as king of Babylon 722–710 BC, and, possibly more shakily, 705–702 BC. Anxious to bolster up his position he set about gathering allies in his rebellion. Chapter 39 records his approach to Hezekiah. But the Lord has already promised (38:6) to deliver Jerusalem from Babylon, so that Hezekiah must now choose either the way of faith or the way of works – rebellion.

Background to Hezekiah's fatal choice

21. And Isaiah had said, 'Let them take a fig poultice and apply it to the boil and he will live.'
22. And Hezekiah had said, 'What is the sign that I will go up to Yahweh's house?'[1]

The fatal decision

I. The envoys and Hezekiah's response

39:1. At that time, Merodach Baladan, son of Baladan, king of Babylon,[2] sent a letter and a gift to Hezekiah – he had heard that he had been ill and had returned to strength.

2. And Hezekiah rejoiced over them and showed them[3] his treasure-house – the silver and the gold and the spices and the fine oil – his whole arsenal and everything that could be found in his treasuries: there was not a thing which Hezekiah did not show them in his house and in all his realm.

[1] These are 'bridge' verses. They conclude the account of Hezekiah's illness and recovery; they prepare for the tragedy that followed. Hezekiah's recovery had come about at Isaiah's direction (the poultice) by the word of the Lord (v. 5); the sign had been asked for (v. 22), promised (v. 7) and fulfilled (v. 8). Thus the Lord's power and faithfulness in keeping his word and promise had been proved – the double promise, of healing and deliverance. The question remains whether Hezekiah will believe this or turn to some other way of deliverance.

2. The Word of the Lord: Choose Babylon and get Babylon

3. And Isaiah the prophet came to king Hezekiah and said to him: 'What did these men say to you, and from where have they come to you?' And Hezekiah said: 'From a distant land they have come to me! From Babylon!'

4. And he said, 'What have they seen in your house?' And Hezekiah said, 'Everything that is in my house they have seen. There is not a thing which I have not shown them in my treasuries.'

5. And Isaiah said to Hezekiah, 'Hear the word of Yahweh of Hosts:

6. Behold, the days are coming when everything which is in your house and what your fathers have treasured away, up to this day, will be taken to Babylon. Nothing will be left, Yahweh has said.

7. And some of your sons who will come from you, whom you will beget, they will take, and they will become eunuchs in the palace of the king of Babylon.'

3. Hezekiah's disappointing reaction

8. And Hezekiah said to Isaiah, 'Yahweh's word which you have spoken is good.' And he said,[4] 'Because there will be peace and truth in my days.'

---

2   Merodach Baladan was a Babylonian patriot, determined to free his city and land from the Assyrian yoke. He actually achieved independence and reigned as king in Babylon 722–710 BC, when he was driven out by Sargon of Assyria, but when Sargon died in 705 Merodach joined in the general rebellion and again became king. This time his success was short lived. Sennacherib defeated him in 702 BC. The embassy to Hezekiah must be dated at some point when Merodach was seeking anti-Assyrian allies.

3   The oddity of Hezekiah's response (when someone visits you on your return from hospital do you show them your bank statement?) can only be explained by assuming that the 'letter' was an invitation to join Merodach in rebellion. But to do so would fly in the face of the Lord's promise that he would deliver Hezekiah and his city from the Assyrians (38:6), a promise confirmed by the astonishing, earth-shaking sign of the sun! This was Hezekiah's choice: faith or works? Trust the Lord or trust Merodach Baladan?

4   Very often in Hebrew a second 'said' like this is equivalent to, 'for he thought/said to himself'. Here outward submission to Yahweh's word is matched by inward smugness.

Thought for the day: Isaiah 38:21–39:8

What a cautionary tale! Beware what you choose –you may get it! Hezekiah chose Babylon, and Babylon was what he got! Yet, over and over again, the Lord graciously stands between us and the consequences of our actions and choices, so possibly we ought to ask what was specially awful about this choice that Hezekiah made. Well, remember 22:14 and why that technological marvel, Hezekiah's tunnel, was the unforgiveable sin. It involved forsaking the way of faith, and choosing the way of 'works', self-salvation. And here is the same Hezekiah at it again: the Lord promised deliverance (38:6), but instead of trusting and waiting, Hezekiah chose deliverance by worldly alliance, human resources, and self-confidence. But the hymn got it right – 'trust and obey; there is no other way'! Now look at the frame of mind that prompted Hezekiah's choice: 'From a distant land … to me!' Just think! The big time rebel of the ancient world, the famous Merodach-Baladan, king of Babylon, inviting little me, Hezekiah of Judah, to join him!! Self-importance – and Hezekiah now had it in spadefuls (v. 8) – is a huge foe of spirituality. How can those who walk with themselves walk with God (Luke 18:11)? The New Testament emphasises the virtue which NKJV translates as 'lowliness' and which Ephesians 4:1 makes the first mark of the 'worthy' life. It should be translated 'humble-mindedness', a correct, realistically lowly estimate of ourselves. When he lost this, Hezekiah lost everything. And how easily the fateful die was cast! We can never tell in advance when the point of no return will be reached. It is a secret locked in the absolute justice of the divine love. We just know that we must flee from every next temptation, and clutch, believingly, patiently, resolutely onto the promises of God.

Day 43   Isaiah 40:1–11

The consolation of the world (40:1–42:17)

Astonishingly, no sooner has Isaiah pronounced judgment on Hezekiah's sin than he is directed to organise messengers of comfort. But (maybe because exile to Babylon prompts thoughts of the wider world) the comfort-message covers all the earth, Israel and the Gentiles.

Consolation for the Lord's people: Voices of consolation

40:1. Console, console my people,[1]
    your God keeps saying.

2.   Speak lovingly to Jerusalem,[2]
    and call out to her,
    that her time of duress has been fulfilled,
    that the punishment of her iniquity has been accepted,
    that she has received from Yahweh's hand
    the exact payment for[3] all her sins.

The first voice: Yahweh coming; worldwide revelation

3.   A voice![4] Someone is calling out:
    In the desert,
    clear a road for Yahweh,
    make straight through the open plain
    a highway for our God.

4.   Every valley must be raised,
    and every mountain and hill lowered,
    and the rough ground must become flat,
    and the mountain chain a pass.

5.   And the glory of Yahweh will be revealed,
    and all flesh will see it together:
    for it is Yahweh's mouth that has spoken.

[1] Plural imperatives. Against the background of the dire prediction of exile and loss, the Lord has such a full message of consolation that not just Isaiah but unnamed others are summoned to bring the consoling word. Far from judgment having the last word (39:6–7) consolation has the first word!

[2] Lit., 'Speak to the heart of' – as of an ardent lover wooing his beloved, Gen. 34:3.

[3] Lit., 'the double', referring to one thing exactly matching another. The preposition 'for' (The Hebrew prefixed preposition b^e) expresses 'price/value/payment'.

[4] See 13:4.

The second voice: Human transience and the permanent Word

6. A Voice! Someone is saying, Call out,
    and someone is saying, What am I to call out?
    All flesh is grass,
    and all its reliability like a flower of the field.

7. Grass withers, flower wilts,
    for Yahweh's Spirit has breathed on it.
    Ah, surely, the people are grass!

8. Grass withers, flower wilts,
    and the word of our God rises up[5] for ever.

The third voice: Good news for Zion

9. To a lofty mountain, up with you,
    Zion, bearer of good news!
    With strength raise your voice,
    Jerusalem, bearer of good news.
    Raise your voice; do not fear.
    Say to the cities of Judah:
    Behold! Your God!

10. Behold –
    as a strong one,
    the Sovereign Yahweh will come,
    his arm[6] ruling for him.
    Behold!
    the wage he has earned[7] is with him,
    and his work is in front of him.

11. Like a shepherd who shepherds his flock,
    in his arm he gathers the lambs,
    and in his bosom carries them;
    those with young he guides along.

5   The literal meaning of *qum*. Used to express not just the continuance of the Word while all else wilts but its certainty of fulfilment and its capacity for active intervention – 'to stand up and be counted'.

6   'Arm' symbolises personal strength. cf., 33:2; 52:10. In 51:9–10 (cf., 53:1) the Lord's arm is personified, and one is therefore tempted to use the upper case here, 'Arm'.

7   Lit., 'his wage', but a pronoun with 'wage' always points to the wage-earner. In ways Isaiah has yet to explain the Lord has worked and earned a wage. The 'work' he has accomplished lies in front of him, i.e., the people who are his flock.

Thought for the day: Isaiah 40:1–11

The most wonderful thing about these verses is not the beauty of their expression (though that in itself would have been enough), nor the attractiveness of what they reveal (though, again, that would suffice), but the place where they come. Doom has been pronounced on Hezekiah (39:6–7), and with it the death knell seems to have been sounded for all Isaiah's glittering predictions of a coming king. At this darkest of moments, the call goes out to speak the word of comfort (v. 1), to proclaim hardship finished and sins forgiven (v. 2), to announce that Yahweh himself is on his way with worldwide significance (vv. 3–5), that his word and promises can never fail (vv. 6–8), and that Zion's people are the flock he has worked for and now holds in his tender care (vv. 9–11). This is the Lord undefeated even by our most grievous sin; the Lord who never calls back the word he has spoken, and who cannot be deflected from its fulfilment! It will all become even more wonderful as Isaiah develops his message in these chapters. We will learn what the Lord's 'arm ruling' means, that it is in truth his 'arm' – the Lord Jesus anticipated in his executive might; we will discover what 'work' he has done to earn the 'wages' he desired – his people, his flock. So much wonder lies ahead, but let us never lose sight of this initial wonder or fail to stand in awe of it. It is what he is towards us as sinners and failures; it is the way his intentions triumph over our frailties. The Sovereign God is never more sovereign than in the work of mercy and salvation, and it is those who know they have most signally erred and strayed from his ways, who, within the blessed arena of salvation, feel most gently the warmth of his shepherding arms around them, and know themselves for sure to be the lambs of his flock.

Day 44 Isaiah 40:12–31

Alongside the tenderness of Yahweh's shepherding care Isaiah now sets the magnificence of his sovereign power and executive rule as Creator. The former expresses the attractiveness and delightfulness of his promises; the latter his irresistible power to keep what he has promised. The climax, therefore, of the present passage is (vv. 27–31) the impossibility that this great Creator should forget or desert his own people.

Wisdom

40:12. Who measured out the waters in the hollow of his hand,
    and adjusted[1] the heavens with his spanned fingers,
    and contained the dust of the earth in a pint pot,[2]
    and weighed out the mountains with a scales,
    and the hills with a pair of balances?
13.   Who adjusted Yahweh's Spirit,
    and, as his consultant, kept him informed?
14.   Whom did he consult so as to help him to discern
    and teach him in the path of judgment,[3]
    and teach him knowledge,
    and inform him of the road to full[4] discernment?

Greatness

15.   Behold! Nations!
    As a splash from a bucket,
    and as dust on a pair of balances
    they are to be assessed!
    Behold! Land masses![5]
    He lifts them up[6] like so much powder!
16.   And Lebanon itself is not sufficient for fuel,
    and its fauna is not sufficient for a burnt offering!

1   Thus, literally, *takan*, to adjust a thing for its place or function, to set something on the right track.

2   The literal meaning seems to be 'a third' and to refer to some standard of measurement; cf., Ps. 80:5–6, lit., 'tears to drink in a "third".'

3   As so often, 'making the right decision'. See 2:4; 26:8.

4   'Discernment' is here a plural of amplification; 'every sort of'.

5   On *'iyyim* see 41:1.

6   Like a person assesses the weight of something with one hand.

17. All the nations are just about nothing placed in front of him!
    Partakers of nonentity and meaninglessness
    they are assessed in comparison with him!

Sole deity
18. And to whom will you liken God*,
    and what likeness will you arrange for him?
19. An image?
    A craftsman casts it!
    A goldsmith plates it with gold
    and with chains of silver a silversmith!
20. The impoverished person for his oblation
    chooses a tree that does not rot;
    a skilled craftsman he seeks for himself,
    to set up an image that will not slip!

King of kings [7]
21. Do you not know?
    Do you not hear?
    Has it not, from the start, been told you?
    Have you not discerned from the foundations of the earth?
22. There is One who sits enthroned over the circle of
    the earth,
    and its inhabitants are like grasshoppers;
    who stretches out like gauze the heavens,
    and has spread them like a tent to live in;
23. who destines people of importance[8] to become nothing;
    earth's judges he makes meaningless.[9]
24. No sooner planted,
    no sooner sown,
    no sooner their stock rooted in the earth,
    than this – he has blown on them,
    and they have withered,
    and, like stubble, a whirlwind carries them off!
25. And to whom will you liken me,
    that I should be on his level,
    the Holy One keeps saying?

7   From here to v. 26 Isaiah turns
    from the work of creation to the
    management of the created world:
    Yahweh's government of 'history'
    (22–24) and of the cosmos (26).

8   Word used six times in OT (only
    here in Isaiah) with a very general
    sense of leaders, high officials.

9   See 24:10. Possibly we could
    interpret it here as 'of no
    further significance'.

26. Lift up your eyes on high
    and see who created these,
    who brings out by number their host,
    calls all of them by name,
    through abundance of power
    and reliable[10] in strength,
    not a single one is missing.

10   See 28:2.

Unforgetting and self-giving
27. Why do you keep saying, Jacob,
    and speaking, Israel:
    'My way has become hidden from Yahweh,
    and from my God my judgment[11] passes away?'

11   See 2:4; 26:8. Here: of the
      authoritative decision his people
      are looking to Yahweh to make
      about them; the sense is of a case
      being constantly dismissed.

28. Have you not known?
    Or have you not heard?
    Yahweh is God Eternal:
    creating the extremities of the earth,[12]
    unfainting and unwearying,
    unfathomable in his discernment,
29. to the fainting giving strength,
    and to the powerless multiplying durability.

12   i.e., 'the earth from one end to
      the other'. 'Creating' could be
      translated 'creator of', but it is in
      fact a participle. The relationship
      between creator and creation is
      ongoing, a perpetual engagement.

30. And young men faint and grow weary,
    and picked men[13] stumble completely,
31. and those who wait confidently[14] for Yahweh
    put on fresh strength;
    they rise up on wings like eagles;
    they run and do not weary;
    they walk and do not faint.

13   'Young men' is the general
      word for the male population
      on its young side; 'picked men'
      most obviously comes from the
      verb 'to choose', those picked
      out for their prowess, those in
      the prime of their strength.

14   See 8:17.

Thought for the day: Isaiah 40:12–31

Even if we wouldn't dream of saying it, circumstances can easily prompt the unbidden thought, Where is God in all this? And why is he not doing something about it? Has he forgotten? There is, of course, a god who is not there when we need him (1 Kings 18:27), but not the Lord God Almighty. He is 'unfainting, unwearying', that is, he lacks neither energy nor commitment; his strength does not ebb away, nor does he tire of the task in hand. It's just that 'he is unfathomable in his discernment' – he sees to the heart of the situation in a way we never can and in ways we are not equipped to appreciate. The sooner we learn that lesson the better. It will meet us again in Isaiah in the famous words (55:8), 'my thoughts are not your thoughts ... your ways are not my ways.' But please remember: our inability to 'discern' does not mean that no discernment is at work; our inability to see point or purpose does not mean there is no point or purpose. The more we exalt the greatness of our God, the more we learn to appreciate our smallness, weakness, incapacity. We need to learn not to fret and fume; we need to accept our limitations of knowledge, wisdom and foresight. Or, as Isaiah tells us, we need to practise 'waiting' for the Lord. Waiting is looking. When Isaiah puts Israel's grousing into words (v. 27) what does he do next? He directs our eyes to the Lord (v. 28). Look away from yourself, *look at him*. Next comes, *expect from him* (v. 29); he is ever the giving God – giving strength to surmount the problem, to run the race, and (best of all) to walk the path (v. 31). But this is not (so to speak) a hypodermic syringe operation – the injection of some transforming serum called 'strength'. It is what the Lord is in himself: the unfainting, unwearying one imparts his own unfainting, unwearying nature (vv. 28, 31).

Day 45 Isaiah 41:1–20

In 40:12–31 Isaiah used the greatness of Yahweh as Creator to guarantee the huge and worldwide promises of 40:1–11. This great God cannot fail to keep his promises and guard his people. In 41:1–20, Isaiah offers a second guarantee: Yahweh is also the world ruler (41:1–7), and in this capacity also he is the guardian of his own people (41:8–20).

Who rules the world?

41:1. Come to me in silence, O wide earth,[1]
　　and let the states[2] put on new strength.
　　When they approach, then they may speak.
　　Let us come near together for judgment.[3]

A case in point

2.　　Who has roused from the sun-rising
　　one whom, in righteousness, he calls to follow him?[4]
　　Before him he gives up nations,[5]
　　and makes him dominate even kings.
　　He gives them, like dust, to his sword,
　　like driven chaff to his bow.

3.　　He pursues them; he passes on in peace.
　　By his feet, along the path, he does not come.[6]

4.　　Who has worked and acted,
　　calling the generations from the start?
　　I, Yahweh, am the beginning,
　　and with the last, I am!

A hopeless reaction: Make new gods!

5.　　The wide earth[7] saw and feared;
　　the extremities of the earth started trembling.
　　They drew together and came.

1　*'iyyim*, sometimes 'island(s)' (e.g., 23:2, 6), is also used by Isaiah for what we would call 'land masses' (40:15), or for a particular, extended area (20:6), or remote places only accessible by water, 'coastlands' (24:15), and, as here, the far flung extent of the earth.

2　See 17:12.

3　See 2:4; 26:8. Here 'judgment' means the decision of a specific question: who rules the world?

4　'To follow him' is lit., 'to his foot'. This is a regular idiomatic use. In vv. 2–4 Isaiah poses a question in principle: if a conqueror arises, who has prompted such a thing and brought it about? As these chapters develop, the picture of the anonymous conqueror becomes the reality of Cyrus the Persian conquering Babylon.

5　i.e., before the advancing conqueror Yahweh gives up nations into his power.

6. Each helps his fellow man,
   and to his brother he keeps saying, 'Be strong'.
7. And the craftsman strengthens the goldsmith,
   the one who smooths with a hammer (strengthens)
   the one striking the anvil,
   saying about the welding: 'That's good!'
   And they made it strong with nails:
   'It can't slip!'

By contrast: Life with Yahweh – three pictures

Picture 1. Victory for the weak

8. And you, Israel, are my servant,
   Jacob, whom I have chosen,
   the seed of Abraham who loves me –
9. you of whom I took hold at the extremities of the earth,
   and at its remotest bounds called you,
   and I said to you:
   You are my servant,
   I have chosen you,
   and I have determined not to spurn you.
10. Do not fear,
    for I am really with you.
    Do not look this way and that,
    for I am your God.
    I will make you resolute:
    more, I will help you;
    more still, I will grip you with the right hand
    of my righteousness.[8]
11. Behold,
    they will reap shame and ignominy – all who are
    enraged against you,
    they will become a veritable nothing and perish –
    those in contention with you;
12. you will seek them and not find them – the men of your strife;
    they will become a veritable nothing and nonentity – the
    men of your war.[9]

6 A horribly wooden, even if literal, translation. The reference is either to some surprise move on the part of the conqueror, not arriving by the way he was expected, or to the speed of his progress – as if his feet did not touch the ground.

7 *'iyyim*, see 41:1.

8 Or 'my righteous right hand'. The 'hand' (see 1:12) is the capacity for personal, intervening action. The Lord's hand puts into effect all his righteous (see 5:7; 26:7) purposes and does what he thinks right for us.

9 i.e., respectively those who strive with you ... those who go to war with you.

13. For I, Yahweh, am your God,
keeping hold of your right hand;
the one who is saying to you:
Do not fear;
I have determined to help you.

Picture 2. Transformation for the negligible

14. Do not fear, Worm Jacob,
mere mortals of Israel.
I have, myself, determined to help you –
and your redeemer[10] is the Holy One of Israel.

15. Behold,
I have decided to make you into a threshing sledge,[11]
Sharpened, new, many-toothed.
You will thresh mountains and pulverise them,
and hills you will make like chaff.

16. You will winnow them
and a wind will carry them off,
and a whirlwind scatter them.
And, as for you, you will exult in Yahweh,
in the Holy One of Israel you will make your boast.

Picture 3. Provision for the needy

17. The downtrodden and vulnerable are seeking water,
and there is none.
With thirst their tongue is dried up.
I, Yahweh, will myself answer them;
the God of Israel, I will not leave them.

18. On bare heights I will open up rivers,
and in the middle of valleys fountains;
I will make a desert into a pool of water,
and a dry land into outflowings of water.

19. I will put in the desert
cedar, acacia, and myrtle, and olive;
in the arid plain I will set
fir, box, and cypress, all together,

10 See 35:9.

11 A heavy wooden platform, weighted down with stones, fitted underneath with anything sharp and cutting. It was dragged to and fro over the reaped corn, to chop up the stalks into stubble ready for winnowing. Imagine a threshing sledge efficient enough to cut mountains down to size!

20. in order that they[12] may see, and know,
pay attention,[13] and understand all at once,
that it is Yahweh's hand which has done this,
and it is the Holy One of Israel who has created it.

---

[12] The downtrodden and vulnerable of v. 17.

[13] Lit., simply 'may set', an ellipsis for 'set the heart (mind) on, give attention to'.

Thought for the day: Isaiah 41:1–20

'Dear young people', said a marvellous lady to our youth group, 'you must never be afraid to come to God. He's so human.' Yes … well! But you can see both what she meant, and that her meaning could not be more true. And the Bible allows us to think like that – to apply human terminology to God – because it's the only way we can think of him. So, Isaiah speaks here of the Lord having a hand! And what a hand it is! A *gripping* hand (v. 10), like the hand Jesus reached out to the sinking Peter (Matt. 14:31), ready and willing to hold us fast while the storm rages. Isaiah says it is 'the *hand of my righteousness*': its intervening action is guaranteed by the inflexible steadfastness of our God who has promised to hold us for all eternity (John 10:28–30), and his 'righteousness' will not allow him to do otherwise. It is the hand that implements his righteous purposes for us, so, come what may, we know that he is in charge and all is well. Isaiah says, too, that it is a *transforming and providing* hand (v. 20). The hymn says, 'Heaven above is softer blue, /Earth around is sweeter green; /Something lives in every hue /Christless eyes have never seen.' On our pilgrimage we walk through his prepared terrain, for he is ever the 'Exodus God', planning ahead to place the wells of Elim on the pilgrims' route, showering manna from heaven, bringing water out of the rock (Exod. 15:27; 16:14; 17:6), or, as Isaiah implies here and has already said (35:1), making the desert blossom as a rose. This hand is *the hand of the Creator* (v. 20), the one who brings everything into being, maintains it in existence, controls it in operation, and directs it to his appointed target. We live in the Creator's hand and walk through the Creator's world.

Day 46 Isaiah 41:21–42:17

There is another – enormous – side to the intentions of the Lord. It would seem that the more Isaiah magnifies the greatness of Yahweh and sees him as the only God, the more the question presses, What does he intend to do about the Gentile world, outside the confines of the chosen seed of Abraham, thus far without revelation of divine truth? To this topic he now turns.

The wider Gentile world

Gentile need exposed

41:21. Bring your[1] case, Yahweh keeps saying.
    Present your strong arguments, Jacob's King keeps saying.
22. Let them present them, and let them declare what is to happen.[2]
    Regarding former things, tell us what they were
    in order that we may give them our attention,[3] and know their outcome;
    or make us hear of things that are coming –
23. tell what are coming afterwards –
    that we may know that you are gods.
    Forsooth! Please do anything, good or bad,[4]
    that we may look in amazement and see, all at once.
24. Behold!
    You yourselves are a veritable nothing!
    And your work is a total puff of air.[5]
    Only an abomination would choose you!

Yahweh by contrast[6]

25. I roused him from the north and come he surely will![7]
    From the sun-rising he will proclaim my name.[8]

1   Verse 23 indicates that this address is to the gods of the Gentiles.

2   The challenge to the 'gods' is to predict the future – either by so understanding what has already happened that they can tell its outcome (i.e., can they interpret the flow and purpose of history), or to predict absolutely what is to happen in the future.

3   Lit., 'set our hearts'. See v. 10.

4   Equivalent to our expression, 'good, bad, or indifferent', i.e., anything at all.

5   A likely rather than a certain meaning. The word does not occur elsewhere.

6   Yahweh ordains what happens (v. 25); he foretold the events before they happened (v 26), and revealed the good news to Zion (v. 27).

And he will come against leaders like so much mortar,
and like a potter treads the clay.

26. Who has told of him from the start so that we may know?
And from earlier on so that we may say, 'He was right'?
Why, no one told!
Indeed, no one gave the news![9]
Certainly, no one heard a single word from you!

27. I first, to Zion – 'Behold, behold them!'[10] –
and to Jerusalem will appoint one bringing good news.

Summary in conclusion: The plight of the Gentile world

28. And I look, and there is no one
even among these, and there is no counsellor –
that I might ask them and they would return a word.

29. Behold!
All of them! A nuisance![11]
Their works a nonentity;
their images, wind and without meaning![12]

The great solution: The Servant's mission to the Gentile world

42:1 Behold!
My Servant whom I uphold,
my Chosen One whom my soul accepts with favour.
I have bestowed my spirit on him;
judgment[13] to the nations he will bring out.

2. He will not shriek out, nor raise,
nor make people hear his voice out of doors.

3. A bruised reed he will not break,
and a smouldering wick he will not snuff out;
in accordance with truth he will bring out judgment.

4. He will not smoulder, nor will he bruise,[14]
until he sets up judgment in the earth.
And for his teaching the wide world waits in hope.[15]

Confirmation by Yahweh of his plan for his Servant[16]

5. This is what the true God*,[17] Yahweh, has said –
creating[18] the heavens and stretching them out,

7   This is the conqueror referred to in principle in vv. 2–4. Yahweh ordains the details of coming events. He (unlike the 'gods') is in charge of the historical process.

8   In the event this conqueror will prove to be Cyrus the Persian who took Babylon in 539 BC, ending the Babylonian Empire and founding the Persian. From Zion's perspective he belongs in the east and, like all Mesopotamian invaders, approaches from the north. He will not necessarily himself know Yahweh, but because everything about him has been predicted his arrival on the scene will be a proclamation of the one and only God.

9   Lit., 'made (people) hear'.

10 The force of this ejaculation is an urgent call to watch out for these things happening.

11 See 1:13.

12 See 24:10.

13 See 2:4; 26:8. Used here (e.g, as in Deut. 5:1 and often) as a summary word for what Yahweh has decided and revealed as his truth to his people. This is the only significance of 'judgment' that suits this context. Gentiles are in a hopeless state for want of divine truth; the Servant comes to bring divine truth to them. We could bring out the meaning of 'judgment' here by translating, '(my) dictates'.

14 The same verbs as in v. 3, except that 'bruise' is here used intransitively, as in our expression 'he bruises easily'.

15 See 8:17.

spreading the earth and its produce,
giving breath to the people on it,
and spirit to those who walk in it –

6. It is I, Yahweh, who have called you in righteousness;[19]
I will grip you by your hand,
and I will safeguard you,
and I will give you to be a covenant for people,
a light for nations;

7. to open blind eyes,
to bring out the bound from confinement,
from the house of restraint those inhabiting darkness.

8. I am Yahweh.
That is my name,
and my glory to another I will not give,
nor my praise to carved images.

9. The earlier things: Behold! They are bound to happen –
and the new things which I am declaring.
Before they sprout I am making you hear.[20]

The world sings in response

10. Sing to Yahweh a new song,
his praise from the extremity of the earth:
Those who go down to the sea, and what fills it,
the wide earth[21] and its inhabitants.

11. Let the wilderness[22] and its cities raise[23] (their voices);
the enclaves Kedar inhabits.
Let the inhabitants of Sela shout aloud;
from the mountain-top let them scream with excitement.

12. Let them ascribe to Yahweh glory,
and in the wide earth let them declare his praise.

The cause for praise

13. Like a warrior, Yahweh will go out.
Like a man of wars[24] he will rouse his passion.
He will give his war-cry;
Oh, yes, he will roar!
Over his enemies he will prove himself to be a warrior.

16 Verses 1–4 are the first of four passages dealing with the Servant of the Lord, usually called 'the Servant Songs'. Each 'song' is followed by verses in which Yahweh confirms his Servant's task – here, speaking as Creator (v. 5), he confirms that his Servant will be light to the Gentiles (vv. 6–7). Thus Yahweh will display his power over the false gods (vv. 8–9).

17 Lit., 'the God*', i.e., the genuine article, the one who is God indeed.

18 On these participles, see 40:28.

19 See 5:7; 26:7. Here 'in pursuance of my righteous purposes'.

20 The 'earlier things' are those related to the conqueror who has been predicted; the 'new things' are the predicted work of the Servant.

21 See 41:1, and v. 12 below.

22 'Wilderness' (*midbar*) can be the barren wilderness (e.g., Deut. 8:15), but equally, as here, the open country dotted with townships. What is called today 'the green belt'.

23 'Lift up/raise' used as an ellipsis for 'raise the voice'. Frequently so.

24 Plural expressing totality, experienced in every branch and art of warfare, battle-hardened.

Yahweh speaks: How he sees his coming actions

14. I have been still from eternity,
    silent, holding myself back.
    Like a girl giving birth I gasp,
    breathing and panting all at once!

15. I will lay waste mountains and hills,
    and all their vegetation I will dry up;
    and I will make rivers islands,[25]
    and pools I will dry up.

16. And I will make the blind walk by a road they do not know,
    by paths they do not know I will make them step out.
    Ahead of them I will make darkness light,
    and rough ground smooth.
    These are the things I have determined to do,
    and I will not leave them undone.[26]

17. They are doomed to be turned back,
    reaping total shame,[27]
    those who trust a carved image,
    who say to a molten image, 'You are our gods'.

25   See 41:1.

26   Or 'and I am determined not to leave them' – the blind who need to be guided home.

27   Lit., 'they will be shamed with shame'.

Thought for the day: Isaiah 41:21–42:17

Everything that speaks of Jesus delights the heart. He identified himself as the 'Servant of the Lord' whom Isaiah foretold. He is the perfect Servant of the Lord, the revelation of truth and light for the whole world, the answer to our hopelessness, darkness and bondage. But, because he is the *perfect* Servant, he is also the *model* Servant, the true pattern for all who, through him, are the Lord's servants today. Very well then – first, the Lord's servants are the Lord's delight (42:1). On the one hand, this is our ambition and target (Col. 1:10), but on the other hand it is the truth about us, for once we belong to Jesus we are the Father's delight, 'accepted in the Beloved' (Eph. 1:6). Secondly, the servant is first and foremost the servant of the Word of God. Do remember that this is what 'judgment' (NKJV, etc., 'justice') means in 42:1, 3, 4: the decisions he has made, the things he has declared to be true (in brief, what he has revealed to his people, what we possess as the Word of God). The servant's task is to bring this Word of truth to those bereft of the truth (41:28–29; 42:1), making sure that it is God's Word in all its truth (42:3) that is being shared, not some merely human opinion, church tradition or personal whim and fancy. Thirdly, the servant of the Lord does not give up on the job, but perseveres till the truth is fully established (42:4). Like Paul said (2 Corinthians 4:1): because we have received mercy we have received ministry, and we must not 'lose heart' (NKJV), that is, leave the work half done, abandon the task, go soft like a decaying apple. How true all this is of Jesus: the Father's delight, in his fidelity to the Word of God, carrying the job through until he could shout 'It is finished'! Every servant covets to be made like the Son of God in everything.

Day 47 Isaiah 42:18–43:21

It's as though, at 42:18, Isaiah realised he had a question to answer. He has described his people, Israel, as 'my servant' (41:8), and in 42:1–4 he has seen the Servant as the Lord's agent in worldwide revelation. Is the nation up to this task? In 42:18–25 he answers with a resounding 'No'. Certainly, in the divine intention, and by title, Israel is the Lord's servant, with a worldwide mission, but as Isaiah looked at them he found them blind (v. 18), spiritually insensitive (v. 20), a failure, and in bondage (vv. 21–22).

A servant who cannot be The Servant

42:18. O deaf ones, hear,
    and, O blind ones, look so as to see!

19.   Who is blind but my servant,
    and as deaf as my messenger whom I send?
    Who is as blind as the reconciled[1] one,
    and as blind as Yahweh's servant?

20.   Seeing many things, you observe nothing;[2]
    opening the ears, he hears nothing.

21.   Yahweh was pleased, for his righteousness' sake,
    that they[3] should magnify the teaching and make
    it majestic,

22.   but this is a people preyed on and plundered,
    trapped in holes, all of them,
    and in houses of restraint hidden away!
    They have become prey, without a deliverer,
    plunder without any to say, 'Restore'.

23.   Who among you will listen to this and hear for afterwards?

24.   Who gave Jacob up for plunder, and Israel to those
    taking prey?

1   A possible translation about which there is no agreement. To be reconciled to Yahweh was Israel's supreme privilege, but, then as now, we who are reconciled live below our dignity.

2   'You' singular, referring to the servant who is no servant.

3   Lit., 'he', singular referring to the blind and deaf servant, the people.

Was it not Yahweh, the one against whom we have sinned?
They were unwilling for walking in his ways,
and did not listen to his teaching.

25. And he poured out on them the rage of exasperation,[4]
and the force of war.
And it set them on fire all round, and they did not know,[5]
and it burned them up and they did not take it to heart.

Yahweh's plans for Israel: (1) Deliverance[6]

Unchanged divine care[7]

43:1. Now then,
this is what Yahweh has said,
who creates you, Jacob, and shapes you, Israel:[8]
Do not be afraid,
for I have determined to redeem you;[9]
I have called you by your name;
mine you are!

2. When you cross waters I am actually with you,
and rivers, they will not sweep you away.
When you walk in fire, you will not be scorched,
and no flame will catch fire on you.

3. For I am Yahweh,
your God, the Holy One of Israel, your Saviour.[10]
As your ransom price, I gave Egypt,[11]
Cush and Seba[12] in place of you.

4. Because you are precious in my eyes,
honoured, and, for my part, I love you,
I would give mankind in your place,
and states[13] in place of your soul.

5. Do not be afraid, for I am actually with you.
From the east I will bring your seed,
and from the west I will gather you,

6. while saying to the north, 'Give',
and to the south 'Do not retain':
Bring my sons from afar, and my daughters from
earth's end,

4 See 5:25.

5 'Know' in the sense of understanding the meaning of what was happening. Isaiah here traces the failure of Israel as 'servant' to a deeper level – failure of spiritual perception, inability to see why they were in such a plight, insensitivity to the work of God.

6 42:18–25 revealed a double need: a people in bondage need deliverance; a people spiritually insensitive need redemption. From 43:1 Isaiah deals with these two needs in turn: liberation (43:1–21); redemption (43:22–44:23).

7 Isaiah pictures the people trailing off into hardship and enslavement, but the Lord is still with them.

8 Participles, see 40:28. To translate 'your Creator … your potter' would be correct but would fail to express the ongoing creatorial and providential care of Yahweh for his people.

9 See 35:9. Here, 'I am determined to be your next-of-kin' – your troubles are mine.

10 A participle expressing unchanging relationship, see v. 1 above.

11 i.e., at the Exodus, Yahweh brought Israel out at the expense of Egypt.

12 The extreme south of Egypt and lands even further south.

7. everyone who is called by my name
   and whom, for my glory, I have created,
   shaped, indeed, made.

No other God; sure promises[14]

8. He has brought out blind people – yet they have eyes! –
   and deaf ones – yet they have ears!
9. All nations have been gathered at the same time,
   and states are being assembled.
   Who among them tells this?
   And can they make us hear the earlier things?
   Let them provide their witnesses in order to be
   proved right;
   let them hear and say, 'It's the truth.'
10. You are my witnesses – this is Yahweh's word –
    and my servant whom I chose
    in order that you might know and believe me,
    and discern that I am he.
    Before me no god* was fashioned,
    and there will be none after me!
11. I, I am Yahweh,
    and, apart from me, there is none who can save.
12. It is I who have declared, and saved, and let you hear,
    and among you there was no one else,[15]
    and you are my witnesses –
    this is Yahweh's word –
    and I am God*.
13. Also, now as always,[16] I am,
    and from my hand none can deliver.
    I work and who can reverse it?

The end of Babylonian bondage: A new Exodus

14. This is what Yahweh has said –
    your Redeemer, the Holy One of Israel.
    For your sake, I have determined to send to Babylon,
    And I will bring down – as fugitives, all of them –
    the Chaldeans,[17] in the ships they shout about.[18]

13 See 17:12.

14 Picture a court assembling.
    Yahweh leads in people who
    are blind and deaf (v. 8; cf.,
    42:18–20), all peoples gather (v. 9)
    and the point at issue is who can
    understand the flow of events in
    history (v. 9b). They are invited
    to produce witnesses so as to win
    their case. Saddled with blind and
    deaf witnesses, however, Yahweh
    must give his own testimony
    that he alone is God and Saviour
    (vv. 10–13). Marvellously, he
    still claims the blind as his own.
    He does not disown them.

15 Lit., 'no alien', no foreign
    or other god.

16 Lit., 'from a day', an expression
    combining 'since time began',
    'today also', and 'henceforth'.

17 A component in the population
    of Babylon, often used as
    synonym for Babylonians.

15. I am Yahweh, your Holy One,
    Creator[19] of Israel, your King.
16. This is what Yahweh has said,
    he who provides a road through the sea,
    and a pathway through strong waters;
17. he who brings out chariot and horse,
    army and force together.
    They lie down; they will not rise;
    quenched like a wick – extinguished!
18. Do not remember those earlier things,
    and on those previous things do not exercise
    your discernment.
19. Behold!
    I am going to do something new;
    now it will sprout up;
    will you not know it?[20]
    Yes, I will make a road in the desert,
    rivers in the wasteland.
20. The wild creatures will honour me,
    jackals and ostriches,
    when I provide water in the desert,
    rivers in the wasteland,
    to give drink to my people, my chosen,
21. the people I shaped for myself
    so that they might recount my praise.

---

18 Lit., 'the ships of their loud shout'.

19 Participle, see v. 1.

20 An affirmation by means of a
   question: 'You cannot miss it.'

Thought for the day: Isaiah 42:18–43:21

John Newton's great hymn 'Begone, Unbelief!' reminds us that 'The heirs of salvation (I know from his Word) / Through much tribulation must follow their Lord.' Consequently, the heirs of salvation face pretty regular temptation to ask that tormenting question, 'Why?' It's not a wrong question, or necessarily a sin to ask it. After all, Jesus cried out 'Why?' (Mark 15:34) – but note that he carefully prefaced it with 'My God'. His question was asked not out of doubt (like ours might be) but within unbroken faith. But as far as we are concerned, Isaiah shows us a better way and a more fruitful question. Envisaging his people defeated and enslaved (42:24) he encouraged them to ask, 'Who gave Jacob up for plunder?' Not 'Why has this happened to Jacob?' but 'Who is responsible?' And that crucial 'who?' brings us into the presence of the great and only God, our Creator, Maker, Potter and Saviour – all the titles that appear in today's reading, and in his almighty, unfailing presence we find refuge and peace of heart. If he is in charge, all is well. It may not be comfortable; it may be far from what we had in mind; but all is well. Old Eli got it absolutely right. Samuel had told him precisely what he did not want to hear – about a future far from what he wished, far from what he wanted for his sons and his priesthood – but when he heard the word of the Lord he said: 'It is the Lord. Let him do what seems good to him' (1 Samuel 3:18). The answer to the question 'Who?' did not alter the unwelcome news but it did bring him peace. We can never exalt the Lord in his total sovereignty too high, or accord to him too great executive and management power and authority over the world and its history, and over our lives and experiences. On every occasion, in every situation, 'It is the Lord.' Therein is our peace.

Day 48 Isaiah 43:22–44:23

In 42:18–25 Isaiah exposed the double need of his people – to be freed from bondage and saved from sin. In this section he turns to the question of sin and forgiveness (cf., 43:25; 44:22).

Yahweh's Plans for Israel: (2) Redemption[1]

Diagnosis: Israel's sin

43:22. It is not upon me that you have called, Jacob,
　　　　rather, you have tired of me, Israel.
23.　　Not to me have you brought lambs as your
　　　　burnt offerings,
　　　　and with your sacrifices you have not honoured me.
　　　　I did not make a slave of you through offerings,
　　　　nor tire you out through frankincense.
24.　　Not for me did you buy fragrant cane at a price,
　　　　and with the fat of your sacrifices you have not
　　　　saturated me.
　　　　You have, however, made a slave of me by your sins,
　　　　tired me out through your iniquities.

Remedy

25.　　I, I am the one who wipes clean your rebellions,
　　　　for my own sake,
　　　　and your sins I do not remember.
26.　　Remind me.
　　　　Let us reach a judgment together.
　　　　Give an account of yourself so that you may be acquitted.
27.　　Your very first father sinned,
　　　　and your representative men rebelled against me
28　　　so that I kept profaning the princes of holiness,
　　　　and consigned Jacob to total destruction,
　　　　and Israel to utter defamation.

1　See the note on 43:1 above.

Unchanged status; coming blessing; glad response

44:1. Now then,

  hear, Jacob, my servant,

  and Israel whom I chose.

2. This is what Yahweh has said –

  your Maker,

  and the one shaping you from birth,

  the one who helps you.[2]

  Do not be afraid, my servant Jacob,

  and Jeshurun,[3] the one I chose.

3. For I will pour water on the thirsty,

  and rivulets on the dry ground.

  I will pour my Spirit on your seed,

  and my blessing on your issue.

4. And they will sprout up in among the grass,

  like willows beside watercourses.

5. One will say: 'To Yahweh I belong',

  and another will proclaim the name of Jacob,

  and another will write with his hand, 'Belonging to Yahweh',

  and take as his surname the name of Israel.

No other God: sure promises[4]

6. This is what Yahweh has said,

  Israel's King and Redeemer,

  Yahweh of Hosts.

  I am the first and I am the last,

  and, barring me, there is no God.

7. And who – as I – can call, and declare,

  and give an ordered account of things,[5]

  since my appointing of the ancient people?

  And, as to coming things, and what are yet to happen,

  can they declare for themselves?[6]

8. Do not be apprehensive and do not be scared.[7]

  Have not I, beforehand, let you hear, and have declared,

  and you are my witnesses?

  Is there a God[8] barring me?

  There is no rock – not that I know of!

2 'Maker' and 'shaping' are participles, see 40:28. 'Helps' is an imperfect tense signifying repeated or recurrent action, here equivalent to 'does always help'.

3 An occasional name of endearment for Israel, e.g., Deut. 32:15; 33:5, 26, related to *yashar*: 'to be right/ upright. The one who has been set right with God.'

4 cf., the parallel passage, 43:8–13. Here, by contrast with the dead 'gods', Yahweh is seen as the only God, and therefore the one whose word must be fulfilled. In this passage Yahweh and Israel (vv. 6–8) at the beginning are balanced by the idols and their devotees (vv. 19–20) at the conclusion.

5 'Call' means start some historical process of events, call them into being; 'declare' here points to predicting them in advance; and 'give an ordered account' (lit., 'set out in order') is the claim that only Yahweh knows what world history is 'all about'.

6 'For themselves' is a 'dative of advantage' – 'so as to do themselves a good turn', i.e, by proving their ability to make absolute predictions.

7 A likely but questioned translation.

9. Those who shape an image are, all of them, meaningless,[9]
   and the things they delight in cannot profit.
   And as for their witnesses, they themselves cannot see,
   and cannot know
   in order to reap shame.
10. Anyone who has shaped a god* and cast an image
   (for no foreseeable profit!) –
11. behold,
   all associated with it – will reap shame!
   The craftsmen themselves are but human!
   Let them gather, all of them;
   stand,[10] become apprehensive, reap shame, all at once.
12. Take a metal worker with his tools.[11]
   He works in the coals
   and shapes it with hammers,
   and with his strong arm he works it.
   He gets hungry too and has no more strength;
   if he has not drunk water he faints.
13. A craftsman in wood stretches out a line,
   outlines it with a marker,
   works at it with planes
   and outlines it with compasses.
   And he has made it like the figure of a man,
   like the beauty of a human,
   to live in a house!
14. He purposed to cut cedars for himself;
   he took tirzah[12] and oak,
   and he grew it strong for himself among the trees
   of the forest.
   He planted laurel and the rain made it grow big.
15. And it is there for a human to burn –
   he takes some of it and gets warm.
   Oh yes, he lights a fire and bakes bread,
   and, yes, he makes a god* and bows in worship!
   He has carved an image and prostrates himself to it!
16. Part of it he has burned in the fire;

8 The word here is *eloah*, the singular of the customary plural *elohim*. This is its only use by Isaiah. It is widely used in Job, sparsely elsewhere. Since Isaiah deliberately used the singular form here it must be significant. Possibly 'not a single God'.

9 See 24:10.

10 As in 'stand up and be counted', take responsibility for their actions.

11 Poetry at its most allusive, but the meaning in context is plain enough: 'Craftsman in iron, a tool'.

12 Unidentified species.

on part of it he prepares food,[13]
cooks a roast and is satisfied.
More, he gets warm,
and says 'Ho, ho! I am warm; I have seen the fire-light.'

17. And what's left of it he has made – into a god*!!
To be his image!
He prostrates himself to it, and bows in worship!
And he prays to it, and says:
'Deliver me, for you are my god*.'

18. They neither know nor discern,
for their eyes are besmeared[14] so that they cannot see,
their hearts so that they cannot appraise[15] the situation.

19. Nor does any take it into consideration[16] –
neither knowledge nor discernment – to say,
'Part of it I burned in the fire,
and, yes, I baked bread on its embers.
I roasted meat and ate it.
And the remainder of it am I to make into an abomination?
To a tree-stump am I to prostrate myself?'

20. Feeding on ashes,
the very heart has been deceived,
has led him off course.[17]
And he cannot deliver his soul,
nor say, 'Is there not a falsehood in my right hand?'

The redeeming Lord

21. Remember these things, Jacob,
and Israel, for you are my servant.
I shaped you.
You are a servant of mine, Israel.
You will not be forgotten as far as I am concerned.

22. I wipe away, like a cloud, your rebellions,
and, like a fog, your sins.
Turn back to me, for I have redeemed[18] you.

23. Shout aloud, O heavens, for Yahweh has taken action;
cry out exultantly, O Earth beneath;

13 Lit., 'eats bread'.

14 Or possibly 'he has smeared their eyes'. To achieve this meaning the vowel of the present verb would have to be adjusted. On the other hand, 'are smeared' would be a singular verb with a plural subject.

15 *sakal*, the capacity for thought, the ability to judge between right and wrong, between the advantageous and the disadvantageous.

16 Lit., 'Bring it back to his heart'.

17 Lit., 'turned him aside'.

18 See 35:9.

burst out, O mountains, in loud shouting,
forest, and every tree in it,
for Yahweh has redeemed[19] Jacob.
And in Israel he displays his beauty.

19   As in v. 22.

Thought for the day: Isaiah 43:22–44:23

Watch out for religion that does not reach God! To say such a thing is miles away from the spirit of this age where all religions equally are roads to God and sincerity is the key to reality. Isaiah thought differently – exposing not just the sheer stupidity of man-made gods (44:9–20) but the tragedy of knowing the true God yet falling into false religion (43:22–24). First, then, are we truly devoted to the God we worship so that the centre of our religion is the longing to come to him (v. 22a), and to revel, unwearyingly, in what he has revealed about himself (vv. 22b)? The old Brethren practice of 'the Gospel on Sunday night' had much to commend it – constant refreshment in the great basic truths of which we should never tire is a mark of true religion. Then again, is our religious practice – our daily devotions in prayer and the Word of God, and our commitment to church fellowship and Sunday 'services' – a bondage to which we have 'enslaved' ourselves (v. 23), or is it an experienced liberation of spirit and a proved means of spiritual growth? And, thirdly (v. 24), is there even the smallest feeling in our hearts that because we are so committed, God 'owes us'; that we have managed to 'put pressure on him', twisted the divine arm, made him obligated, secured him as our 'slave' to do our bidding? There is a narrow dividing line between giving our all in devoted service to Jesus, and finding our all in devoted service as such. Is it not for this reason that many full-time ministers find it hard to retire? They have lost that to which they were devoted. No wonder John exhorts us to keep ourselves from idols (1 John 5:21). The previous verse says, 'The Son of God has come'! Nothing must replace or displace that central, basic, essential fact. Jesus alone is worthy.

Day 49 Isaiah 44:24–45:7

Look back. Since 42:18 Isaiah has covered two topics in parallel. (1) The first is the political, circumstantial needs of Israel, bondage to a foreign power, named in 43:14 as Babylon. The Lord promises to deal with this (42:18–43:21). (2) The second is Israel's spiritual need. It was sin and disobedience that brought them into enslavement, but the Lord will deal with this also (43:22–44:23). Now, in 44:24–55:13, Isaiah turns to the 'how?' The solution to their circumstantial plight is the Persian Emperor, Cyrus (44:24–48:22); and the solution to their spiritual plight is the Servant of the Lord (49:1–55:13).

The Lord's 'Cyrus Plan': 1. The plan announced; the agent named

44:24. This is what Yahweh has said;
    your Redeemer,[1]
    and the one who shapes you from birth.
    I am Yahweh, doer of all:
    by myself stretching out the heavens;
    spreading out the earth by my sole will and deed;[2]

25.   invalidating the signs of the pretentious talkers,[3]
    and the one who bemuses fortune-tellers;
    turning the wise back to front,
    and the one who makes their knowledge an insight into folly;[4]

26.   implementing the word of his servant,
    and the one who brings to fulfilment the advice of his messengers;
    who says about Jerusalem, 'It will be inhabited,'
    and of the cities of Judah, 'They will be built,
    and its desolations I will raise up';

[1] See 35:9.

[2] Owing to textual variation, the Hebrew here is either 'from myself', meaning 'as something decided by me alone', or 'Who was with me?', meaning 'I alone am the agent'. Hence the 'will and deed' rendering.

[3] A possible though uncertain rendering, referring to fortune-tellers and astrologers and their proud claims.

[4] Isaiah apparently here combines two verbs ('to have insight' and 'to be foolish') into one compound.

27. who says to the deep, 'Be waterless,
    and your streams I will dry up';
28. who says about Cyrus, 'My shepherd –
    and all my pleasure he will fulfil',
    even to say about Jerusalem, 'It will be built,'
    and about the temple, 'Its foundation will be laid.'

2. The plan confirmed: For Cyrus, Israel, and the whole world

Cyrus[5]

45:1. This is what Yahweh has said to his anointed, Cyrus,
    whose right hand I have gripped,
    in order to beat down the nations before him,
    and that I should ungird the loins of kings;
    in order to open double doors before him,
    and that gates should be unbolted.
2. Ahead of you, I will myself go,
    and I will smooth out upraised barriers.[6]
    I will shatter doors of bronze,
    and I will cut through bars of iron,
3. and I will give to you the treasures of darkness,
    and things concealed in hiding places,
    in order that you may know that it is I, Yahweh,
    who is calling you by your name, the God of Israel.

Israel

4. It is for the sake of Jacob my servant,
    and Israel my chosen,
    that I have called you by your name,
    I surname you,
    And you do not know me! –
5. I, Yahweh, and no other,
    besides me – no God!
    I gird you –
    and you do not know me!

5   King of Anshan (S. Iran), a vassal within the Median Empire who revolted against his overlord and seized the empire in 550 BC. He proceeded with astonishing speed to take all Mesopotamia into his power, and entered Babylon in 539 BC, bringing the Babyonian Empire to an end and establishing the Persian.

6   Uncertain but possible translation.

The world

6.   It is in order that from where the sun rises to where it sets
     they may know that there is nothing besides me –
     I, Yahweh, and no other!

7.   Shaping light and creating darkness,
     making peace, and creating evil[7] –
     I, Yahweh, doing all these things!

7   'Peace'and 'evil' are both versatile
words needing to be interpreted
in context. Here the context is the
differing circumstances that can
be present in earthly experience
– now the circumstances that
allow the storing up of treasures;
now the advent of a despoiling
conqueror. Hence 'peace' and
'evil' have there the sense of
'prosperity' and 'calamity'.

Thought for the day: Isaiah 44:24–45:7

We can well imagine the trepidation with which the exiled people of Judah in Babylon would have viewed the advent of a conqueror powerful enough to sweep all before him and, in the end, enter mighty Babylon unopposed. 'Bad enough,' did they say, 'to be gripped by Babylon's power'? 'What price, the power of Babylon's conqueror?' And we often feel the same today – at the mercy of powerful forces in the present, and trembling at what enormities the future will bring. Isn't that why the Lord had, in grace, given them the message of Isaiah, spoken one hundred and fifty years in advance of Cyrus? To possess and read the Word of God is to be forewarned and forearmed. Oh, yes, Cyrus is on his way; and, yes, he is seemingly invincible, but – yes, also – he is in the hand of the Lord, called according to the Lord's purposes, and (note this specially) 'for the sake of' the Lord's people. For our encouragement, we also know the end of the story: it was the greater conqueror, seeming to bring the threat of a more irreversible captivity, who proved to be the liberator who would send the people back home with his imperial mandate to rebuild the temple (Ezra 1:1–3). Isaiah put the message superbly in his own inimitable words: Whether it is light or darkness, prosperity or calamity, 'I Yahweh, do all these things.' We can never overemphasise or over-exalt the sovereignty of God. Isaiah depicts him as in full, operational charge of his world and of its every circumstance. This is our security; it is the pillow on which we lay our heads; it is why Psalm 121:2 found a place of repose in the God 'who made heaven and earth', for, as the Bible reveals the Creator, he not only originates everything but also sustains, and controls everything, and directs everything to his appointed goal: a God who is God indeed!

Day 50   Isaiah 45:8–25

Having announced and confirmed the Lord's plan to use Cyrus to deliver his exiled people, to rebuild Jerusalem, and refound the temple, Isaiah now envisages two contrasting reactions. One reaction is to pray for it to happen (v. 8); but others find the plan is abhorrent (vv. 9–13) and want to argue against it. To them the Lord first insists that what he has planned will happen (v. 13), but then he goes on to reassure them that using a Gentile conqueror like this does not change Israel's primary place in his worldwide purposes (vv. 14–25).

Two contrasting reactions

Reaction 1: Let it happen

45:8. Shower down, O heavens, from above,
    and let the very clouds drizzle righteousness!
    Let the earth open up,
    so that salvation and righteousness may be fruitful.
    Let it blossom all at once.
    I, Yahweh, have myself determined to create it.

Reaction 2: Objection overruled [1]

9.   Woe to the one who brings a case against his Potter –
    a potsherd among earthen potsherds!
    Can clay say to its potter,
    'What are you making?'
    and, 'Your work shows no skill'? [2]

10. Woe to the one who says to a father,
    'What are you begetting?'
    and to a woman,
    'With what are you in labour?'

11. This is what Yahweh has said –
    the Holy One of Israel, and his Potter –

[1] Israel's difficulty over the Cyrus-plan is understandable. To return to their land under a Gentile overlord left their subordinate, puppet position unchanged. They did not want Cyrus but David and the promised eternal, worldwide kingdom (Ps. 89:27–29).

[2] Lit., 'your work has no hands'. We still use 'handy' meaning 'skilful'.

'Regarding things to come, question me!
About my sons, and about the work of my hands,
do command me!'

12. It is I who made the earth,
and humankind on it I created.
It is I who, with my own hands, stretched out the heavens,
and all their host I commanded.

13. I am the one who, in righteousness, roused him,[3]
and all his ways I will make straight.
He is the one who will build my city,
and send away my captives –
not for a price and not for pay,
Yahweh of Hosts has said.

The great reassurance[4]
The submission of the world

14. This is what Yahweh has said:
The toil of Egypt and the profits of Cush,
and the Sabeans – tall as they are –
will pass over to you and will become yours.
Behind you they will walk:
in chains they will come over,
and to you they will reverently bow;
to you they will supplicate.
'Only among you is God*;
and there is no other; no god at all!'

The Lord's hidden ways

15. Ah, surely you are a God* hiding yourself,
God of Israel, Saviour.

16. They are sure to reap shame and ignominy,
all of them.
Together, they are doomed to walk in ignominy,
craftsmen of images.

17. Israel, however, is sure to be saved by Yahweh,
a truly[5] eternal salvation.

3   The anonymous conqueror of 41:2,
now named as Cyrus (44:28; 45:1).

4   Using military imagery – but
in the same sense that the New
Testament uses its pictures of
soldiers, armour and warfare
to depict life in and for the
gospel, Isaiah sees the nations
willingly accepting their place
as Israel's conquered foes. This
is offered as reassurance that,
notwithstanding the Lord's use of
a Gentile deliverer, his worldwide
plans for Israel, his promises
to David, have not changed.

5   'Truly'; reflects the plural – 'a
salvation of everlastings'.

They will reap neither shame nor ignominy
to the everlastings of eternity.

The salvation of the world: The Creator – one God over the whole earth

18. For this is what Yahweh has said,
creator of the heavens: it is he who is God,[6]
shaping and making the earth; he it is who made it secure.
Not meaninglessly[7] did he create it;
for inhabiting he shaped it –
I, Yahweh, and there is no other.

The God who speaks, making himself known

19. Not under cover have I spoken
in some dark place of the earth.
I did not say to the seed of Jacob,
'Seek me pointlessly.'
I am Yahweh, speaking righteousness,
declaring what is straightforward.

The one and only God; the righteous Saviour

20. Assemble and come,
bring yourselves near, all together,
you escapees from the nations.
They know nothing who carry about the tree of
their carved image,
and make their prayer to a god* unable to save.
21. Declare and present[8] –
of course they may consult with one another!
Who made anyone hear of this beforehand,
declared it earlier on?[9]
Was it not I, Yahweh?
And there is no other God barring me,
God*, righteous and saving.
None besides me!
22. Turn to me and be saved,
all earth's remotest bounds,
for I am God* and there is no other.

6   Lit., 'The God', i.e., God indeed, the genuine God compared with pretenders.

7   See 24:10 – the word is used again in v. 19.

8   i.e., as in a courtroom, 'Speak up and present your case.'

9   'This' and 'it' refer to the Cyrus-plan. The conqueror was himself predicted – by name (44:28; 45:1) – that he would sweep to victory and send Judah home to build the temple. No other god has done or can do such a thing; Yahweh uses his power to predict (and to control the flow of history so as to fulfil his word) as proof of his sole deity.

Affirmation: The worldwide Israel

23. By myself I have sworn on oath.
    In righteousness the word has gone out of my mouth,
    and it will not turn back,
    that to me every knee will bow,
    every tongue swear on oath.[10]

24. 'Only in Yahweh,'
    each will surely say regarding me,
    'is full righteousness[11] and strength.'
    Right up to him such will come,
    and all who are outraged at him will reap shame.

25. It is in Yahweh they will find righteousness and utter praise,
    all the seed of Israel.[12]

_____

10   i.e., its oath of loyalty, commitment.

11   Lit., 'righteousnesses': plural of amplification, righteousness in full and plenty, the genuine article in all its fullness.

12   i.e., the whole worldwide gathering, the escapees of the nations, all who confess Yahweh and find righteousness in him are reckoned 'the seed of Israel': Ps. 47:9; 87:4–6; Gal. 6:16; etc.

Thought for the day: Isaiah 45:8–25

Without question we have become so used to the fact that the Lord fulfils his predictions that we fail to see how important it is. Oh yes, we say, Micah predicted the Messiah would be born in Bethlehem, and so it was. But to Isaiah this proved that the predicting God exists and is the only God. He did not take it lightly; it was the clear proof of Yahweh's sole deity and of the non-reality of the gods who could not predict. How Isaiah would have rejoiced in the abundance of predictions made about the Messiah and the pinpoint accuracy of their fulfilment in Jesus! For 'fulfilment' is not just a matter of stepping in at the right moment and doing what was promised centuries before. The Lord's fulfilments come about, so to speak, within the flow of world history. Like Cyrus: Cyrus was a standard imperialist conqueror, reaching Babylon stage by stage, battle by battle. Likewise Babylon was ready for collapse according to the processes of decline and fall that work in history. The Lord's fulfilments show not only his faithfulness to his pledged word, but his sovereign control and direction of the whole world and all its events until they reach his desired and appointed end. Jesus' birth in Bethlehem came about because Micah had predicted it, but it actually happened because Caesar Augustus made the appropriate decree at the appointed time (Luke 2:1): the Word of God is in the Lord's hands, to make it happen; the rulers of the world are in the Lord's hands to accomplish what he has decreed. The cross of Jesus came about by sovereign decree, but it actually happened through the hands of wicked men (Acts 2:23); Herod, Pilate, the Gentiles and Israel assembled in Jerusalem 'to do whatever your purpose determined' (Acts 4:28). Prediction and fulfilment call us to wait patiently on the faithfulness of God – 'Has he said and will he not do it?' (Numbers 23:19). They also call for restful confidence in the God who has the whole world in his hands.

Day 51   Isaiah 46:1–13

In the next three chapters Isaiah rounds off his prediction that Babylon will fall (43:14). In chapter 46 we see, imaginatively, the mighty idols of Babylon, being tipped over and being loaded up for transportation out of the doomed city; in chapter 47 a fine poem foretells the fall of Babylon and explains the causes of it; and in chapter 48 Israel leaves Babylon for home, and Isaiah dwells on the spiritual state of the returning people. The chapters are, however, much more than an exercise in historical prediction. They are a reassurance: Isaiah has foreseen his people going into Babylonian captivity (39:6), and he is now allowed to assure them that they will return. But just as the return will not change their political situation – they will still be a puppet kingdom in a pagan empire– neither will it see them altered spiritually. They are still rebels, far from righteousness, needing salvation.

Contrast 1: The gods who are a burden, and the burden-bearing God

46:1. Bel has bowed down;
>   Nebo is toppling.
>   Their statues now belong to animal and beast.
>   What you lifted up is loaded up –
>   a burden for the weary.[1]

2.   They have bowed, toppled[2] together,
>   unable to rescue the[ir] burden,[3]
>   and they themselves[4] have gone into captivity.

3.   Give me a hearing, house of Jacob,
>   and all the remnant of the house of Israel –
>   you who have been loaded up[5] from birth,
>   who have been carried from the womb.

[1] 'Bel' (cf., the name 'Belshazzar', Dan. 5:1) and 'Nebo' (as in the name 'Nebuchadnezzar', Dan. 2:1) were the patron 'deities' of Babylon. What a 'god' and 'patron', which itself needs to be the first to be evacuated from the doomed city! (Isaiah writes as though watching it happen.) The great effigy of Bel has already bowed (perfect

4. And right up to old age I am the same.
   And right up to grey hair I will myself shoulder the weight.
   It is I who made,
   and it is I who will carry,
   and it is I who will shoulder the weight –
   and rescue!

Contrast 2: The gods who cannot save and the God who saves

5. To whom can you liken me and equate me,
   and compare me, that we should be alike?
6. There are those who lavish gold out of a purse,
   and with a balance weigh out silver,
   hire a metal-worker – and make it into god*!
   They prostrate themselves!
   Yes, they bow in worship!
7. They carry it on their backs;
   they shoulder it
   and put it down on its spot –
   and it stays there.
   It cannot shift from its place.
   Indeed, even when someone shrieks out to it
   it does not answer;
   from his trouble it does not save him.
8. Remember this and reason it out;[6]
   take it to heart, rebelling ones.
9. Remember earlier things, long ago.
   For it is I who am God*, and there is no other;
   God, and without compare.
10. At the beginning declaring the end,
    and beforehand what has not been done;
    saying,
    'It is my plan which will be implemented;
    every bit of my pleasure is what I will do;
11. from the east calling a bird of prey,[7]
    from a far land my planned man.'[8]
    Yes indeed I have spoken!

tense), secured by ropes, tipped over, lowered from its pedestal; Nebo is toppling (imperfect tense). Far from protecting their city, they need protecting, and even the pack-animals are tired of them! 'Weary' is feminine singular, referring back to the feminines, 'animal and beast'.

2. When Hebrew uses two verbs together like this, without connecting particle, the second carries the main thought and the first is adverbial to it: 'Bowingly, they have toppled.'

3. The gods' 'burden' of responsibility was the city. Far from helping it to escape, they are the first to leave it – and had to be helped to escape! They are the burden!

4. Lit., 'their souls'.

5. In context, loaded on to Yahweh.

6. The Lord calls his people to remember his unbroken faithfulness as the God who carries them, but he finds them rebellious (v. 8), stubborn and far from right with him (v. 12). In a word, they are still resistant to the Cyrus-plan for their return home – understandably so, in that it leaves them still beholden to a foreign ruler. 'Reason it out' is an interpretative translation, the best that can be made of a unique verb.

7. The predatory Cyrus.

8. The Hebrew has either 'a man of my plan' (i.e., who is my

Why then, I will bring it about!
I have shaped it;
why then, I will do it!

12. Give me a hearing, stubborn-hearted ones,
    far from righteousness.

13. I have determined to bring my righteousness[9] near;
    it will not be distant;
    and my salvation will not be tardy.
    And in Zion I will place salvation,
    for Israel my beauty.

planned man) or 'a man of his plan' (one who will succeed in whatever he plans).

9   What I believe to be right and that which expresses my righteous ways.

Thought for the day: Isaiah 46:1–13

In the hymn, 'How firm a foundation,' Richard Keen captured the very essence of Isaiah's teaching: 'E'en down to old age all my people shall prove/My sovereign, eternal, unchangeable love/And then when grey hairs shall their temples adorn/Like lambs they shall still in my bosom be borne.' Yes indeed! The prophet said it, and he meant it. There are only two sorts of religion in the world: the religion of human effort, of service directed to some 'god', of toil, trouble and bother, of deaf gods and unsolved problems; and the religion of a serving God who cares and carries, hears and answers, sees and saves. To put it another way: religions of works and the religion of grace. What labour went into producing the statues of Bel and Nebo! What effort in hauling them into position! What nonsense, bowing to a god that can't even move – of course it can't, the devotees themselves cemented it into position! And then, by contrast, the living God. Look back, cries Isaiah, take a thoughtful view. Has he not carried you? Have you not almost felt his hand under your elbow when your foot threatened to slip? And is not his ear open to your shriek for help, and his salvation at the ready? Remarkably and wonderfully, this same passage which underlines the burden-bearing God equally emphasises our unworthiness, our meritless lack of deserving. We are the rebels who are far from righteousness. Our position on his burden-bearing shoulders is totally down to him. All is of grace, and because it is 'of grace' it is 'for perpetuity'. Just as on the one hand it cannot be earned, on the other hand it cannot be forfeited. Here is Richard Keen again: 'The soul that on Jesus has leaned for repose/ He will not, he cannot desert to its foes/That soul, though all hell should endeavour to shake/ He'll never, no never, no never forsake.'

Day 52 Isaiah 47:1–15

Step by step, from 44:24, Isaiah foresees the rescue of the captives from Babylon: the liberator (44:24–45:7); the evacuation of Babylon's 'gods', and the Lord's continued 'carrying' of his people (46:1–4). Chapter 47 imaginatively foretells the fall of Babylon, and chapter 48 the return home of the exiles in spite of their unworthiness and lack of peace with God.

The fall of Babylon

Divine vengeance applied

47:1. Come down and sit in the dust,
    virgin daughter of Babylon.
    Sit on the ground – no throne! –
    daughter of the Chaldeans.
    For you will never more have people calling you
    delicate and dainty.
2. Take mill-stones and grind corn.
    Remove your veil;
    strip off your billowing skirt;
    expose your legs;
    cross rivers;
3. let your nakedness be exposed –
    also your shame will be seen.
    I will take vengeance,
    and come to terms with no one.[1]
4. Our redeemer!
    Yahweh of Hosts is his name.
    The Holy One of Israel.

Divine vengeance explained

5. Sit in silence and go into darkness,
    daughter of the Chaldeans,

1   Lit., 'I will meet no human.' Possibly like our expression 'to meet someone half way'.

The verb is used in the sense 'to meet with favour' (64:5).

for you will never more have people calling you
mistress of kingdoms.

6. I was exasperated with my people;
I profaned my possession,
and I gave them into your hand.
You did not offer them compassion.
Upon even the elderly you made your yoke very heavy.

7. And you said:
'For ever I will continue,
mistress for ever!'
You did not take these things into your consideration;[2]
you did not remember how it would end.

[2] 'Set these things in your heart'.

Diagnosis: things meriting judgment

8. Now then, hear this,
pampered one,
sitting in complacency,
one who says in her heart,
' I, and no one else besides! –
I will not sit as a widow,
nor will I know bereavement!'

9. And they will come to you, these two,
in an instant, on one day,
bereavement and widowhood –
in their full reality they will come upon you,
in spite of the abundance of your magic arts;
in spite of the great strength of your spells.

10. And you trusted in your evil,
and you said:
' There is no one to see me.'
Your wisdom and your knowledge –
that is what turned you around,[3]
and you said in your heart,
'I, and no one else besides!'

[3] cf., Ezek. 38:4 where the same verb ('to turn someone back') is used in the sense of leading them up the wrong path.

11. And evil[4] will come upon you:
you will not know its dawning –

[4] See 45:7.

and disaster will fall upon you;
you will not be able to buy it off,
and, suddenly, devastation will come upon you –
you will not know!

The religion that failed
12. Stand, then, through your spells
     and through the abundance of your magic arts
     at which you have toiled since your youth.
     Perhaps you will be able to gain advantage.
     Perhaps you will strike terror.
13. You have grown tired through the abundance of your plans.
     Now let them stand, and let them save you
     (those who divide up the heavens, who see visions by
     the stars,
     providing knowledge month by month)
     from what will come upon you.
14. Behold,
     they have become so much chaff;
     fire has burned them;
     they do not deliver even their own souls from the
     hand of the flame.
     No coals, these, for getting warm!
     No firelight to sit by!
15. This is what they have become for you –
     those on whom you have toiled,
     making a trade of you from your youth –
     each making his own exit, they wander off;
     no one to save you!

Thought for the day: Isaiah 47:1–15

We don't like the word 'vengeance' and we do like the word 'redemption'. In the Bible, however, in Isaiah, and in verses 3–4 of today's reading, they belong together. Our hesitation about 'vengeance' is understandable. In human experience it ordinarily includes vengefulness, and brings with it a whole cluster of sinful emotions and (often) over-reactions. Not so with the Holy God! His law is not something separate from himself; it is another way of thinking about him; it is his holy nature written down in commandments. Sin, therefore, is both breaking the law (for which the penalty must be paid), and offending and alienating the Law-giver (requiring reparation and reconciliation). Precisely these two things are solved by redemption. As to the broken law, one of the Hebrew words translated redemption (e.g., 35:9–10) points to the payment of the price that covers the debt. It is exactly as when we pay for our purchases at the counter or the check-out: the money handed over 'covers' the debt incurred. So the Lord God, the Holy One himself, knows (as we might say) 'to the last penny' what price must be paid, and, as our Redeemer, sets about paying it on our behalf. He does not look to us to assess the price and find the wherewithal! He weighs our sins in his own balances and looks to himself to cover them. For the other side of the notion of 'redemption' (the word used in v. 4) is 'next-of-kinship': the right of our nearest kinsman to take on himself our needs as if they were his, to pay our debts as if it were he who had incurred them. In the case of the Lord God it is the right to establish a next-of-kin relationship between himself and us by cancelling the hurt and offence our sin has caused, bridging the gap and alienation it created, bringing us to himself as his sons and daughters, making peace (Isa. 53:3–5; 54:10; Rom. 4:25–5:1; Eph. 2:15–18).

Day 53   Isaiah 48:1–22

This is a hugely important chapter. It completes Isaiah's prediction of the 'Cyrus-plan' – the fall of Babylon (ch. 47) and the return of the exiles (ch. 48). But it has also an additional function: in what spiritual condition do they return home? Verse 1 says they have forfeited the right to be called 'Israel', and verse 22 affirms that there is no peace to the wicked. Within these brackets Isaiah leaves no stone unturned to expose the spiritual needs of the Lord's people, and in this way he prepares for chapters 49–55 and the revelation of saving work of the Servant of the Lord.

Home, yet not home[1]

Unreality: no right to the name

48:1. Hear this, House of Jacob,
   those who call themselves by the name 'Israel',
   and have issued from the waters of Judah;[2]
   who swear oaths by the name of Yahweh,
   and keep the God of Israel in memory.
   Not in truth and not with right!
2.   Though they call themselves after the holy city itself,
   and claim the support of the God of Israel,
   Yahweh of Hosts is his name.

Determined unbelief and self-sufficiency: former predictions[3]

3.   As to former things:
   I declared them in advance;
   from my mouth they issued,
   and I made you hear of them.
   Suddenly I took action and they happened!

1   This summarises the message of the chapter: home from exile, but a change of address does not bring about a change of heart, and they are not yet at home with the Lord; cf., vv. 1, 22.

2   The line of descent pictured as a river with a source. cf., the 'fountain' imagery in Deut. 33:28; Ps. 68:26.

3   The 'former' predictions are those that foretell the rise and conquering career of Cyrus. The argument is that prediction long before the event forbids that unbelief should attribute the fulfilment to an idol.

4. Because of my knowledge that you are difficult –
   your neck an iron sinew, and your forehead bronze –
5. I declared them to you in advance;
   before anything happened I let you hear,
   in case you should say,
   'My idol did them,
   and my carved and my molten image commanded them.'
6. You did hear. View the whole thing!
   And for your part, will you not declare it?

New predictions[4]
   I have made you hear new things,
   belonging to now, and kept in reserve,
   and you had not known them.
7. Now they have been created, and not previously:
   before today you had not heard of them,
   in case you should say:
   'Behold, I have known them!'
8. But indeed you had not heard;
   but indeed you had not known;
   but indeed from beforehand your ear did not open.
   For I know that you are utterly deceitful,
   and 'Rebelling' has been your name from birth!

The Lord's motive
9. It is for the sake of my name that I keep my temper,[5]
   and for the sake of my praise that I restrain it for you,
   so as not to cut you down.
10. Behold,
    I have refined you, but not as is the case with silver;
    I chose you in the furnace of affliction.[6]
11. For my own sake, for my own sake I act,[7]
    for how should it be profaned?[8]
    And my glory to another I will not give.

The sovereign, all-commanding Lord[9]
12. Listen to me, Jacob, and Israel my called one.

4   The predictions about the Servant
    of the Lord – a novel turn of
    events, whereby no one can
    dismiss them as 'old hat' or too
    well known to be remarkable.

5   I usually translate this word
    'exasperation' (see 5:25) but,
    coupled with the verb 'to prolong',
    it is impossible to resist the
    obvious 'keep my temper'.

6   With silver, the refining process
    goes on till all dross is removed,
    but since, with Israel, the silver
    has become dross (1:22) the end
    would be total destruction. In the
    crucible, the Lord renewed his
    choice (as the verb 'to choose' can
    be translated, Zech. 1:17; etc.).

I am the same;
I am the first; and, yes, I am also the last.

13. Why, it was my hand founded the earth,
and my right hand that apportioned out the heavens,
I but start calling to them;
at once they stand.[10]

The Cyrus-plan affirmed[11]

14. Gather together, all of you, and hear.
Who among them declared these things?[12]
He whom Yahweh loves will do his pleasure against Babylon,
and his arm against the Chaldeans.[13]

15. It is I, I, who have spoken;
indeed, yes, I called him,
brought him along and he will make his way prosper.

The Servant-plan affirmed[14]

16. Come near to me.
Hear this.
From the outset, not under cover, I spoke.
At the time it happens, I am there.
'Now then, the sovereign Yahweh
has sent me, endowed with his Spirit.'[15]

A problem solved; A problem raised

17. This is what Yahweh has said,
your Redeemer,[16] the Holy One of Israel.
I am Yahweh, your God, teaching you to profit,
directing you in the way you should go.

18. If only you had paid attention to my commands!
Your peace would have been like a river,
and your righteousness like the rollers of the sea.

19. And your seed would have been like the sand,
and the offspring of your body like its grains.
Their name would not have been cut down;
and would not have been destroyed before me,

7   Or 'keep acting'. Imperfect tense denoting customary action.

8   'It' refers to Yahweh's name or praise, or, in general, to what touches his 'sake'.

9   These verses form the 'heart' of the chapter. No matter how they fall short or rebel, the Lord remains sovereign. He *will* have his way in both political (vv. 14–15) and spiritual (v. 16) salvation.

10 'Stand' at the ready, the position of the waiting servant, cf., 6:2; Gen. 18:8.

11 Cyrus is not named here but the content of vv. 14–15 indicates that he is meant: the one whom the Lord has called to conquer Babylon will succeed. Thus the 'former things' (vv. 3–6a) will be fulfilled.

12 i.e., the false gods who cannot predict what is to happen.

13 i.e., 'his [Cyrus'] arm [will be] against ...'

14 As well as the Cyrus-plan for release, there is the Servant-plan for spiritual redemption. It was foretold and it will be accomplished. The voice of the Servant attests his calling.

15 Lit., 'sent me and his Spirit' – the Spirit-endowed Servant (42:1).

16 See 35:9.

20. Go out from Babylon;
    fly from the Chaldeans.
    With loud-shouting voice declare.
    Make them hear this;
    make it go out to the ends of the earth;
    say:
    'Yahweh has redeemed[17] his servant Jacob.'   17   See 35:9.
21. And they did not thirst in the deserts he led them through.
    Water from the rock he distilled for them:
    he split the rock and the water flowed.
22. 'There is no peace,'
    Yahweh has said,
    'to the wicked.'

<hr />

Thought for the day: Isaiah 48:1–22

No, we cannot ever lose 'peace with God' but we can lose what Isaiah calls 'peace like a river' (v. 18). Our blood-bought peace (Col. 1:20), the peace with God which justification brings (Rom. 5:1), the peace which is Christ's gift (John 14:27), the peace which, indeed, is Jesus himself (Eph. 2:14) – nothing can touch that! But a river belongs in this world, making its way from source 'through all the changing scenes of life' until it discharges into the sea and, unless we are careful, it can become clogged and polluted, and the cares and blows of the world take over and we lose our peace. It need not be so; it ought not to be so. Think of deeply, steadily, silently flowing waters, the same whether the scene on its banks is turbulent, whether under sunny or lowering skies, whether through fertile fields or through barren lands. On it flows, serene, calm. Margaret was the wisest member of our home-group, usually also the least talkative, but once the question came up how we could make an effective impact on the world around us. Margaret simply said, 'Peace'. Everyone said, 'Tell us more,' and she replied: 'There are eleven flats in this block besides mine, they are all facing the difficulties, challenges, trials of life. What they need to see, more than anything else, are people facing the same issues but enjoying an unshaken peace.' Maybe you don't think that is the whole answer. But it has to be part – even a big part – of the whole answer, doesn't it? A distinctiveness that would make our testimony magnetic to a troubled society. So here, then, is Isaiah's thought for today: they lost their life of peace, their testifying peace, because they forsook their obedience to the Word of God (v. 18). Think of it! We can still have the invisible reality of peace in the heart, peace with God, but it is by constantly saying 'Yes' to the Word of God that the invisible starts visibly shining.

Day 54   Isaiah 49:1–13

The Servant's task revised (49:1–13)
This is the second of what are called 'The Servant Songs'.
In the first (42:1–4) the Lord revealed his Servant as the
answer to the world problem of lack of knowledge of the
one and only God. Isaiah became at once aware (42:18–25)
that Israel as he knew it could not be the Lord's Servant to
the world, and this awareness came to a climax in 48:1–22.
Israel will return from Babylon with the problem of sin
unresolved, and without peace with God (48:22). The
Servant tells how he has been called and prepared for a
double task: to bring Israel back to God, and to be the
Lord's salvation worldwide.

The Servant's testimony (vv. 1–6)
The first testimony: The prepared servant and his name
49:1. Give me a hearing, wide-spreading world![1]

    Pay attention, you states[2] afar off!
    From birth Yahweh himself called me,
    from my mother's womb he kept my name in remembrance.
2.   And he made my mouth like a sharp sword;
    in the shadow of his hand he concealed me.
    And he made me into a polished arrow;
    in his quiver he kept me under cover.
3.   And he said to me:
    'You are my Servant,
    Israel in whom I will show my beauty.'

The second testimony: Despondency and a larger job-description
4.   As for me, I said,
    'For emptiness I have toiled;

[1]   See 41:1.

[2]   See 17:12.

without sense[3] or substance I have exhausted my strength.
However,
my judgment[4] is with Yahweh,
and my achievement is with my God.'

5. Now then, Yahweh has said –
he who has been fashioning me from birth to be his Servant,
to bring Jacob back to him,
and that Israel might be gathered to him
(I am honoured in Yahweh's eyes,
and my God has proved to be my might!) –

6. he has said:
'It is too trifling for you to be my Servant
to raise the tribes of Jacob,
and to bring the preserved ones of Israel back:
I will appoint you to be the light of nations,
to be my salvation to the ends of the earth.'

The Lord's confirmation: Worldwide success (vv. 7–13)

Yahweh's first testimony to his Servant

7. This is what Yahweh has said –
Israel's Redeemer,[5] his Holy One –
to one heartily despised,[6]
to one nationally abhorrent,[7]
to a servant of rulers:
'Even kings will see and rise;
princes too, they will bow in reverence,
for the sake of Yahweh who proves himself faithful,
the Holy One of Israel indeed,
he chose you.'

Yahweh's second testimony to his Servant: 1. The people

8. This is what Yahweh has said:
'At the favoured time I have determined to answer you;
and at the day of salvation I have determined to help you.[8]
I will preserve you,
and I will appoint you

3 See 24:10. As the Servant reviews his career to date it doesn't add up to anything.

4 i.e., the decision about me. See 2:4.

5 See 35:9.

6 Lit., 'to a despising of soul', i.e., either 'utterly despised', or 'heartily despised'.

7 This is the meaning required here; the Hebrew as spelled in Masoretic Text is 'to one abhorring the nation'.

8 'Answer' and 'help' are perfect tenses, treated here as perfects of certainty, the Lord's pledge to his Servant.

to be a covenant of the people,
to raise up the earth,
to make them possess possessions lying desolate,
9.   to say to those who are bound, "Come out",
to those in darkness, "Show yourselves".'

Yahweh's second testimony to his Servant: 2. The world
'Along the roads they will find pasture,
and on all bare heights their pasture-land.
10. They will neither hunger nor thirst,
and neither parching heat nor sun will strike them down,
for he who has compassion for them will himself lead them,
and by outgushings of water he will guide them,
11. and I will make all my mountains into a road,
and my highways will be uplifted.
12. Behold!
From far off these will come;
and, behold!
These from north and west,
and these from the land of Sinim.'9
13. Shout aloud, heavens, and exult, earth.
Burst out, mountains, in loud shouting,
for Yahweh has determined to comfort his people,
and on his downtrodden ones he will have compassion.

9   Only mentioned here. There is no certainty of location. Intended to suggest remoteness – even if they are in lands you haven't heard of, the Lord knows them and will bring them.

Thought for the day: Isaiah 49:1–13

Who but Jesus fulfils Isaiah's portrait of the Servant? Yet it is not easy to match the despondency of 49:4 with any incident or period recorded in the Gospels, though, since he was 'in all points' tested as we are (Heb. 4:15), the Lord Jesus must have walked this path as well. How comfortingly and helpfully this reaches out to us. Jesus knows! Maybe some of us are more prone than others to being 'down in the dumps', fed up with ourselves, in despair over our present as well as our past, but few will fail to identify (to whatever extent) with 'For emptiness I have toiled' (v. 4). The old hymn rightly says, 'Those who fain would serve thee best are conscious most of wrong within' – yes, and of downright failure, incompetence and general uselessness. We set out like Peter with great promises and it all ends in tears (Matt. 26:35, 75). So how do we counter the dumps? First, reaffirm our basic position of faith: see how the disconsolate Servant of the Lord speaks of 'Yahweh … my God'. Not even our direst failure, our uttermost uselessness, can unpick the relationship of trust. We are not saved by success or dismissed by failure. Within that intimacy of believer and Lord, leave all to him; let him be the judge ('my judgment') and let him decide the outcome ('my achievement'). He is neither dependent on our competence nor derailed by our incompetence; he is sovereign in the accomplishing of his own will. Whatever he desired from my unworthy efforts, he will himself unfailingly achieve, and even turn disaster to triumph, bringing his good pleasure out of and in spite of my disasters. But there is also a second aspect to this position of faith. Despondency would anchor us in the past, but the Lord is able and waiting to open up for us the future, to say to us as to his perfect Servant, 'I will appoint you to be my salvation.' He does not give up on us.

Day 55 Isaiah 49:14–50:3

The Servant of the Lord bears the name 'Israel' (49:3). What does this mean? In 49:14–50:11 Isaiah sets up a contrast. On the one hand the actual Israel – spoken of here as the desolate Zion – is irretrievably despondent (49:14), and utterly unresponsive to the Lord's voice (50:2), whereas, by contrast, the Servant hears and obeys the Lord's voice (50:5) and faces his consequent suffering with buoyant faith (50:7, 9). Just as 42:18–25 began to show that the nation cannot do what the Lord requires of his Servant, so here the Servant stands out in all his individuality of faith and character in contrast to the nation.

Countering despondency: The four promises

1. The unforgetting Lord

49:14. And Zion has said:
'Yahweh has left me;
and, Sovereign though he is, he has forgotten me!'

15. Does a woman forget the infant at her breast,[1]
so as to fail in compassion for the son of her body?
Even these may forget!
But as for me, I will not forget you.

16. Behold!
On my palms[2] I have engraved you;
your walls are constantly in front of me.

2. The gathering family

17. Certainly your sons will hurry.
Those who demolish and devastate you,
they will go right away from you.

18. Raise your eyes all round and see.[3]
All of them will surely come gathering to you.

---

[1] Lit., 'her sucking child'.

[2] See 1:15.

[3] Feminine singular imperatives, addressed to despondent Zion.

As I live –
this is Yahweh's word –
all of them, like ornaments, you will wear,
and fasten them on like a bride.

19. For, as to your devastated and desolate places,
    your demolished land,
    why now you will be too cramped for the inhabitants,
    and those who were swallowing you whole will be far away.

20. Once more in your hearing the sons of your
    bereavement will say,
    'The place is too cramped for me.
    Make room for me so that I may take up residence.'

21. And you will say in your heart,
    'Who begot these for me?
    As for me, I was bereaved and barren,
    deported,
    turning this way and that,
    and these!
    Who reared them?
    Behold,
    for my part, I was left on my own.
    These!
    Where were they?'

3. World dominion

22. This is what the Sovereign Yahweh has said:
    Behold!
    I will lift up my hand for the nations,
    and for the peoples I will raise high my banner,
    and they will bring your sons in [their] bosom,
    and your daughters too –
    they will be carried shoulder high.

23. And kings will be your foster-parents,
    and their princesses your wet-nurses.
    Faces to the ground they will bow in reverence to you,
    and even lick the dust under your feet,

and you will know that I am Yahweh:
those waiting confidently[4] for me will not be disappointed.[5]

4. Deliverance

24. Can what a warrior has taken be taken back
    or can what is lawfully captive be released?[6]
25. But this is what Yahweh has said:
    'Even what a warrior has taken captive will be taken back,
    and what terrifying power has taken will be released.
    And your case at law I will myself argue,
    and your sons I will myself save.'
26. And I will make your oppressors eat their own flesh,
    and with their blood, as with new wine, they will
    become drunk.
    And all flesh will know that I am Yahweh,
    your Saviour and Redeemer,[7] the Potentate[8] of Jacob.

Ransom[9]

50:1. This is what Yahweh has said:
    'Wherever is your mother's divorce certificate
    with which I have put her away?
    Or who is it among my creditors to whom I sold you?
    Behold,
    in payment for your iniquities you were sold,
    and in payment for your rebellions your mother was
    put away.
2. On what ground is it that when I came there was no one,
    when I called there was no one to answer?
    Is my hand utterly too short to ransom,[10]
    or is there no power in me to deliver?
    Behold,
    by my rebuke I can make the sea dry,
    I can make rivers into a desert!
    Their fish stink because there is no water,
    and die of drought.
3. I clothe the heavens with blackness,
    and I make sackcloth their covering.'

4 See 8:17.

5 In the Hebrew this line is expressed not (as here) as a separate fact but as an attribute of Yahweh – 'Yahweh whom those waiting for me will not be disappointed.' It is not just what happens to us but more what he is like.

6 Two separate issues are raised in v. 24. First the matter of power – how can this 'warrior' be overcome? Secondly the matter of legality: if he lawfully holds what he has taken the law must be satisfied in order for the captive to be released.

7 See 35:9.

8 See 1:24; 10:13.

9 The problem of legality is faced here. On the one hand there has been no legal separation between Yahweh and his people. He has every right to intervene on their behalf. On the other hand, he is ready to pay the ransom price to settle whatever legal claim might be made against them. But Yahweh says and promises all this against the background of sheer unresponsiveness on his people's part.

10 See 1:27; 35:10. The 'hand' symbolises personal ability to intervene and act. Often used of (financial) resources, e.g., Deut. 16:17; lit., 'according to the giving of his hand', consequently suitable here to express the 'payment' aspect of 'ransom'.

Thought for the day: Isaiah 49:14–50:3

'Talking to yourself,' we used to say, 'is the first sign of madness.' Far from it, rather it's an important sign of Christian commonsense – depending, of course, on what we are saying to ourselves. Paul puts it another way when he says that we are transformed by the renewing of our mind (Rom. 12:2) – and, of course, the mind is only renewed by thinking of new and renewing topics. If we talk to ourselves about worldly things we develop a worldly mind; if we focus on things above we develop a heavenly mind (Col. 3:1–2). We can cultivate the mind of the flesh or the mind of the Spirit (Rom. 8:6). Every thought entertained disposes our minds in that direction. It matters what we talk to ourselves about! And today, in particular, what do we say to ourselves when things go from bad to worse and despondency takes over? The natural tendency – and it often seems strong beyond resistance – is to 'retire hurt', and moan to ourselves how terrible and unfair life is, to 'chew the fat'. Go that way and despondency feeds on itself, and deepens and darkens by the minute. Don't do it, Isaiah would counsel us. Feed your mind on the promises of God, tell yourself all he has pledged to do, hold on to his Word. Look at the four promises in today's passage: he never forgets us (14–16); he will increase his church (17–23); he will give it victory over the world (24–26); and he will ransom us from every alien power (1–3). Somewhere in that list you can position yourself in every situation. The Lord's therapy is to bring us, by means of his Word, pondered and understood, out of depression and the downcast face (Luke 24:17) into the burning heart, the buoyant step, and the assured testimony (Luke. 24:32–35).

Day 56 Isaiah 50:4–11

The Lord has been expostulating with his unresponsive people (vv. 1–3) when suddenly a single voice cuts in – Remember me? I have responded, haven't I? We are listening to the voice of the Servant of the Lord (see v. 10), the single, only one perfectly obedient to the will of the Lord – and suffering dreadfully for it.

The voice of the Servant of the Lord

50:4. The Sovereign Yahweh
    has given me the disciples' tongue,[1]
    so as to know to speak a word in season[2] to the fainting one.
    He rouses,
    morning by morning,
    he rouses my ear[3] to hear,
    as is the case with disciples.
5.   The Sovereign Yahweh
    opened my ear,
    and, for my part, I did not prove mutinous:
    I did not slip away backwards.[4]
6.   My back I determined to give to the floggers,
    and my cheeks to those who pluck them bare,
    not to cover even my face from any ignominy and spitting.
7.   The Sovereign Yahweh
    will help me,
    therefore I will not be abashed;[5]
    therefore I have set my face like flint,
    and I know that I will not reap shame.
8.   Near is the one who pronounces me righteous.
    Who will make out a case against me?

1   Lit., 'the tongue of those being taught.' A disciple is a person under instruction.

2   The verb *'ut* is not found elsewhere. Some say it means 'to incline towards', in the sense 'to console'. Simplicity says it is related to the noun *'et*, a 'season', hence 'to be seasonable', appropriate to the situation. 'To be seasonable in a word' gives the traditional rendering 'to speak a word in season', which suits the context completely.

3   More lit., 'he rouses for me the ear', i.e., for my advantage or good. The same in v. 5.

4   cf., the colloquial expression, 'to back off'.

5   'Ignominy' (v. 6) and 'abashed' (v. 7) are the same word, noun and verb. The sense therefore is 'any ignominy ... I will not fail before ignominy'. The Servant is confident in the face

Let us stand in court⁶ together!
Who will prove master of my case?
Let him approach me!
9. Behold,
the Sovereign Yahweh
will help me.
Who can declare me guilty?
Behold,
all of them – like clothes, they will wear out!
Moths will eat them!

Comment: Yahweh's Servant, exemplary and decisive⁷
10. Who among you fears Yahweh,
pays heed to the voice of his Servant?
Whoever walks in any sort of darkness⁸ and has no
glimmer of light,
let him trust in the name of Yahweh,
and lean upon his God.
11. Behold,
all of you who kindle fire,
surrounding yourselves with flashing flames,
walk by the light of your fire,
and by the flashing flames you have ignited.
By my hand this will happen to you:
In a place of pain you will make your bed!

of whatever comes his way as
he obeys the will of Yahweh.

6   The verb 'to stand' used in
the forensic sense 'to face
one another in court'.

7   The alternatives are clear: the way
of faith (v. 10), or works, facing
life in the light of the fire we
have ourselves made (v. 11). The
Servant is thus the Example for
believers to follow. Just as he is
not the nation itself, neither is he
a personification of the believing
remnant within the nation.
Rather he is the Example for such
to follow. To refuse the Servant is
to lie down in pain. He is not only
Example but is also the deciding
factor between life and death.

8   Lit., 'in darknesses',
plural of multiplicity.

Thought for the day: Isaiah 50:4–11

The difficulties and sufferings of life take us by surprise, but they should not. Jesus said, 'If they persecuted me, they will persecute you' (John 15:20), or, as the hymn puts it, 'It is the way the Master went, /Shall not the servant tread it still?' All too often trials make us retire to the sidelines and 'retire hurt', but Isaiah teaches 'No'. 'Time of trial, time for trust, /Not time to leave but time to lean.' That's the Jesus-way. Walking in darkness is no fun; it is a high risk situation and we seriously need the electric torch, or even the homely candle. So far so good, but is it the torch of our own abilities, the candle of our own best efforts ('I can cope')? Yes indeed, the time of trial may demand our utmost efforts if we are to get through, but not effort arising from self-reliance. The effort called for is that seen in the Servant, determination to stay the course, constant come what may, but only doing so in the 'strength that God supplies', confident in his God, still walking in the time of trouble, but walking because trusting, walking because leaning. Four times over, and with tremendous emphasis in Isaiah's Hebrew, the great divine title and name sounds out: 'the Sovereign Yahweh'. He is in total command. If we are 'in the soup', then it is he who has decided what sort of soup it is! And at what temperature we must endure it! And how long it will last! He is a God who is truly God, *Sovereign* at all times, in all places, over all forces, in all circumstances. But he is always the Sovereign *Yahweh*, the God of all grace, who hears our cries of distress, knows our sorrows, and comes down to deliver (Exod. 3:7–8). The old prayer got it right: he 'declares his almighty power most chiefly in showing mercy and pity'. A God worth knowing, and trusting, an arm to lean on.

Day 57 Isaiah 51:1–16

51:1–52:12 is a lengthy 'run up' to the final Servant Song (52:13–53:12), a forecast of what the Servant will accomplish. We find six 'calls' – double calls in each case – three to listen (51:1, 4, 7) and three further calls, to 'awake' (51:17; 52:1) and to 'depart' (52:11). The 'listen' calls are promises of what the Lord purposes to do; in the 'wake up' and 'get out' calls the work has already been done and is available to enjoy. But we are not told how the promises will be fulfilled or how the work has been done until Isaiah says, 'Behold, my Servant' in 52:13. Between the two sets of three calls there is an interlude – a prayer calling on the Lord to act (51:9–11), and a 'briefing session' in which the Lord speaks in turn to those involved (51:12–16).

Three promises
The first promise: Comfort for Zion

51:1. Give me a hearing,
> you who pursue righteousness,
> who earnestly seek Yahweh.
> Look at the rock you were carved from,
> and at deep excavation[1] you were dug from.

2. Look at Abraham your father,
> and at Sarah who endured your birth-pangs.
> For he was but a sole individual when I called him,
> and I kept blessing him and multiplying him.

3. For Yahweh has determined to comfort Zion;
> he has determined to comfort all its wastelands,
> and to make its wilderness like Eden,
> and its barren plain like the garden of Yahweh.

1 Lit., 'excavation of a pit'.

Happiness and rejoicing will be found in it,
thanksgiving and the sound[2] of music.

The second promise: Worldwide revelation

4. Pay attention to me, my people;
   my own folk,[3] listen to me.
   For from me teaching will go out,
   and I will bring my judgments[4] to rest as light for the peoples.
5. My righteousness is near;
   my salvation has gone out,
   and my arms[5] will judge[6] the peoples.
   For me the wide world waits confidently,[7]
   and for my arm they wait in hope.
6. Lift your eyes to the heavens,
   and look to the earth beneath,
   for the heavens are destined to be dispersed like so
   much smoke,
   and the earth will wear out like clothes,
   and, likewise, its inhabitants will die.
   And my salvation will continue in being for ever,
   and my righteousness will not be shattered.

The third promise: Lasting salvation

7. Give me a hearing, you who know righteousness,
   people in whose heart is my teaching.
   Do not fear the rebuke of mortal man,[8]
   and do not be shattered by their revilings,
8. for, like clothes, a moth will eat them,
   and, like wool, a grub will eat them.
   And my righteousness will continue in being for ever,
   and my salvation to all succeeding generations.

Interludes

The threefold promise of the preceding verses is met by a dramatic cry to the arm of the Lord to bring in this great salvation. The terms used are those of the Exodus: the

---

2 Lit., 'the voice of music', possibly 'singing voices' but see also 33:3.

3 *le'ummim*, cf., 17:12.

4 See 2:4.

5 Plural of amplitude, the fullness of divine personal action. The plural 'arms' is only elsewhere used of Yahweh in Deut. 33:27, but what was exclusive to one nation is now for the world.

6 'Set everything to rights for' as in 2:4.

7 See 8:17 for both 'wait confidently' and 'wait in hope'.

8 See 8:1; 13:7.

---

overthrow of Egypt (v. 9); the crossing of the Sea (v. 10); and arrival in the promised land (v. 11).[9]

Interlude: 1. Prayer

9. Wake up, wake up, put on garments of strength,
    arm of Yahweh.[10]
    Wake up as in earlier days, generations long ago.
    Was it not you who cut Rahab[11] in pieces,
    piercing the monster?

10. Was it not you who dried up the sea,
    the waters of the abundant deep,[12]
    who made the depths of the sea a road
    so that the redeemed[13] might cross over?

11. And Yahweh's ransomed ones will return,
    and they will come to Zion with loud shouting.
    And eternal rejoicing will be upon their heads.
    And they will overtake happiness and rejoicing,
    and sorrow and sighing will flee away.[14]

Interlude: 2. Reassurance[15]

Yahweh's reassurance for all those involved in the coming salvation

12. It is I, I who bring you comfort.

Reassurance for desolate Zion[16]

Who are you to be afraid of frail mortal humans,
and of a son of mankind to be classed as grass!

Reassurance for the helpless captives[17]

13. And you have forgotten Yahweh, your Maker –
    stretching out the heavens and founding the earth –
    and constantly, all the day,
    you are apprehensive of the rage[18] of the oppressor,
    while he is preparing to bring ruin;
    and where is the rage of the oppressor?

14. The cowering one will surely hasten to be untied,
    and he will not die, consigned to the pit,

9   Like the similar prayer for the promise to be fulfilled in 45:8, this prayer is anonymous. Who is praying? It typifies the proper reaction of the Lord's people to the Lord's promises: prayer for their prompt enjoyment.

10   See 40:10.

11   cf. 30:7. In Babylonian religion 'Rahab' was the restless sea-monster, ever opposed to the ordered creation. The 'creator', Marduk, had to engage in a pre-creation battle with Rahab before the field was clear for the creative task to proceed. By contrast, Yahweh's victories over opposing 'forces' are historical, performed before witnesses (Deut. 1:30; 6:22; Josh. 4:23).

12   'Sea' and 'deep', the ocean habitat of 'Rahab', but the sea (*yam*) was also 'personified' and worshipped in Babylon, again as the opponent whom the creator-god subdued before performing the work of creation. Notice the absence of any hint in Genesis 1 or the Old Testament of a pre-creation combat.

13   See 35:9.

14   See 35:10.

15   The Hebrew Text in these verses raises questions which different people have answered in different ways. In v. 12a 'you' is masculine plural; in v. 12b it is feminine singular; in vv. 13–16 it is masculine singular, and defined as 'a cowering one'; in vv. 15–16 'you' is again masculine singular but the wording used

and his bread will not be lacking:
I am Yahweh, your God,
15. cleaving the sea,[19] though its waves roar!
Yahweh of Hosts is his name!

Reassurance for the Servant[20]
16. And I have put my words in your mouth,
and with the shadow of my hand I have covered you,
in order to plant the heavens,
and to found the earth,
and to say to Zion, 'You are my people.'

16 Cities are treated as feminine in Hebrew. In these chapters 'Zion' (cf., 52:1) is the target of the Lord's salvation and the most obvious candidate for the feminine singular in v. 12b.

17 In 39:6 Isaiah predicted wholesale deportation to Babylon: in 43:14 he foresaw the Lord mounting a rescue operation, cf., 48:20–22, but from 49:1 onwards he is concerned with the return to Yahweh of the captives of sin and death.

18 See 5:25.

19 As in the case of the Red Sea, removing whatever barrier blocked the way of his people. Note how this little section begins with heaven and earth (v. 13) and ends with sea (v. 15), the all encompassing power of Yahweh over every possible situation.

20 The Servant is not referred to by title in these verses, but the gift of words and the sheltering hand are reminiscent of 50:4; 49:2.

recalls the Servant of the Lord. The view taken here is that the text should not be emended and that, after the word of comfort to them all in v. 12a, different people are addressed in turn.

Thought for the day: Isaiah 51:1–16

A man who figures so prominently throughout the Bible demands our close attention. For Paul (Rom. 4:18–25) Abraham exemplifies for us how a true faith rests without wavering on the promises of God; Hebrews finds in him the steadfastness of faith under trial (11:8–12,17–19); and, to James, Abraham is evidence that real faith proves itself in consequent works (2:21–24). Big lessons. Isaiah's point about Abraham is that, on the one hand, being a single, solitary individual is of no significance, and, on the other hand, that the single, solitary individual is of great significance. Our solitariness imposes no limitation on the Lord; our faithfulness as single individuals is of the utmost importance to him. Well, just suppose Abraham had said: 'What's the point of my emigrating from Ur? I'm just one, childless, person! What can I do, or how can I matter?' No fulfilment of divine promises, no people of God, no messianic line into which Jesus can be born, no worldwide salvation and blessing! All this may be classed as 'humanly speaking' for the Sovereign Lord has his own ways of achieving what he wants, but, humanly speaking, it's true. Like when the Lord called Ananias to go to Paul: he told him Paul was expecting a man named Ananias (Acts 9:11–12). The 'Ananias Plan' was the only plan! No one else would 'do'. The unknown man – the man we have not heard of before and will not hear of again – is the only one who can set the great world-missionary on his feet! And, take Abraham, he must have spent many years – if not most of his life – wondering what it was all about. He had to wait thirteen years for the birth of Isaac, and, even after Isaac was born there was no great flurry of divine activity, was there? Hebrews picks out that aspect of Abraham – the 'what's it all about? When will it happen?' aspect – by saying he looked for a city and lived in a tent (11:9–10). But he mattered! My word, how he mattered!

Day 58 Isaiah 51:17–52:12

The tone now changes from listening to promises (51:1, 4, 7), to waking up to benefits already achieved (51:17; 52:10) and embarking on a new life (52:11). Nothing is yet said how these benefits have come to be available, of how it is that a new life is there to be embarked on. We await the 'behold' of 52:13, and the saving work of the Servant of the Lord as the required explanation.

The first benefit: The end of wrath

51:17. Rouse yourself, rouse yourself!
    Get up, Jerusalem!
    You who have drunk from Yahweh's hand the cup
    of his rage;[1]
    the bowl of the cup of intoxication you have drunk
    to the dregs.[2]

18.   No one to guide her of all the sons she bore;
    and no one to grip her by the hand of all the sons she reared.

19.   Two things have happened to you;
    who will console you?
    Spoliation[3] and shattering;
    famine and sword.
    Who am I to comfort you?[4]

20.   Your sons – they lie in a swoon at the top of every street,
    like a netted antelope,[5]
    themselves full of the rage[6] of Yahweh,
    the rebuke of your God.

21.   Therefore do hear this,
    downtrodden one, and drunk but not with wine!

22.   This is what your Sovereign, Yahweh has said –
    your God who argues the case of his people:

1   See 5:25.

2   Two elements here of duplication: 'the bowl of the cup' = the full large cup; 'you have drunk, you have drained' = 'drunk to the last drop'.

3   See 13:6. "Shattering', lit., 'breaking', is chosen to reflect the alliteration here in the Hebrew: *shod washeber*.

4   The prophet speaking. This is a situation beyond human ability to help.

5   An animal mentioned in Deut. 14:5, identification uncertain.

6   See 5:25, also 'rage' in v. 22.

'Behold,
I have determined to take from your hand
the cup of intoxicant,
the bowl of the cup of my rage.
You will not drink it ever again.

23. And I will put it into the hand of those who distress you,
who said to your soul:[7]
"Down with you so that we may walk over you."
And you made your back like the ground,
and like a street-pavement for them to walk over.'

The second benefit: Holiness

52:1. Wake up, wake up,
dress yourself in your strength, Zion!
Dress yourself in the garments of your beauty,
Jerusalem, city of holiness!
For there will never again come into you
the uncircumcised and the unclean.[8]

2. Shake yourself free of the dust!
Get up!
Sit in the throne, Jerusalem!
Unloose yourself from the fetters on your neck,
captive one, daughter of Zion.

Preview: Divine action to deliver and save[9]

3. For this is what Yahweh has said:
'For nothing you were sold,
and it is not for silver that you will be redeemed.'[10]

4. For this is what the Sovereign Yahweh has said:
'It was to Egypt my people went down at the start,
to seek asylum there;
and it is Assyria which, latterly, oppressed them.

5. And now,
what have I here –
(this is Yahweh's word!) –
that my people have been taken for nothing?

7 More than simply 'said to you', 'spoke in a way that pierced right into your heart'.

8 cf., Heb. 12:22–24; Rev. 21:27. 'Circumcised', those within the covenant of God, touched by his grace, recipients of his promise; 'clean', those fitted for his presence.

9 The call to Zion to enter into holiness and purity leads Isaiah to launch into an explanation: behind the call to enjoy (52:1–2) lies divine action. The Lord will speak the decisive word (v. 6) and perform the decisive action (vv. 9–10).

10 See 35:9.

Those ruling them[11] wail –
this is Yahweh's word –
and continually, all the day, my name is spurned.

6. Therefore my people will know my name –
therefore, in that day,[12]
that I am the Speaker![13]
Behold me!'

News of an accomplished salvation

7. How lovely on the mountains the feet of one bearing
good news!
Letting folk hear of peace!
Bringing good news of something good!
Letting folk hear of salvation!
Saying to Zion:
'Your God is King!'

8. Listen! Your watchmen![14]
They have raised their voice!
Together, they shout aloud!
For, in plain view,[15] they look at Yahweh's return to Zion.

9. Explode in loud shouts, all together, waste places
of Jerusalem,
for Yahweh has comforted his people;
he has redeemed[16] Jerusalem.

10. Yahweh has bared the arm of his holiness
before the eyes of all the nations,
and all the ends of the earth will see the salvation of our God.

The third benefit: Freedom, separation[17]

11. Move on, move on, go out from there.
The unclean – do not touch it!
Go out from within it.
Show yourselves to be pure, bearers of the vessels of Yahweh,

12. for without trepidation you will depart,
and in flight you will not go,
for Yahweh will actually go ahead of you,
and your rearguard will be the God of Israel.

11 Isaiah had seen Hezekiah's helplessness in the days of the Assyrian attack, and here he envisages a similar despairing helplessness on the part of those who should be their people's leaders and protectors.

12 It is obvious that 'they will know' is to be understood from the previous line, but to repeat it pedantically would spoil the way Isaiah rushes on to his climax.

13 It is the Lord who 'has the say'. It is for him to speak the decisive word what will happen.

14 Lit., 'The voice of your watchmen!' On 'voice' see 13:4; 40:5–6.

15 Lit., 'eye to eye'. But 'seeing eye to eye' now means 'to agree'. In Hebrew, just as 'to shout a shout' means to shout loudly, so to see 'eye to eye' means to see with total clarity.

16 See 35:9.

17 Using the picture of Babylonian captivity, Isaiah foresees bondage ended, entry into freedom, a holy people walking in holiness. This is consequent on the Lord 'rolling up his sleeves' (v. 10), but is about to be achieved by the saving work of the Servant who is himself Yahweh's arm (53:1).

Thought for the day: Isaiah 51:17–52:12

The great objective – fight, too – of the Christian life is to be what we are. Not seeking or striving after some future blessing but exploring and experiencing ever more fully the complete salvation given to us in Jesus. Does not the Bible call him our 'righteousness, sanctification and redemption' (1 Cor. 1:30)? What more is there? Does not the Bible say that the Father has blessed us (past tense) with every spiritual blessing in Christ (Eph. 1:3)? So what more is there to give? Salvation is like a great hamper filled full of every possible blessing of God, and our task is to discover – personally, progressively, ceaselessly – what has thus been given to us once for all. Suppose someone is pronounced 'cured' after a long, weakening illness. Convalescence lies ahead with the constant choice between acquiescing in the body's experienced feebleness, or acting resolutely, maybe even painfully, certainly progressively on the expert diagnosis, and slowly entering into new-found health. That is where we meet Isaiah today. In effect he is saying wrath is over (v. 17), holiness is yours (v. 1), new life awaits (v. 11), so wake up to what you are and have, and gird your loins for a new Exodus. Believe that his wrath is a thing of the past, dress yourself in your new robe of righteousness, start walking the separated pathway. Yahweh has himself taken away his wrath (v. 22), himself accomplished the total work of salvation (v. 10), and himself will accompany you protectively on your journey (v. 12). Let us ask ourselves why Romans 8:30 says that the Lord 'glorified us', using the same past tense as when it says he 'justified' us? Or why does Ephesians 2:6 speak of us as already seated in the heavenly places? Or Colossians 3:1 that we 'were raised with Christ'? This is a divine expert diagnosis like the doctor's pronouncement 'you are cured'. We feel our weakness; we are summoned to lay hold on our strength.

Day 59 Isaiah 52:13–53:12

Isaiah has let us into the secret that Yahweh himself has 'bared his holy arm' – as we might say 'rolled up his sleeves' – for the task of worldwide salvation (52:10). Now he allows us to meet 'the Arm of the Lord' in person (53:1), the one whom Yahweh will presently call 'that righteous one, my Servant' (v. 11). The opening 'Behold' of 52:13 calls us to watch the work of salvation being accomplished.

Enigma: Success through suffering

52:13.   Behold!

My Servant will succeed.

He will be raised, and uplifted, and exalted indeed!

14.   Just as many were shocked over you –

(his appearance – such disfigurement beyond anyone else
and his physical form, beyond humankind!)[1] –

15.   exactly so he will sprinkle[2] many nations.

Kings will shut their mouths over him

for what had not been recounted to them they will see,

and what they had not heard they will discern.

The man who is God: unrecognised, misunderstood

53:1.   Who believed what we heard?

And Yahweh's Arm, to whom was it revealed?

2.   Seeing that like a delicate plant he grew up before him,[3]

and like a root out of arid soil.

He had no physical form, and no splendour, that we
should look at him,

and no looks that we should take pleasure in him.

3.   Despised and lacking in men,

a man of sorrows, and familiar with sickness,[4]

[1] 'Anyone ... humankind' involves the contrast between *'ish* and *'adam*, the individual person and the common run of people. The thought is that his suffering left him more damaged than any other ever had been, and indeed prompted the question whether what remained could even be human.

[2] 'Sprinkle' or 'startle'? Neither is totally free of difficulty. The verb 'to sprinkle' is familiar in the Old Testament but elsewhere its direct object is the substance sprinkled, and that on which the sprinkling is made is governed by a preposition ('on'). Here that on which the sprinkling is made is a direct object. 'To startle' is derived from an Arabic verb, not elsewhere

and, as with a hiding of face from him, despised!
And we thought nothing of him.

Suffering explained

4. Ah but surely it was our sickness he himself bore,
   and our sorrows which he shouldered.
   As for us, we thought him
   plagued, struck down by God and humiliated.
5. As for him, pierced because of our rebellions,
   crushed because of our iniquities,
   the correction bringing us peace was upon him,
   and at the cost of [5] his wounds healing for us! [6]
6. All of us,
   like sheep we strayed.
   We each
   to his way turned aside.
   And Yahweh!
   He brought together upon him the iniquity of us all.

Self-submission; voluntary acceptance of undeserved death

7. He let himself be brutalised,
   and himself accepted humiliation,
   and did not open his mouth.
   Like a sheep to the slaughter he was led off,
   and like a ewe, before its shearers, stays dumb!
   And he did not open his mouth.
8. From custody and without justice he was taken away,
   and, among his contemporaries, who was pondering
   that he was cut down from the land of the living
   because of the rebellion of my people to whom the
   blow belonged?
9. And they assigned [7] his grave with wicked men,
   and with a rich man [8] in his wondrous death,
   though he had done no violence at all,
   nor was there deceit in his mouth.

exemplified in the Old Testament. This would not be an insuperable difficulty, but in Arabic, we are told, the verb means literally 'to jump' and is never used in the emotional sense 'you made me jump'. Thus 'startle' would be an unexemplified meaning in every way. The huge balance of probability lies with 'to sprinkle'.

3   'He' is the Arm of Yahweh, the Servant; 'him' is Yahweh.

4   We are left at this point to make what we can of the references to sorrow and sickness. Presently it transpires (v. 4) that Isaiah is referring to the Servant's voluntary identification with our sinful condition.

5   The preposition *be* expresses instrumentality, 'by his wounds', but it is also the '*be*' of price and value, 'at the expense of'.

6   Lit., 'it has been healed for us.' The impersonal and passive wording looks away from the agent in order to emphasise the result, that has been objectively achieved.

7   Lit., 'he/someone'. Hebrew uses the singular for an indefinite subject where we use the indefinite 'they'.

8   The reference to wicked men and rich man remained without

The enigma explained: Suffering and triumph both the act of Yahweh

10. And Yahweh was himself pleased to crush him:

he made him sick.[9]

If and when you make his soul a guilt offering[10]

he will see seed;

he will lengthen days;

and in his hand[11] Yahweh's pleasure will flourish.

11. Arising from the toil of his soul he will see, be satisfied.[12]

By his knowledge

that righteous one, my Servant,

will provide righteousness[13] for the many:

their iniquities he will himself shoulder.[14]

12. Therefore,

I will apportion out to him the many,

and the mighty ones he will apportion as spoil,[15]

as an exact result of the fact that he poured out his

soul to death,

and allowed himself to be counted with those in rebellion:

he bore the sin of many himself,

and for those in rebellion[16] he interposed.

explanation until it was fulfilled (Matt. 27:57–59). 'Death' is a plural of amplification, hence 'wondrous death' (cf., 2 Kings 22:20), lit., 'your graves', 'your impressive tomb'.

9   The sickness in question is that of v. 4; the reference to a direct action of Yahweh looks back to the last element in v. 6.

10 Or, 'If and when his soul makes a guilt-offering', or 'If and when you (O Lord) make his soul a guilt-offering.' The last is the least likely since it requires some additional note that the subject is Yahweh. The rendering preferred above is the most obvious, and a reference to a true response to the Servant's death would nicely counterbalance the erroneous responses recorded in vv. 2, 4, 8. For guilt-offering, see Lev. 5:1–6:7. Its distinctiveness is an insistence on minute exactness between sin and remedy. It is the 'total satisfaction' offering.

11 i.e., 'by his personal agency'. The Servant who died for the salvation of sinners lives to administer the salvation he accomplished.

12 The Hebrew idiom of co-ordinate verbs: 'be satisfied with what he sees'.

13 A form of words not found elsewhere in the Old Testament justifying this rendering.

14 This line opens with 'and' in Hebrew. A regular way of adding an explanation. Represented throughout this translation by the colon at the end of the preceding line.

15 The traditional rendering of these lines makes them say something which is impossible – that the Servant is, after all, only one victor among many, sharing his spoil with the strong! The true meaning is, 'I will give him the many as his portion' –'the many' being the whole company for whom the Saviour died. What John 6:37 calls 'the whole thing the Father gives me'. And 'he will share out the mighty ones as his spoil' – the spoiling of the strong by the stronger (Mark 3:27).

16 'In rebellion' in each case in this verse is a plural participle. Not a noun 'rebels' but those engaged in rebelling.

Thought for the day: Isaiah 52:13–53:12

Holy ground indeed! It feels irreverent to attempt a 'thought for the day' from this awesome passage. Why not just read and re-read it? But if a 'thought' must be offered, consider the opening of verse 10: 'It was Yahweh's pleasure to crush him.' Many a Christian parent has known heartfelt joy when a dear child is called into the Lord's service, and has also accepted with (tearful) joy the departure of the child to distant – even menacing – places, demanding suffering and sacrifice. But there comes a point where tears remain and joy ends! Consider, therefore, 'the love that drew salvation's plan', finding pleasure in sending the beloved Son; finding pleasure too when 'by the carefully planned intention and foreknowledge of God' (Acts 2:23) he was 'delivered' into lawless hands to crucify and put to death. No, that is a love beyond our possibility of experience, yet, says John (1 John 4:9–10, 14), 'this is what love is – he loved us and sent his Son to be the propitiation for our sins'. It is not only God's peace that is 'past understanding', beyond our powers of heart and mind; far more so his love. The hymn-writer asks, 'Jesus, what didst thou find in me that thou has dealt so lovingly?' Change the wording from 'Jesus' to 'Father'. The answer remains the same – he loved us because he loved us because he is love. The response is not to question, not to raise unintelligent questions prompted by our deficient, sin-impaired logic but, as Wesley should have written, that we should be '*found* in wonder, love and praise.' In this place, too, we discover how marvellously secure we are in Christ. Through him as Mediator we come to the Father, and, knowing partially but terrifyingly, all that unfits us for his presence and fits us for his wrath, we find ourselves in the presence of love beyond anything known on earth, and the voice which says, 'I was delighted when my Son died for you – and I am still delighted.'

Day 60   Isaiah 54:1–17

In two chapters Isaiah now spells out the consequences of the death of the Servant.[1] The promised (51:4–6), divinely-accomplished (52:10), universal salvation has been achieved, and now the call goes out to the two groups (49:5–6) to whom the Servant was sent. First the call to Zion (54), and then the invitation to the whole world (55).

Joy for Zion: Five pictures of benefit (54:1–17)

Increase: The barren woman and her growing family

54:1. Shout aloud, barren one –
    she who has not given birth.
    Break out into loud shouts and scream[2] –
    she who has not writhed in labour.
    For many[3] are the sons of the desolate one,
    more than the sons of the married woman,
    Yahweh has said.

2. Enlarge the place of your tent,
    and let them spread out the curtains of your dwelling.
    Do not check them!
    Lengthen out your ropes and make your pegs strong.

3. For right and left you will burst out
    and your seed will take possession of even nations;
    they will inhabit devastated cities.

Transformation: the deserted wife and everlasting love

4. Do not be afraid for you will not be disappointed,
    and do not be abashed for you will not be disgraced.
    For you will forget the shame of your youth,
    and the reproach of your widowhood you will not
    remember again.

[1]   Each 'Servant song' is followed by verses offering a comment on what has been revealed of the Servant. 42:1–4 is affirmed in 42:5–13; 49:1–6 in 49:7–13; 50:4–9 is applied in vv. 10–11. So here Isaiah's command to Zion (54) and his invitation to all (55) spell out again what the Servant has done.

[2]   See 12:6.

[3]   'Many' links back to 52:14–15; 53:11–12, those who were the object of the Servant's atoning work.

5. For your Maker is your husband.
   Yahweh of Hosts is his name.
   And your Redeemer[4] is the Holy One of Israel.
   He is called the God of all the earth.
6. For like a wife abandoned and grieved in spirit
   Yahweh has called you –
   a young wife when she is scorned –
   your God has said.
7. For a tiny moment I left you,
   and with great compassion[5] I will gather you.
8. In a rush of impatience[6] I hid my face momentarily
   from you,
   and with everlasting devotion I have set myself to show
   you compassion,
   your Redeemer[7] Yahweh has said.

Peace: Wrath is past; peace is covenanted

9. For to me this is the waters of Noah:
   exactly as I swore that Noah's waters not cross the
   earth again,
   so I have sworn not to be impatient with you,
   and not to rebuke you.
10. For the mountains may slip away and the hills slide
    but my devotion will not slip away from being with you,
    nor will the covenant of my peace slide,
    Yahweh who shows you compassion[8] has said.

Security: a city walled and founded

11. Downtrodden, tempest-tossed, unpitied,[9]
    behold!
    I am going to set your stones in mascara,[10]
    and lay your foundations in sapphires.
12. And I will make your suns[11] rubies,
    and your gates of fiery red stones,[12]
    and all your boundary of pleasing stones.
13. And all your sons will be Yahweh's disciples[13]
    and abundant the peace of your sons.

4   See 35:9.

5   'Compassion' and 'devotion'
    (v. 8) are the two sides of the
    divine love. 'Compassion',
    related to the word for 'womb',
    is surging, maternal love (cf.,
    1 Kings 3:26). It is the love of
    being 'in love'; love centred in the
    emotions and heart. 'Devotion'
    (*chesedh*) is love centred in
    the will; a determination
    and commitment to love.

6   See 5:25.

7   See 35:9.

8   See 30:18.

9   Three feminine singulars.

10 Here meaning that mortar
    is mixed with black pigment
    to enhance the beauty
    of the stonework.

11 A literal translation, usually taken
    to refer to features of the city
    reflecting the sun – pinnacles
    or battlements or (cf. Song 4:4)
    shields hung round the walls

14. In righteousness you will be made secure;
be far[14] from oppression – for you will not fear –
and from anxiety – for it will not approach you.

Protection: the Sovereign Creator
15. Behold,
someone is sure to pick a quarrel, wholly without me.
Anyone who quarrels with you will desert[15] to you.
16. Behold,
it is I who create a craftsman,
fanning the coals in the fire, and producing a tool
for its purpose,
and it is I who create a destroyer to work ruin.
17. Not a single tool fashioned against you will flourish!
and every tongue which rises to bring a case against you[16]
will prove guilty.
This is the possession of the servants[17] of Yahweh,
and their righteousness is straight from me.[18]
This is the word of Yahweh.

_____

12   to symbolise the strength (and, here, the beauty) of the city.

12   'Stones' in these two lines in the jewellery sense.

13   See 50:4.

14   The Hebrew idiom of an imperative expressing a sure consequence.

15   Lit., 'will fall (away) to you.' For 'fall away to' = change sides, desert to; cf., 2 Kings 25:11. Not even those who come with hostile intent will be able to resist the impulse to join you.

16   Lit., 'rises with you for judgment'.

17   After ch. 53 'servant' is only used in the plural. The saving work of the Servant makes 'servants'.

18   See 53:11. The Servant provides righteousness. It is what Paul will call 'a righteousness from God' (Phil. 3:9), imputed to the Servant's 'seed' (53:10), the 'sons' of 54:13.

Thought for the day: Isaiah 54:1–17

The truth about God the Creator runs far beyond what happens in Genesis 1:1–2, yet so often that is where our thinking stops: God the Creator started everything off. Well of course he did, but in the Bible the Creator not only *begins* everything, he also *maintains* everything in its existence – which is why Isaiah speaks of him as 'the creating One';[19] he also *controls* everything in its operation (54:16–17), and *guides* everything to his intended goal (65:17). He *begins, maintains, controls, guides* – everything, all the time. He is God, in truly executive rule of his world. This is why it is important in Psalm 121:1–2 to remember that, when we face coming dangers, we do so in the Creator's world – help comes from Yahweh, maker of heaven and earth (also 124:8; 134:3). It all happens 'on his patch', 'on his watch'. The problem, danger, trouble we face is part of what he *begins, maintains, controls, and guides.* So to speak, it is 'all in hand' – in his hand – which is also where we are eternally secure (John 10:28–29). In the same way Paul assures us that nothing touches us but what he has weighed and measured as suitable for us, and it does so under his controlling management (1 Cor. 10:13). As the Creator's children in the Creator's world we are a protected species in a planned environment and destined for a glorious future that is already ours. Remember how Jesus went straight from his command not to be troubled to his assurance about our prepared place in the Father's house (John 14:1–3). Just as we are 'in Christ' by divine determination, planning, and intention (Eph. 1:4), so, already, in that same divine mind, we have been glorified (Rom. 8:30) and made to sit with Christ in heavenly places (Eph. 2:4–6). He who is the Alpha and the Omega is also all stations between!

---

19   See 40:28, 'Day 44. Isaiah 40:12–31', footnote 12 (page 193).

Day 61   Isaiah 55:1–13

The great invitation now goes out to everyone without exception. The servant was given a double task, one part of which was to 'be my salvation to the ends of the earth' (49:6). The terms in which that invitation is now extended indicates how completely the Servant has done his work.

The whole world invited into the New World (55:1–13)

Free provision

55:1. Ho there! Every thirsty one,
    come[1] to the waters!
    Whoever has no money
    come, buy and eat!
    Yes, come, buy – for no money, at no cost –
    wine and milk.

2. Why do you weigh out money for what is not bread,
    your hard-earned cash for what brings no satisfaction?
    Listen – just listen – to me and eat[2] well,
    and your soul will find delight in rich fare.

Welcome to the blessings of David's Kingdom: Equal citizenship

3. Incline your ear and come to me.
    Hear so that your soul will live.
    And I will inaugurate for you an eternal covenant:
    the trustworthy love-pledges made to David.[3]

4. Behold:
    I have appointed him a witness to the peoples,
    a captain and commander of the peoples.

5.[4] Behold,
    you will call even a nation you do not know,

[1] Plural imperative. The singular ('every one') points to individual responsibility; the plural ('come') points to sufficient provision.

[2] Imperative of assured result = and you will assuredly eat well.

[3] The plural of *chesedh* (see 16:5) occurs here, as in Ps. 89:1, 49. The psalm defines this plural by two occurrences of the word in the singular (89:24, 28). David was promised a universal and eternal kingdom. Into this kingdom all are now invited, to a free citizenship.

and a nation who does not know you will come running
to you,
  on account of Yahweh your God,
  and for the Holy One of Israel because he has beautified you.

*The invitation of verse 1 now stated in plain terms: Coming back
to Yahweh*

6. Seek Yahweh while he permits himself to be found.
  Call him while he is near.
7. Let the wicked man leave his way,
  and the immoral man his thoughts,
  and let him turn back to Yahweh so that he may show
  him compassion,
  and to our God, for he will multiply forgiveness.
8. For my thoughts are not your thoughts,
  and your ways are not my ways.
  This is the word of Yahweh.

The supernal Yahweh and his efficacious word [5]

9. For as the heavens are higher than the earth
  so my ways are higher than your ways
  and my thoughts than your thoughts.
10. For just as the rain and the snow come down from heaven,
  and do not return there but, to the contrary, saturate
  the earth,
  and make it germinate and sprout,
  and give seed for the sower and bread to the eater,
11. so is my word which goes out of my mouth:
  it does not come back to me empty,
  but to the contrary is bound to do what I please
  and to flourish where I have sent it.

New Exodus, new world

12. For with rejoicing you will go out,
  and in peace you will be conducted along.
  Mountains even and hills will break out before you

[4] The change from a statement in v. 4 to an address in v. 5 can only be explained by making v. 5 refer to the Servant. He inherits David's international status (v. 4) and is internationally recognized as such (v. 5). In the case of the Servant the 'beautification' came with the resurrection, ascension and heavenly session of Jesus: the threefold exaltation predicted in 52:15.

[5] This section contains two 'explanations', note the explanatory 'for' which opens vv. 9–10. The former calls attention to the fact that Yahweh is highly distinctive in the way his mind works ('thoughts') and in his characteristic actions ('ways'). That he is so ready to forgive, so generous in forgiveness, and that he does so on the simple ground of repentance 'stands to reason' – not our reason but his. Furthermore his call to repentance is guaranteed by the fact that is it the unfailing Word of God, and those who rely on it will find it effective.

into loud shouts,
   and the very trees of the field will all clap hands.
13.   In place of the thorn-bush, fir will come up;
   in place of nettles, myrtle will come up.
   And it will make a name for Yahweh,
   an eternal sign not to be cut off.

———————————————————————

Thought for the day: Isaiah 55:1–13

Looking back is not always a tonic! A Sunday school class years ago, with not much evidence of results; a Bible class or club for youngsters, with memories of difficulties but not much to show for all that effort. Maybe door to door visitation: what a hard and stoney furrow! Did anyone listen? Was anyone won for Christ? Of course that is never the whole story, but some days it seems so – and when those days come, where are we to turn? Turn to Isaiah 55:11. Let it be never so true that we tried to share the Word of God and saw nothing for it, and our opportunity is now long since gone and irrecoverable: the Word we shared is not ours but his; our chance is gone, not his. No one loves the Word of God more than the God whose Word it is, and he, the eternal, almighty, impeccably faithful Lord, has pledged that his Word will never be fruitless, never come back empty handed. When we speak of God's Word as a 'living Word', this is the reality of which we speak. First, it comes from his mouth: like the 'Let there be light' of Genesis 1:3 – 'and there was light!' His Word is full of his creative power to achieve what the Word expresses. Secondly, God's Word is his personal messenger. It goes where he 'sends' it and achieves what he commands it. Thirdly, it cannot but hit its target, do its work. So then, those children, young people and door-openers of long ago, those passers-by at the open air meeting, that 'chance' fellow in the next seat in the bus who accepted a tract, that seemingly cold, unresponsive congregation in hall or church – did they hear the Word of God? From his mouth, through us, was the great messenger sent? Have no fear: as with Jeremiah (1:12), so with us, the Lord 'is ever wide awake, watching over my word to perform it'. All will be well, indeed, more than well.

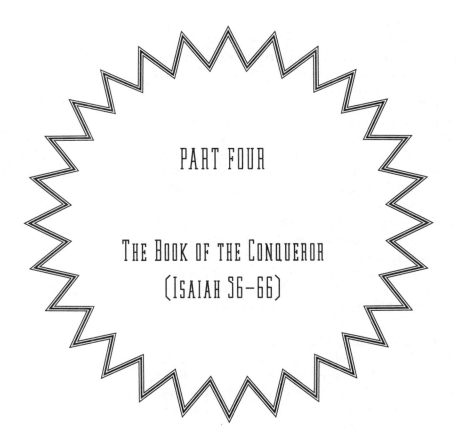

PART FOUR

The Book of the Conqueror
(Isaiah 56–66)

Day 62 Isaiah 56:1–12

From the point of view of history, in chapters 38–55 Isaiah predicted the Babylonian captivity of his people and foresaw their return. Now he looks further forward into the circumstances and experiences of the returnees. This gives him the canvas on which to paint his third portrait of the Messiah. There is still one great achievement of the Servant's saving work which has to be put into effect: his taking of the strong as his spoil (53:12), the consummation of his victory over all his foes. This work of conquest will be performed by the anointed Conqueror whom we meet in 59:14–63:6. In other words, the situation Isaiah depicts matches what we ourselves now experience. Suppose we think of ourselves standing at 56:1. We look back to 52:13–53:12, a completed work of salvation, yet, as 56:1 says, we are still awaiting salvation. Isn't that exactly 'us' – possessing salvation and awaiting salvation? Placed like this, we are called to obedience (56:1) while we await the coming of the Conqueror, the final showdown with the hostile powers (63:1–6) and the New Heaven and New Earth (65:17).

The ideal and the actual (56:1–59:13)

The vision of an ideal world-wide community of the Lord's 'Sabbath-people' (56:1–8) is balanced by the very different actuality of a 'mixed bag' of the righteous and compromisers (56:9–57:21). In 58:1–14 the Sabbath ideal is again set out, only to be followed by a confession of failure (59:1–13).

The waiting people (56:1–8)

Blessing to come

56:1. This is what Yahweh has said:

'Keep judgment[1] and do righteousness,[2]

[1] See 2:4; 26:8. 'Judgment' here has the same meaning as in

for my salvation is near, at the point of coming,
and my righteousness is ready to be revealed.'

2. Blessed[3] is the mortal[4] who does this,
   – the human[5] who takes a grip on it,
   keeping the Sabbath so as not to profane it,
   and keeping his hand from doing anything evil.

Inclusiveness: Two cases in point, one united people[6]

3. And the son of an alien who joins himself to Yahweh
   must not keep saying,
   'For certain Yahweh will exclude me from belonging
   to[7] his people.'
   And the eunuch must not keep saying,
   'Behold, I am a dry tree.'

4. For this is what Yahweh has said:
   'To the eunuchs
   who keep my Sabbaths,
   and choose what pleases me,
   and are taking a firm grip on my covenant:

5. I will give to them,
   in my house and within my walls,
   monument[8] and name better than sons and than daughters.
   An everlasting name I will give to each,
   one which will not be cut off.'

6. And as for the sons of an alien[9] who join themselves to
   Yahweh –
   to minister to him,
   and to love the name of Yahweh
   to become his servants;
   everyone keeping the Sabbath so as not to profane it,
   and those who take a firm grip on my covenant –

7. I will bring them to the mountain of my holiness,
   and I will make them rejoice in my house of prayer;
   their burnt-offerings and their sacrifices
   suitable for acceptance on my altar.
   For my house will be called a house of prayer for all
   the peoples.

Deut. 5:1 – the authoritative decisions, governing truth and conduct, which Yahweh has made and revealed to his people.

2 See 5:7; 26:7. 'Righteousness', as always that which is right with God, is here a comprehensive word for living so as to please him (cf. Col. 1:10).

3 See 30:18.

4 See 8:1; 13:7.

5 Lit., 'son of Adam/mankind'

6 'The son of an alien' had always been welcome into the covenant (e.g., Gen. 17:13; Exod. 12:48–49; Num. 9:14; Deut. 16:11). Deut. 23:1 bans eunuchs from the covenant assembly – probably meaning those who have been castrated for the service of a false god. In any case Isaiah, in the Lord's name, counters the spirit of exclusivism which would bar 'foreigners' and teaches that, in the light of the universal salvation accomplished by the Servant, the exclusion of eunuchs has now had its day – in the same way that Jesus taught concerning food laws (Mark 7:19).

7 Lit., 'from upon'. The preposition *'al* used to express 'addition to'.

8 The word here is 'hand', used as in 1 Sam. 15:12.

9 See note 6.

8. This is the word of the Sovereign, Yahweh,
   the gatherer of Israel's scattered ones:
   Yet more will I gather to them in addition to their[10]
   gathered ones.

The actual: 1. At the top – the failure of the ruling classes[11]

9. All living things of the field,
   come and eat,
   all living things in the forest.[12]
10. Their watchmen are blind, all of them:
    they know nothing!
    All of them are dumb dogs:
    they are unable to bark!
    Breathing heavily, asleep, loving to doze!
11. And the dogs have powerful appetites:
    they do not know what it is to be satisfied!
    And these are shepherds –
    they do not know to exercise discernment!
    They, all of them, turn to their own way,
    each in his entirety devoted to his own extortionate gain.
12. 'Come, I will fetch wine.
    Let us get drunk on beer,
    and tomorrow will be the same as today.
    Much, much more than enough!'

10 'Them … their', lit., 'him … his', the singular referring to Israel. For the thought, John 10:16.

11 Isaiah's picture of the united, worldwide, spiritual community (56:1–8) is the logical outcome of the accomplishment of worldwide salvation (53) and the double invitation (54–55). The actual situation is very different. The leaders are meant to be watchmen and shepherds but are actually self-absorbed, leaving the people open to attack by wild forces.

12 'Field … forest', i.e., animals 'in the wild'. cf., Lev. 26:21–22; Deut. 28:26; 2 Kings 17:25.

Thought for the day: Isaiah 56:1–12

Peter asked (2 Pet. 3:11–12) 'what manner of persons' we ought to be as we await 'the day of God'. That is exactly what Isaiah is concerned about in chapters 56–66: how we live as we await the coming salvation. He lays enormous emphasis on keeping the Lord's Day (56:4, 6; 58:1–14; 66:23). We will think about this when we reach chapter 58. But even here it is clear that keeping Sabbath with the Lord (v. 4) as a pure day (v. 6) is given greater prominence than is common at present. Alongside keeping the Lord's Day what marks the waiting people? First, personal decision ('joined himself to the Lord', vv. 3, 6), and love of his name (v. 6), then determination to go the Lord's way ('choose', v. 4). And what does it mean to 'take a firm grip on my covenant'? Two things: his 'covenant' is first and foremost his outreach to us in grace and love, his gracious promises made our personal possession, and then secondly, as a result, our life of obedience, living for his good pleasure (Col. 1:10). Our hearts, given to the Lord and full of love for all he has revealed about himself (his name); our wills, committed and choosing what we know will please him; our lives, as their basic principle, resting on his grace, living out his Word. We are joined to the Lord himself in spiritual union; pondering, loving and revelling in his revealed truth; committed to going his way; saved by grace; obedient in life. These are the things that bind us into the shared reality of being the one, universal people of the Lord, the blessed company of all believers, what Paul will call 'the Israel of God' (Gal. 6:16). We need to give careful attention to all that unites, and to be wary of things that make differences and divide.

Day 63   Isaiah 57:1–21

Isaiah turns from the top echelons of society to the grass roots. He discerns two 'families' in tension – the family of the prostitute and the family of the Lord – with the latter often seeming to be at the receiving end of hostility and loss. The truth of the matter is that those who are right with God are in fact the ones who are secure in the enjoyment of peace. This truth brackets the section.

The actual: 2. Divided society

Peace for the righteous

57:1. It is the righteous who perish,[1]
    and no one at all takes it to heart.
    And men of steadfast love[2] are being gathered away,
    without anyone discerning
    that it is from trouble the righteous have been gathered away.[3]

2.   Each enters
    into peace;
    they rest in their beds –
    each who walks in his uprightness.

The prostitute, her family, her ways and end

3.   As for you, come near – over here!
    Sons of a witch,
    seed of an adulterer and a working prostitute.[4]

4.   Against whom are you delighting yourself?
    Against whom are you smirking broadly,[5]
    sticking out your tongue?
    Are you not children of rebellion,
    seed of falsehood?

5.   You who inflame your passions in among the oaks,
    under every luxuriant tree;[6]

1   Probably the best way to understand these words. 'Righteous' is singular, understood here as the name of a class, those who are 'right with God'. The verb is perfect tense, understood here as expressing a standing truth. In the society Isaiah describes 'the righteous' always seem to come off worst.

2   'Men of *chesedh*', see 16:5, i.e., first those on whom Yahweh has set his changeless love, then, secondly, those who have pledged their fidelity back to him.

3   The first 'gathered' is plural, a general truth; the second is singular, covering each individual case.

4   Lit., 'and she who practises prostitution' – imperfect verb describing customary behaviour.

5   Lit., 'making a wide mouth'.

butchering the children in the river-valleys,
under the caves in the cliffs.⁷

6. Your portion is the pebbles⁸ of the river-valleys:
they, they are yours by lot.
Also it is to them you have poured a libation,
sent up an offering!
Should I be at ease over these things?

7. On a mountain, high and uplifted you placed your bed.⁹
There too you have gone up to offer sacrifice.

8. And behind the door and the doorpost you placed
your memorial,¹⁰
for, from being with me, you exposed and went up –
you made your bed wide,
and you got covenant promises in your favour from them.¹¹
You loved their bed.
You took note of ready money!¹²

9. Off you went, in perfume, to the king¹³ –
indeed you multiplied your cosmetics!
And you sent your envoys to distant parts,
and abased yourself to Sheol!

10. Through the plethora of your journeying¹⁴ you grew weary.
You never said 'Hopeless!'
You found personal resilience,¹⁵ therefore you did
not weaken.

11. About whom did you feel anxiety and were you afraid
that you proved false, and did not remember me,
did not take it to heart?
Have not I kept still – even for ever! –
and you did not fear even me.

12. I will myself declare your righteousness,
and, as for your deeds, they will not profit you!

13. When you shriek out let your gathered resources¹⁶
deliver you –
and, all of them, the wind will carry off,
a breath will take away!

6 Evergreen trees, treated as symbols of endless life, were favoured as the scene for orgiastic rites; cf. 1:28–30.

7 Lit., 'the clefts of the cliffs', the identical words used of the cave Samson lived in (Judg. 15:8). Here, to suit the preposition 'under', maybe 'the overhangs of the cliffs'.

8 Lit., 'smooth ones', only here of stones worn smooth by water. 'Pebbles' tries to reflect the assonance in Hebrew with 'portion'. The picture is of the stony barrenness of false religion.

9 The contrast with the river-valley is deliberate: the whole land engaged in false religion – totality expressed by contrast. The bed on a mountaintop depicts open, blatant practice.

10 A literal translation, but what does it mean? Possibly Deut. 6:9 helps – no public affirmation of loyalty to Yahweh; all is 'under wraps'. This at least suits the following accusation of departing from Yahweh.

11 Lit., 'you inaugurated a covenant for you from them'.

12 Very speculative rendering of 'you observed a hand'. 'Hand' does, however, mean 'available resources' (Lev. 5:7, 11; 14:21).

13 Isaiah foresees future disloyalty in terms of the 'flirting' with heathen powers which was a cardinal sin of his day.

14 'The abundance of your road'.

Yahweh and his family

But whoever takes refuge in me will possess the land,
and take possession of the mountain of my holiness.

14. And someone will say:[17]
'Build up, build up; make the road plain.
Take up any obstacle from my people's road.'

15. For this is what he has said –
the high and uplifted One,
dwelling[18] eternally;
his name is holy –
'In the high and holy place I dwell
and with anyone crushed and lowly in spirit,
to give life to the spirit of the lowly ones,
and to give life to the heart of the crushed ones.'

16. For not for ever will I argue my case,
nor perpetually will I be impatient,
for before me spirit would flag
– the breathing things I myself made.

17. In payment for the iniquity of his extortionate gain[19]
I grew impatient.
And I cut him down, going into hiding, and I
continued impatient,
and he increased in backsliding in the way of his heart.

18. I have seen his ways and I will heal him and guide him,
and I will give perfect comfort to him and to his mourners,

19. creating the fruit of the lips.[20]
Peace, peace[21] to the one far off and to the one nearby,
Yahweh has said,
and I will heal him.

The impossibility of peace for the wicked

20. And as for the wicked –
like sea that is tossed about,
for it is not able to enjoy quiet,
and its waters toss up mire and muck.

21. There is no peace,
my God has said, to the wicked.

15 'The life/vitality of your hand'. 'Hand' means personal intervention and action.

16 Lit., 'your collection', referring to 'righteousness' (what you are) and 'deeds' (what you have done) – the things that those who hope for self-salvation rely on.

17 Hebrew uses a third person singular verb as an indefinite, when it wishes just to hint at the agent. Here, the voice of Yahweh summoning his people home.

18 In, e.g., Exod. 25:8; 29:45 the verb (*sakan*) is used of Yahweh's gracious 'dwelling' among his people in the Tabernacle. The intention here is that what once happened at the Exodus will be eternally so: Yahweh dwelling among his people.

19 *bets'a* has the general meaning of unscrupulous gain for oneself: in business, unprincipled 'profiteering'; in personal life, 'covetousness', grasping after more, as in Isaiah 33:15; 56:11. Sadly, here, that which characterises the failed rulers (56:11) also mars Yahweh's family. Nevertheless the present passage includes such as those whom Yahweh is leading home (vv. 14–15), and to whom he will bring healing and peace (vv. 18–19).

20 i.e., the capacity to respond to Yahweh.

21 Hebrew uses duplication to express a superlative (the most perfect peace) or to state the total truth about the topic in question (unbroken peace).

Thought for the day: Isaiah 57:1–21

Isaiah would have been distinctly uneasy with today's folk religion and its pseudo comfort that Grandma who has just died is 'still with us', even 'watching over us', 'looking out for us like she always did'. He shared the biblical understanding that the dead are elsewhere, as he said 'gathered away' (v. 1), like Genesis 25:17 says Abraham was 'gathered away to his people'. Furthermore he shares the Bible's view that there is no such thing as an untimely death – a truth even believers find hard. But there it is: the very verb 'gathered away' teaches it, does it not? It points to a Gatherer, his decision, timing and action, just as Paul speaks (literally in 1 Thess. 4:14) of those who 'have fallen asleep through Jesus' and are safe with him until, when he comes, they come with him. It is in Jesus' keeping we are safe – and they! Isaiah is not yet finished with this properly tearful, deeply wonderful topic. The question forces itself: 'But why?' His answer here is not, of course, the whole answer. But whether death comes (humanly speaking) early or late, it is always true that we are 'gathered away' from evil into peace. What further suffering has our beloved dead been spared, what calamity that would have proved too much? At this point, as at every other, our loving Lord says 'No' to the trial which would be too much (1 Cor. 10:13), and 'Yes' to the bliss that, 'Precious in the sight of the Lord is the death of his saints' (Ps. 116:15) – 'precious' like a priceless jewel purchased at inexpressible cost, something he longs to give to those he loves. And he gives it thoughtfully, foreseeingly, protectively – 'Come, my people, hide yourself … until the indignation passes…' (26:20). In John 14:1–3 this security of the Father's home belongs to those who 'trust in God, trust in me'. Isaiah thinks of the other side of the coin: those who are 'righteous' – 'right with God' – covered by the Servant's provision (53:11). They are possessed of a righteousness from God (54:17; Phil. 3:9).

Day 64   Isaiah 58:1–14

The Sabbath is a leading idea in Isaiah's vision of the waiting people. The Lord's salvation is near, the full demonstration of his righteousness (56:1). Keeping the Sabbath marks out those who join themselves to the Lord (56:3–6). Even when he envisions the New Heaven and New Earth, Isaiah uses the patterns of his own time to describe the future: the Sabbath is still of the essence (66:23). In chapter 58 he states the Sabbath ideal. But chapter 58 has another part to play also. In chapters 56–57 the Sabbath ideal was contrasted with the rather sad actual state of Yahweh's waiting people (56:1–8 compared with 56:9–57:21). Now the ideal (ch. 58) will be contrasted with a very different actuality (59:1–13), a people conscious of their failings. This, in turn, prepares for the grand vision of what the Lord proposes to do (59:14–63:6). The Lord's earthly people, even though they look back to their great salvation (52:13–53:6), still toil in their sinfulness and weakness and still await the crowning fulfilment of all that salvation means.

The voice of rebuke

58:1. Cry out with a full throated cry![1]
    Do not keep silent!
    Like a trumpet, raise your voice
    and declare to my people their rebellion
    and to the house of Jacob their sin!

Fasting without blessing: the unreal exposed

2. And[2] day after day they keep seeking[3] me,[4]
    and keep delighting in the knowledge of my ways –
    like a nation that has committed to righteousness
    and had not forsaken the judgment[5] of its God.

---

1   Lit., 'cry out with the throat'.

2   The use of the conjunction to introduce an explanation; equivalent to 'for' or 'see how'.

3   See 8:19.

They keep asking me for judgments of righteousness,[6]
and they go on delighting in the nearness of God.

3. 'Why have we fasted and you have not seen it?
Abased our souls and you do not know?'
Behold!
In the day of your fasting you are finding delight![7]
And you act as taskmasters to all your suffering workers![8]

4. Behold!
It is to quarrelling and argument that your fasting leads,
and to hitting out with the clenched fist of wickedness![9]
You will not fast like today to make your voice heard on high!

5. Is it like this – the fast I choose –
a day for someone to abase his soul?[10]
Is it for bowing his head, like a rush,
and making a bed of sack-cloth and ashes?
Is this what you call a fast,
a day acceptable to Yahweh?

Yahweh's chosen fast: 1. Social emphases

6. Is not this the fast I choose –
to undo the fetters of wickedness –
to unfasten the straps of the yoke –
and to let the crushed go free –
and that you should fracture every yoke?

7. Is it not to break your bread for the hungry,
and to give shelter to the downtrodden[11] homeless?
When you see the naked, cover him!
And from your own flesh do not hide yourself.[12]

Yahweh's chosen fast: 2. Personal and spiritual rewards

8. Then[13] your light will break out like the dawn,
and your renewal[14] will quickly flower.
And your righteousness[15] will go before you,
Yahweh's glory will guard you from behind.

9. Then you will call out and Yahweh himself will answer;[16]
you will call for help and he will say 'Here I am'.

4   'Me' is given strong emphasis in the Hebrew here.

5   See 2:4; 26:8.

6   i.e., decisions of particular issues ('judgments') which enshrine the principles of divine righteousness, what is right with God.

7   Not, that is, delighting in fasting but, rather, the fast day used as a day of pleasure.

8   A likely rendering but still a surmise. The basic verb means 'to be in pain'; Ps. 127:2 uses a related word in the sense of 'taking pains' over life's duties. Here, coupled with the 'taskmaster' verb, the idea of the employer taking a day off for allegedly religious reasons while the work-force is as driven as ever.

9   The family come to blows, forced together by the 'day off' but irritable through fasting!

10 i.e., to engage in formal exercises of self-humbling. We could translate 'to suppress his appetite', i.e., the mere abstaining from food seen as itself meritorious.

11 See 3:14.

12 For this use of 'hide yourself', meaning 'fail to help', see Deut. 22:1, 4. 'Your own flesh' (as we would say, 'your flesh and blood'); not to forget that kindness and charity begin at home.

13 Here and at the opening of v. 9 'then' is an emphatic particle of time.

Yahweh's chosen fast: 3. Social emphases
>   If you take away the yoke from among you,
>   pointing the finger[17] and speaking mischievously;[18]
> 10.   and if you give yourself[19] to the hungry,
>   and satisfy the soul of the downtrodden,

Yahweh's chosen fast: 4. Personal and spiritual rewards
>   your light will flash out in the darkness,
>   and your gloom will be like noonday.
> 11. And Yahweh will guide you constantly,
>   and satisfy your soul even in the driest conditions,
>   and he will equip your bones,[20]
>   and you will be like a well-watered garden,
>   and like an outflow of water whose waters do not prove false.
> 12. And some of your own will build the ancient ruins,
>   the foundations of generation after generation you
>   will raise up,
>   and you will have the name: 'Rebuilder of the Breach',
>   'Restorer of Paths to Inhabit'.

A feast with a blessing
> 13. If you keep back your foot from the Sabbath,
>   the doing of your own pleasure on the day of my holiness,
>   and call the Sabbath 'Delight',
>   what is holy to Yahweh 'Truly Honoured',
>   and you honour it by not doing your ways,
>   by not finding your pleasure,
>   and talk for talk's sake,[21]
> 14. then you will experience delight in Yahweh,

The voice of promise
>   and I will make you ride on the high places of the earth
>   and make you eat the possession of your father Jacob.
>   For Yahweh's mouth has spoken.

14 The word means the new flesh that grows where there has been a wound; e.g., Jer. 8:22; used of repair work on a broken wall, Neh. 4:1.

15 cf., the 'breastplate of righteousness' (Eph. 6:14); our clothing in Christ, cf., Rom. 13:14.

16 Two imperfect verbs expressing constancy or custom: 'whenever you call …' or 'as you call …'

17 Innuendo, a 'nod and a wink', the 'unattributable leak', cf., Prov. 6:12–14.

18 See 1:13.

19 The verb means 'to totter', 'to meet', 'to let meet, grant'. 'If you grant your soul', presumably: if your help to the hungry is not mere conformism but heartfelt. Possibly even, 'If you grant to the hungry what you desire for yourself' (lit., 'your own soul/appetite/longing').

20 i.e. 'make you physically equipped to face life.'

21 Lit., 'speaking a word'. Only elsewhere in Deut. 18:20 of words not authorised by Yahweh.

Thought for the day: Isaiah 58:1–14

That remarkable eighteenth-century character Dean Swift – he of *Gulliver's Travels* – said of the fashionable ladies of his day that 'they were so busy being religious they had no time to say their prayers'. Isaiah would have identified with that. He saw the sort of punctiliousness in sabbath-keeping that forgot what the Sabbath was all about. Very different from our day when the world – and how many Christians? – have devised a week ending with two Saturdays and a 'Lord's Day' observed between 10.30 a.m. and 12.00 noon. Jeremiah (17:24–25) would have joined Isaiah in making the Sabbath a test case of spiritual reality and a divinely intended means of blessing. How many of us today would come with good marks out of that test? And Isaiah did not mean 'old-style' Sabbatarianism with its negativity, a no-work day of often boring idleness. He looked for a day of concern for the welfare of those we influence (v. 3), making sure that we do not exploit others so that we may 'keep the Sabbath': a day so kept that it excludes family strife (but, on the contrary, encourages family harmony [v. 4]); a day to care for the needy, the homeless, the underdogs – including our needy relatives (v. 7); a day to work for social amelioration and reformation (v. 6). Quite a busy day, you might well say! So we had better recall, for example, the work-free day of rest and refreshment in Exodus 23:12 and so many other verses. If we end the Lord's Day tired out we have not kept the Lord's Day. So then, Isaiah is not writing a programme but indicating preferences and possibilities, offering typical diary entries, and we do well to listen. Sunday is not a second Saturday, nor is it a day of penal boredom. It is one of the Lord's intended 'means of grace', bringing 'renewal' (v. 8), a cure for depression (v. 10), promoting spiritual refreshment (v. 11) and elation (v. 14), and bringing the promise of security (v. 8) and answered prayer (v. 9).

Day 65   Isaiah 59:1–19

In contrast to the 'ideal' in chapter 58, here is the sad 'actual'. Having held up the mirror of God's Word with its requirement of a conformed life (ch. 58), Isaiah turns now to see how the Lord's people look in the light of the call to obedience. Accusation (vv. 2–3, note 'your') is followed by description (vv. 4–8, note 'they', 'their'), and this leads to confession (vv. 9–13, note 'we', 'us', 'our'). The passage, however, begins with a statement of Yahweh's ability to save (v. 1), and this theme is taken up in verses 14–19, where Yahweh himself dresses in garments speaking of his commitment and ability to save, to implement his own righteous purposes, and to deal with his foes.

The saving Yahweh

59:1. Behold,

     Yahweh's hand[1] is not short so that he cannot save,

     nor his ear insensitive so that he cannot hear!

Accusation

2.   On the contrary your iniquities

     cause a division between you and your God,

     and your sins have hidden his face from you,

     so as not to hear.

3.   For your hands[2] are polluted with blood,

     and your fingers with iniquity.

     Your lips have spoken falsehood;

     Your tongue murmurs[3] wrong[4].

Description

4.   There is no one calling out in righteousness[5]

     and there is no one arguing a case with fidelity[6] –

1   As well as 'hand' signifying effective ability to intervene, it also means 'available resources' (see 57:8). Yahweh's ability to save is thus within his competence and within his resources.

2   More accurately, 'your palms' or the 'grip of the hand'. See 1:15.

3   See 8:19. Here of what is said 'under the breath', i.e., the tongue as expressing the real thought of the heart.

trusting in what is meaningless,
and speaking falsehood,
conceiving trouble and giving birth to mischief.[7]

5. They hatch viper's eggs,
and weave spider's webs –
whoever eats any of their eggs will die,
and from the broken shell[8] an adder[9] breaks out.

6. Their webs will not make a garment,
nor will they cover themselves with their works:
their works are works of mischief,
and the doing of violence is in their hands.[10]

7. Their feet run to evil,
and they hurry to shed innocent blood.
Their thoughts are thoughts of mischief-making;
spoliation[11] and shattering lie along their highway.

8. The way of peace they do not know,
and there is no judgment[12] in their tracks.
Their paths they have made crooked for themselves.
No one at all travelling on it will know peace.

Confession

9. Therefore judgment[13] is distant from us,
and righteousness does not overtake us.
We wait confidently for light, and – behold – darkness!
For a glimmer of light – we walk in a fog!

10. We grope along the wall like the blind –
like people without eyes we grope.
We trip up in noonday as if in twilight,
among the vigorous, like the dead!

11. We growl like bears, all of us,
and like doves – how sadly we coo![14]
We wait confidently for judgment[15] and there is none,
for salvation – it is distant from us.

12. For our rebellions are many before you,
and our sins answer against us.
For our rebellions are with us,
and as for our iniquities, we know them!

4 What is deviant or perverted from the right/straight. The verb occurs in 26:10.

5 Taking a public stand for righteousness.

6 The use of legal process for illegal ends.

7 See 1:13, also on 'mischief' (v. 6) and 'mischief-making' (v. 7).

8 Lit., 'what is broken/ the broken thing'.

9 'Viper' and 'adder' are uncertain renderings.

10 See. 1:15.

11 See 13:6; 51:9.

12 See 2:4; 26:8.

13 See 2:4; 26:8. For 'judgment' and 'righteousness' used together, 5:7.

14 See 8:19. 'Sadly' is introduced here to secure the meaning – the mournful sounding 'coo' of a dove.

15 See v. 9.

13. Rebellion,
    and deception against Yahweh,
    and backsliding from following[16] our God.
    Speaking oppression and stubborn rebellion.
    Conceiving and muttering[17] from the heart words
    of falsehood.

Yahweh's final action – the coming salvation – the revelation of the Anointed Conqueror (Isaiah 59:14–63:6)

This section constitutes the heart of Isaiah 56–66. At 56:12, the people are told that salvation is near. Against the background of all that is wrong with his people (59:1–13) Yahweh now undertakes for them, himself donning the garments of salvation and also of vengeance, for he purposes to deal finally, too, with all who oppose him. The section 59:14–19 is an introduction to this, and sets the background for the revelation of the covenant-maker (59:20–21), the one anointed to comfort and exact vengeance (61:1–3). It is, in fact, this Anointed One who in the event is robed in the garments of salvation (61:10–62:7), and who, alone, performs the work of salvation and vengeance (63:1–6).

Yahweh prepares himself to save and to avenge

Situation

14. And judgment[18] is made to slip away back,
    and righteousness stands at a distance.
    For truth has stumbled in the street,
    and uprightness is not able to come in.
15. And truth continues to be missing,
    and anyone who turns from evil makes himself a prey.

Reaction

    And Yahweh saw,
    and it was evil in his eyes
    that there was no judgment.
16. And he saw that there was no man,
    and he felt appalled that there was no one to interpose,

16 Lit., 'from after'. The preposition 'after' used idiomatically of the position taken up by a loyal follower.

17 See 8:19.

18 See 2:4; 26:8. On 'judgment' and 'righteousness' together, see 5:7.

and his arm accomplished salvation for him,
and his righteousness[19] was what sustained him.

17. And he dressed in righteousness as a breastplate,
and on his head as a helmet salvation.
And he dressed in garments of vengeance for clothing,
and, like a cloak, wrapped himself in zeal.[20]

18. In accordance with exact recompense,[21] so he will pay in full:
rage[22] to his adversaries;
recompense to his enemies.
To the wide earth[23] he will pay recompense in full.

The outcome

19. And in the west they will fear the name of Yahweh,
and in the sun-rising his glory.
When an adversary comes like a river,[24]
Yahweh's Spirit raises a banner against him.

_____

19 His commitment to his own righteousness nature, purposes and promises.

20 See 9:7.

21 'Recompenses', a plural of completeness.

22 See 5:25.

23 See 41:1.

24 As we might say 'comes streaming in'.

Thought for the day: Isaiah 59:1–19

Repentance is a marvellously powerful thing. In Psalm 51:1–3 David testifies to its simplicity and effectiveness. He uses all three main Hebrew words – sin (the specific offence), iniquity (the hidden defect of nature), and rebellion (wilful flouting of God's way) – and we know that behind these words lie the death-dealing offences of adultery and murder (2 Sam. 12:9), yet he seeks mercy and cleansing simply by repentance: 'For I know my rebellions, and my sin is ever before me.' 'To know', of course, means here 'to acknowledge', and the same verb comes in today's Isaiah reading, verse 12, again linked with the trio of sin, rebellion, and iniquity. But where David underlines the effectiveness of repentance in securing mercy and cleansing, Isaiah underlines the way repentance triggers divine reaction on our behalf, for, in response, the offended Lord now girds himself for the work of salvation. This is a work which displays and accords with all his righteous demands and standards (v. 16; cf., 45:21; Rom. 3:24–26) – and at the same time pledges the powerful action of the Holy Spirit to stop our enemy in his tracks (v. 19). And all because we are ready to say we 'know' our iniquities. Do you remember how Isaiah invited us who have no money to 'buy' the wine and milk of salvation (55:1)? The penniless can only 'buy' if someone else gives them the purchase-price. Repentance, in all its simplicity, is only free and effective for us because the Servant of the Lord has 'paid the price of sin'. But though repentance is 'simple' we need to be careful not to let it become 'easy' or superficial, for sin consigns us to the darkness (v. 9), and makes self-salvation impossible (v. 10); repentance must run deep and be heartfelt (v. 11), and our 'knowing' must include how grossly we have offended the Lord (vv. 12–13). Yet it is for just such people the Lord dresses himself for salvation, and to just such hopeless cases he promises the armed intervention of his counter-attacking Spirit.

Day 66 Isaiah 59:20–60:22

With the same 'suddenness' as the first appearance of the Servant of the Lord in 42:1, a personage endowed with the Spirit and the Word enters the scene, the Mediator and Exemplar of the Lord's covenant with his people.

Yahweh's Agent, endowed with his Spirit and his Word[1]

20. And to Zion will come a redeemer[2] –
    to those who turn back from rebellion in Jacob.[3]
    This is Yahweh's Word.

21. And as for me, this is my covenant with them,
    Yahweh has said:
    My Spirit who is on you[4],
    and my word which I have put in your mouth,
    will not move from your mouth
    and from the mouth of your seed
    and from the mouth of your seed's seed,
    Yahweh has said,
    from now and for ever.

Comment: The Lord's universal city; blessing for the world[5]

The Lord in Zion

60:1. Get up, be alight,
    for your light has come,
    and Yahweh's glory has flashed out upon you.

2. For, behold!
    The darkness covers the earth,
    and heavy clouds the peoples,[6]
    and upon you[7] Yahweh will flash out,
    and upon you his glory will be seen!

1 As unexpectedly (and mysteriously) as the Servant of the Lord in 42:1, an anonymous Agent appears, in covenant with Yahweh; one whose 'seed' will, through him, inherit the same Spirit and Word everlastingly. On 'seed', cf., 53:10. This is the first appearance of one who will be progressively portrayed as the anointed Conqueror up to 63:1–6. Verses 59:16–17 have not prepared us for such an Agent. Yahweh himself dresses for the saving work – clothing, as always, expressing character and commitment. But in 61:10 Yahweh transfers the garments to his great Agent.

2 See 35:9.

3 cf., 1:27.

4 'You' is masculine singular, referring to the unnamed 'redeemer'; cf. 42:1; 61:1.

5 As with the Servant Songs in chapters 40–55, each of the poems looking forward to the Lord's covenant Agent, the anointed Conqueror, is followed by a passage of confirmation. The Lord promised a universal (59:19), Zion-centred (59:20) work of salvation

3.   And nations will travel to your light,
     and kings to the gleaming light of your outshining.

The world in Zion

4.   Lift up your eyes all round and see:
     all of them come gathering to you.
     From a distance your sons[8] will come,
     and your daughters will be nursed along on the hip.

5.   Then you will see and beam radiantly,
     and your heart will be awed and swell,
     for the abundance[9] of the sea will be turned over to you;
     the resources of the nations will come to you.

6.   The profusion of camels will cover you,
     young camels of Midian and Ephah.
     They will come from Sheba, all of them,
     gold and incense they will carry,
     and tell the good news of Yahweh's praises.

7.   All the sheep of Kedar will be gathered to you;
     the rams of Nebaioth will minister[10] to you.
     They will go up with acceptance on my altar,
     and I will beautify the house of my beauty.

8.   Who are these who fly like a cloud,
     and like doves to their windows?

9.   For it is for me the wide earth[11] will wait confidently[12] –
     the ships of Tarshish first –
     to bring my sons from a distance,
     their silver and their gold with them,
     to the name of Yahweh your God,
     and to the Holy One of Israel,
     for he has beautified you.

The city of destiny[13]

10. And the sons of the alien will build your walls,
     and kings will minister to you,
     for it was in my impatience[14] that I struck you,
     and with my acceptance I am determined to
     have compassion[15] on you.

(59:16). Isaiah 60 beautifully portrays the glorified Zion as the centre for world-pilgrimage.

6   See 17:1.

7   'You' is feminine singular, i.e., Zion. The lifting of the universal cloud-cover starts at Zion. cf. 25:7; Matt. 5:14; Heb. 12:22.

8   Not to be understood of scattered Israelites coming back but of the nations of v. 3 coming in full family membership into the glorified Zion; cf. Ps. 87:1–6.

9   See 5:13 ('masses'). 'The abundance of the sea' is all the riches that can come by sea to Zion. This is the least complicated understanding. 'Turned over' usually has a literal meaning, but Lam. 5:2 shows that it can be used of changing ownership of property.

10   'To minister' is used mostly of levitical, priestly ministry in worship. Only here applied to the animals which provided the material of such service. To 'go up' is technically used of the burnt offering.

11   See 41:1.

12   See 8:17.

13   The International City, the theme of vv. 4–9, continues here at the heart of this great Zion Poem, but there is the added thought (in the central v. 12) that attitudes to Zion determine destiny.

14   See 5:25.

11. And they will open your gates continually –
    by day and night they will not be closed –
    to bring in to you the resources of the nations,
    and their kings conducted along.
12. For the nation and the kingdom which does not serve
    you will perish,
    and the nations will be totally a wasteland.
13. To you will come the glory of Lebanon,
    fir, pine and box together,
    to beautify the place of my sanctuary:
    I will glorify the place for my feet.
14. Crouching down, they will come to you –
    the sons of those who humbled you,
    and they will bow in reverence at the soles of your feet –
    all who scorned you.
    And they will call you 'City of Yahweh',
    'Zion of the Holy One of Israel'.

Zion transformed and enriched

15. In the place of your being forsaken and hated,
    and no one passing through,
    I will make you into an eternal pride,
    a delight for generation after generation.
16. And you will suck the milk of nations,
    and you will suck the breast of kings,
    and you will know that I am Yahweh,
    your Saviour and your Redeemer,[16]
    the Potentate[17] of Jacob.
17. In the place of bronze I will bring gold;
    and in the place of iron I will bring silver;
    and in the place of timber, bronze;
    and in the place of stone, iron.
    And I will make your officialdom peace,
    and your overseers righteousness.
18. Violence will not be heard again in your land,
    spoliation and shattering in your territory,

15 See 9:17; 30:18; 54:7

16 See 35:9. A 'Saviour' deals with the threat, of whatever nature

it may be; 'Redeemer' describes how he does it, by making it his own; 'Potentate' is his absolute power to do whatever he wills.

17 See 1:24.

and you will call your walls 'Salvation',
and your gates 'Praise'.

Yahweh in Zion

19. You will not any more have the sun for light by day,
    nor for gleaming light will the moon illuminate you –
    you will have Yahweh for everlasting light,
    and your God will be your beauty.
20. No more will your sun set,
    nor your moon be removed,
    for you will have Yahweh for everlasting light,
    and the days of your mourning will be completed.
21. And your people, all of them, will be righteous.
    For ever they will possess the earth,
    the shoot of my plantation,
    the work of my hands,
    that I may display my beauty.
22. The little will become a thousand,
    and the small a mighty nation.
    In its time, I, Yahweh, will hasten it.

———————————————————————

Thought for the day: Isaiah 59:20–60:22

John Newton, as usual, got it right. He sang, 'Saviour, if of Zion's City, I, through grace, a member am'. There is this great Zion, the fulfilment of everything the historic Zion was meant to be and never was, the city of those saved by grace, the city of the people of Jesus. Psalm 87 glimpsed it, in a poetic, slightly enigmatic way; Isaiah caught its radiance more fully than anyone else in the old covenant; Paul saw it as the 'mother' of the children of promise in Christ (Gal. 4:26–31); Hebrews 12:22 described it as the city we now inhabit by right, the city of the firstborn, its registered citizens, sheltered under the blood of Jesus, safe and accepted in the presence of God the Judge; John was privileged to watch its eternal fulfilment in the city descending from heaven, the bride of the Lamb (Rev. 21:9–10), exclusive to those whose names are in the Lamb's book of life (Rev. 21:27). 'The city' is one of the Bible's pervasive themes. In Genesis 11:1–9 a 'city' was humankind's remedy for the divisiveness of sin and the ever-threatening world sin had created – a human organisation for salvation and security. Isaiah foresaw the whole world organised into a 'global village', and called it 'the city of meaningless' (24:10), sharply contrasting with the 'strong city' of salvation (26:1–4), the city of peace and of believers. Philippi (Acts 16:12) was a 'colony', a prized privilege in Roman days, for citizens of a 'colony' were actually enrolled on the citizens' lists in Rome, the capital itself, and, in distant Philippi, lived by and enjoyed the privileges of the capital city itself. 'Our citizenship' – Paul reminded the Philippians – is in heaven; our names are enrolled there. In our far off, earthly 'colony' we enjoy the privileges of the eternal city which is now our home, and which will be so everlastingly. We read Isaiah 60 and say – with wondering delight – these joys are my joys, these privileges mine.

Day 67 Isaiah 61:1–62:12

This passage comprises the second and third poems about the Anointed One (61:1–3; 61:10–62:7). Each is followed by verses of comment and application (61:4–9; 62:8–12). Like the second Servant song (49:1–6), the Anointed One (61:1) has a double task – good tidings and vengeance. As in the third Servant Song (50:4–9), the Anointed One speaks with his own voice and tells how he is joyfully committed and equipped for the work of salvation, wearing the garments which (in 59:16–17) Yahweh himself wore, and thus willingly taking on himself and doing Yahweh's will.

The Anointed One and his transforming work (61:1–9)

Testimony: transformation and vengeance

61:1. The spirit of the Sovereign Yahweh is upon me –
    because Yahweh has anointed me.
    To bring good news to the downtrodden he has sent me:
    to bandage the broken-hearted,
    to proclaim liberty to captives,
    a real opening-up[1] to those who are bound,
2.   to proclaim a year of acceptance belonging to Yahweh,
    and a day of vengeance belonging to our God,
    to comfort all who are mourning,
3.   to assign to Zion's mourners –
    to give them – a head-dress in place of ashes,
    oil of delight in place of mourning,
    a wrap of praise in place of a spirit of listlessness.
    And they will be called 'Oaks of Righteousness',
    'Yahweh's Plantation',
    that he may display his beauty.

1   The parent verb here is specifically 'to open the eyes'. In form this noun is reduplicated for emphasis. Possibly, retaining the implied reference to the eyes, 'a real access to the light for …', or possibly a general emphasis, 'a real eye-opener'.

Comment: transformation confirmed

4. And they will build the long-standing wastes,
   and raise what were previously desolations,
   and renew cities laid waste,
   desolations from generation to generation.

5. And foreigners will stand and shepherd your sheep,
   and the sons of the alien will be your ploughmen and
   your vine-dressers,

6. and you yourselves will be called 'Yahweh's Priests';
   'Ministers of our God' will be said to you.
   The resources of the nations you will eat,
   and in their glory you will make your boast.[2]

7. In place of your shame, double!
   And ignominy? – they will shout aloud in their portion.
   Therefore,
   in their land they will possess twice as much:
   they will have everlasting joy.

8. For I, Yahweh, love judgment,[3]
   hate robbery in a burnt offering,[4]
   And I will pay their wage in truth,[5]
   and I will inaugurate for them[6] an everlasting covenant.

9. And their seed will be known in the nations,
   and their offspring among the peoples.
   Everyone seeing them will recognise them,
   For they are seed Yahweh has blessed.

Further personal testimony: The Anointed One equipped to save, and joyfully committed to restore Zion (61:10–62:12)

Joy in the work of salvation

10. I truly delight in Yahweh;
    my soul will exult my God,
    for he has dressed me in the garments of salvation,
    in a robe of righteousness he wraps me,
    like a bridegroom puts on his priestly head-dress,[7]
    and like a bride pins on her jewels.[8]

2 Conventional translation with doubt attached.

3 See 2:4; 26:8. Not the narrow meaning of 'justice', social and legal exactitude, but the right decision made in every situation, God's revealed truth received and applied.

4 This statement is so unusual that commentators often alter the Hebrew text (see NIV), but the sense is clear even if unexpected. The burnt offering expressed total self-offering. How easily, like Ananias, we keep back part of the price and pretend we give all (Acts 5:2). The Lord who loves his truth looks for a wholehearted commitment from his people.

5 i.e, Yahweh who looks for his people's total commitment will himself hold nothing back from them.

6 In the vocabulary of the covenant, 'for them' means 'in their interest/ for their advantage'. The eternal covenant is the way Isaiah defines the true wage of the preceding line, how the Lord delights to 'reward' his redeemed.

11. For like the earth produces its sprouts,
    and like a garden sprouts with what is sown in it,
    so the Sovereign Yahweh will make righteousness[9] sprout,
    and praise, in front of all the nations.

Zeal for Zion's glory

62:1. For the sake of Zion I will not be quiet,[10]
    and for the sake of Jerusalem I will not be still.
    Until its righteousness issues out like a flash of light,
    and its salvation burns like a torch.
2. And the nations will see your righteousness,
    and all kings your glory.
    And you will be called by a new name,
    which Yahweh's mouth will pick out.
3. And you will be a crown of beauty in Yahweh's hand,
    and a turban of kingliness in the grip[11] of your God.

Transformation: New names, new status

4. No more shall it be said of you, 'Forsaken',
    and of your land it will no more be said, 'Desolate',
    for you will be named, 'My pleasure is in it',
    and your land, 'Married'.
    For Yahweh's pleasure is in you,
    and your land will be married.
5. For as a young man marries a young woman,
    your sons will marry you;
    and like the delight of a bridegroom over a bride,
    your God will delight over you.

The praying guardians[12]

6. Upon your walls, Jerusalem, I have appointed guardians.
    Every day and every night, continually, they will not be quiet.
    You who keep Yahweh mindful,
    have no rest yourselves!
7. Give him no rest,
    until he establishes –
    until he makes Jerusalem a praise in the earth.

7   Lit., 'acts as a priest regarding his head-dress'. Basically a reference to the sacredness of marriage in biblical thinking. In context, just as carefully as a couple dress for their wedding, the Lord's Anointed Agent is prepared for the work of salvation – and with like joy (Heb. 12:2)!

8   Lit., 'ornaments herself with her things'.

9   'Salvation' (v. 10) is the actual work of rescue and deliverance; 'righteousness' (vv. 10–11) is the spirit in which it was carried out, the motive which prompted it, and the way in which it conformed to all the righteous requirements of the holy God.

10 The verb (*chasah*) applies as much to inactivity as to silence. Combined with 'to be still' (*shaqat*) it describes the Anointed One as ceaseless in intercession and action.

11 See 1:15.

12 Parallel with vv. 1–3 in which the Anointed One commits himself to prayer until the full reality of salvation is consummated, here he appoints intercessors to the same ministry.

The great oath, the great call, and the great promise[13]

8. Yahweh has sworn by his right hand and by the arm
   of his strength:
   that I will no more give your corn as food for your enemies,
   and the sons of the alien will not drink your new wine
   on which you toiled,

9. for those who gather it will eat it,
   and they will praise Yahweh;
   and those who collect it will drink it,
   in the courts of my holiness.

10. Pass through, pass through the gates!
    Clear the road for the people!
    Heap up, heap up the causeway!
    Rid it of stones!
    Lift high a banner for the peoples![14]

11. Behold!
    Yahweh has himself announced to the ends of the earth,
    'Say to the daughter of Zion,
    Behold,
    your salvation is set to come.
    Behold,
    the wage he has earned is with him,
    and his work is in front of him.'[15]

12. And they will call them
    'The people of holiness',
    'The redeemed[16] of Yahweh',
    and to you the name will be given,[17]
    'Sought',
    'The city not forsaken'.

13 Verses 8–12 are the 'tail-piece' or concluding comment on second poem of the Anointed One (61:10–62:7). Yahweh now speaks, first (vv. 8–9), going on oath to secure Jerusalem in its inheritance, he then summons his worldwide people to pilgrimage (v. 10), and, finally (vv. 11–12), their full salvation in Zion is promised.

14 See 5:26, a banner as a rallying point; 11:12, the Davidic Messiah as the rallying point for Yahweh's worldwide people.

15 See 40:10.

16 See 35:9.

17 Lit., 'to you it will be called'; 'you' is feminine singular, referring to Zion.

Thought for the day: Isaiah 61:1–62:12

How blithely we read that 'for the joy that was set before him he endured the cross ...' (Heb. 12:2), and many have been heard to say that the 'joy' in question was the crown that awaited him. Very likely so, but Isaiah says it was the joy of saving us. We think of the intended humiliation and actual pain of the crown of thorns, but to the Lord Jesus it was a bridegroom's priestly head-dress (61:10). We picture the bedraggled and bloodstained seamless robe that he wore to Calvary, but to him it was a wedding garment! His Calvary-joy was wedding-day joy. He was winning his bride. Just as 'we may not know, we cannot tell what pains he had to bear', neither can we enter into that joy, but we can be awed by it; our hearts can be moved and our tears flow. This is how much we mean to him. His wedding garments were 'salvation' and 'righteousness', says Isaiah (61:10). In the Bible, clothing speaks of capacity and commitment. When the Lord showed himself to Joshua as an armed man (Josh. 5:13), it was to display his warrior might and his commitment to win the Lord's wars. Jesus was dressed in 'salvation' because he alone has power to save (Acts 4:12), and because he is personally committed to the work of saving us (John 18:11; Heb. 10:7, 9). He wore the robe of righteousness, first, because he is the perfectly righteous Jesus who knew no sin (2 Cor. 5:21), did no sin (1 Pet. 2:22), and in whom there was no sin (1 John 3:5). Only the sinless can bear the sins of others. Secondly, he was committed to doing the righteousness – the righteous will – of God, to 'fulfil all righteousness' (Matt. 3:15). And thirdly, the salvation he has accomplished is itself a righteous work: the whole law of God is totally satisfied in the price paid, the penalty accepted and endured. Righteousness without salvation would mean our eternal condemnation; salvation without righteousness would not be acceptable to the inviolable holiness of God. Jesus is all-perfect, all-sufficient – all-loving.

Day 68   Isaiah 63:1–14

The last of the poems of the Anointed One brings together the themes of salvation and vengeance with awesomeness and clarity. This is what Yahweh clothed himself to achieve (59:17); it is what the covenant Agent of 59:20–21 was anointed for (61:1–2). The salvation/righteousness theme dominated the third poem (61:10; 62:1), and now, the warrior figure, 'mighty to save' (63:1), acting in the 'year of my redeemed' (63:4), himself alone exacts Yahweh's vengeance (63:3–4, 6). Now, at last, the whole work has been done. The counterpart in the New Testament is the wrath of the Lamb (Revelation 6:16), and the treading of the winepress of the wrath of God (Rev. 14:17–20).

The final poem of the Anointed Conqueror

63:1. Who is this coming from Edom,[1]
    in vivid[2] garments from Bozrah? –
this one majestically adorned in his clothing,
    swinging along in the abundance of his strength?[3]
I speak in righteousness;
    abundant to save![4]

2.   Why[5] is there red on your clothes,
    and your garments are like someone treading
    in the winepress?

3.   The winepress[6] I have trodden on my own,
    and from the peoples there was no one with me.
And I was treading them in my exasperation,[7]
    and trampling them in my rage,[8]
    and their splashing blood was sprinkling on my garments,
    and I was polluting all my clothing.

4.   For the day of vengeance was in my heart,
    and the year of my redeemed[9] had come,

1   'Edom' represented inveterate opposition to the Lord and his people. Starting in Gen. 27:41, Num. 20:14–21 shows its continuance, and Amos 1:11 condemns its perpetuity. David conquered Edom (2 Sam. 8:14; 1 Kings 11:15). For these two reasons the prophets see the 'last battle' as against Edom and in Edom, when the second David comes to fight and win (Isa. 34; Ezek. 35; Amos 9:11–12; Pss 60 and 83). 'Bozrah' was a chief city of Edom. The word 'edom' means 'red'; 'bozrah' means 'vintage'. Isaiah purposely picks up and develops these ideas.

2   'Sharpened', in the sense that we speak of 'sharp' colours. As the watchmen see the approaching figure, all they can yet discern is brightness, vividness.

5. and I looked,
   and there was no helper,
   and I was appalled,
   and there was no one offering support.
   And my arm acted for me savingly,
   and it was my rage gave me support.
6. And I was crushing peoples in my exasperation,
   and making them drunk in my rage,
   and I kept bringing their blood splashing down
   on the ground.

Prayer and response

Chapters 65 and 66 can be considered as the 'tail-piece' following the final poem of the Anointed Conqueror (63:1–6). In 62:6, the Anointed One appointed intercessors who would keep Jerusalem's future before the Lord. Isaiah 63:7–64:12 records just such a prayer, and 65:1–66:24 is Yahweh's response: the promise of the New Jerusalem.

The remembrancer's prayer (63:7–64:12)

Recollection[10]

7. I will bring to remembrance the ever-unchanging loves[11] of Yahweh,
   the praises of Yahweh,
   in accordance with all that Yahweh has so fully done for us,
   an abundance of good to the house of Israel,
   which he so fully did for them,
   according to his compassion,
   and according to the abundance of his ever-unchanging loves.
8. He said:
   'Indeed they are my people.
   My sons –
   they will not play false.'
   And he became the Saviour they needed.[12]
9. In all their adversity he experienced adversity,[13]
   and the Angel of his face[14] saved them.

3 A single figure could mean a fugitive from a defeat – hence David's comment on the single running figure of Ahimaaz (2 Sam. 18:27). But the dress and gait of this figure speak of majesty and vigour. No bedraggled fugitive this!

4 In answer to the 'who?' of v. 1, the marching figure replies. 'Righteous' always means 'right with God'. On a battlefield the one 'right with God' is the one who is granted the victory. This victory is that of the Saviour.

5 Expressed by *maddu'a*, 'why?' asks for an explanation, not a purpose. The dignified marching figure has obviously come nearer the city gates. The watchmen now see the vivid colour to be red, but clothing thus splashed with red needs an explanation.

6 A different word from that in the previous line, without a distinguishable meaning.

7 See 5:25, also 'exasperation' in v. 6.

8 See 5:25, also 'rage' in vv. 5–6.

9 See 35:9.

10 Typically of Bible praying, this prayer begins by 'telling God about God', dwelling on what he is and has done.

11 The plural of *chesed*, see 55:3. On *chesed*, see 16:5.

12 Lit., 'a Saviour for them', i.e., 'for their welfare' (dative of advantage), 'their Saviour' (dative of possession').

In his love[15] and in his forbearance[16] he redeemed[17] them,
and lifted them and carried them all the long days of old.[18]

10. And they, for their part, mutinied,
    and they hurt his Holy Spirit,
    and he turned right round to be their enemy:
    himself, he made war with them.

11. And he remembered the long days of old,
    Moses!
    His people!
    Where is he who brought them up from the sea,
    with the shepherds of his flock?[19]
    Where is he who placed his Holy Spirit among them,

12. causing the right arm of his beauty to go at Moses' right hand,
    dividing the waters before them to make for himself
    an eternal name,

13. making them go through the deeps?
    Like a horse in the wilderness they did not stumble.

14. Like a herd goes down into the valley,
    Yahweh's Spirit was giving them rest.
    Thus you led your people,
    to make for yourself a name of beauty.

---

13   Or 'no adversary he!' – it was not he who opposed them, nor did he stand aloof from them when adversity came.

14   The Angel who was himself the personal, recognisable presence of Yahweh.

15   *'ahabah*, only here in Isaiah, is the tenderness of love between those devoted to each other (e.g., Gen. 29:20; Deut. 7:8; 1 Sam. 18:3).

16   *Chemlah*, only here in Isaiah; the verb occurs in 9:19 ('spares'); 30:14.

17   See 35:9.

18   Lit., 'days of eternity', also v. 11.

19   cf., Ps. 77:19–20.

Thought for the day: Isaiah 63:1–14

The Bible is meant to be our teacher in everything, and just as we search it to know the truth, and to know how to behave, so we should seek to learn from it how to pray. Think, for example, of Psalm 139. The last five verses reveal that David is 'up against it', facing such hostility as can only be solved by asking for the destruction of his foes. Yet, pressing and deadly though the danger is, it takes him eighteen verses to get around to asking about it – eighteen verses telling God about God! Eighteen verses filling his mind with the glories of the God to whom he speaks! How very different is this prayer (v. 1, 'O Lord, you …') from the rush we so often make into the presence of God with 'O Lord we …', or 'O Lord, I…'! It would seem that, in Bible prayers, the first concern is the truth about the God to whom we would bring our needs. In Isaiah, starting with today's passage, the proportions are not the same as in Psalm 139; eight verses of meditation on the Lord (63:7–14), followed by nineteen verses of request (63:15–64:12), but the truth about prayer is the same. Start with God: his abundant goodness (v. 7), his loving claim of his people (v. 8), his identification with us in our needs (v. 9), his forbearance (v. 10), and his faithfulness now to what he was then (vv. 11–14). Now that we know him we are better placed to speak to him of our needs, to know what to ask, and to be confident of a hearing. And does not 'the Lord's Prayer' reveal the same pattern: first, God's name, kingdom and will; then our needs – food, forgiveness and protection? The great man who would rather call himself 'poor George Muller' would kneel daily with open Bible, read, and turn what he had read into godly meditation and praise, before ever mentioning his own need and that of two thousand orphans in his care. Lord, make me like that!

Day 69 Isaiah 63:15–64:12

The Guardian on Zion's walls (62:6) now turns to asking. Like us, he sees the city of God in earthly disarray and longs for such a divine intervention as will set all to rights.

Where is the Lord's love?

15. Look from heaven,
     and see from your mansion of holiness and beauty.
     Where are your zeal[1] and your warrior strength,
     the turbulence of your feelings, and your compassion
     for me –
     have they held themselves back?
16. For you are our Father,
     though Abraham does not know us,
     and Israel does not recognise us.[2]
     You, Yahweh, are our Father;
     from long since our Redeemer[3] is your name.

Why does the Lord remain estranged?

17. Why, Yahweh, have you made us stray from your ways,
     hardened our heart from fearing you?
     Turn back for your servants' sake,
     the tribes of your possession.
18. For a little, your holy people were in possession;
     our adversaries trample on your sanctuary.
19. For long years we have become those you did not rule,
     those not called by your name.

Why has the Lord not acted?

64:1. If only you
     had torn the heavens!

1   See 9:7.

2   Referring back to 48:1 where the Lord's earthly people no longer merit the name 'Israel'. Here, in confession, they acknowledge the correctness of this, and yet plead that Yahweh is not limited in his affections as even their greatest forebears may be.

3   See 35:9. The parallelism here of 'father' and 'redeemer' brings to the fore the 'next-of-kin' aspect of redemption.

Had come down!
That the mountains
had quaked at your presence!

2. Like fire kindles brushwood;
fire makes water boil!
To make your adversaries know your name;
so that before you nations might tremble –

3. while you do awesome things we were not expecting!
Had come down;
mountains had quaked at your presence![4]

Is there still hope?

4. And from for ever they have not heard,
they have not listened.
No eye has seen a God besides you,
who takes action for the one who waits expectantly[5]
for him.

5. You meet with the one who delights and
practises righteousness,
those who remember you in your ways.
Behold,
you were personally exasperated,
and we sinned!
In them for ever![6]
And are we to be saved?

Helplessness and hopelessness

6. And we – all of us – have become like something unclean,
and all our righteousnesses like a soiled garment.
And we – all of us – have withered like foliage,
and like a wind our iniquities carry us off.

7. And no one calls on your name,
rousing himself up to grip onto you,
for you have hidden your face from us,
and you have melted us down through our iniquities.[7]

4 Note how (typically) Isaiah makes this little poem end where it began in v. 1. I have not tried to 'smooth out' his designed abruptness. In v. 3 'Had come' picks up the 'if only' clause of v. 1.

5 See 8:17. In v. 3, I usually translate the verb there 'confidently await' but 'confidently' (like 'expectantly' here) is no more than a way of differentiating between synonymous verbs and would be out of place.

6 'In them for ever' is just as abrupt and allusive as Isaiah's Hebrew at this point. In its immediate reference 'them' refers to the Lord's exasperation and our sin.

7 'Melt' is metaphorical of depriving of strength, loss of 'get up and go', listlessness in the

The unchanged God

8. Now then Yahweh,
   you are our Father.
   We are the clay and you are the Potter,
   and all of us are the work of your hand.
9. Do not utterly lose patience with us, Yahweh,
   nor for ever remember our iniquity.
   Behold!
   Please look!
   We are, all of us, your people.

Can love still be withheld?

10. The cities of your holiness are destined to
    become a wilderness!
    Even Zion is destined to become a wilderness!
    Jerusalem a desolation!
11. Our house of holiness and beauty,
    where our fathers praised you,
    is destined to become a conflagration of fire,
    and all our pleasant things are destined to become a waste.
12. Yahweh, on account of these things will you hold
    yourself back,
    keep quiet,[8] and humble us exceedingly?

face of any and every challenge;
e.g., Josh. 2:11. 'Through' is
'by the hand of', as of an agent
used to perform a task.

_____

8   See 62:1

Thought for the day: Isaiah 63:15–64:12

Did you notice the telling similarity of wording in 63:15 ('your mansion of holiness and beauty') and 64:11 ('our house of holiness and beauty')? The former is the Lord's heavenly habitation, the latter the earthly house where he promised to live among his people (cf., Exod. 25:8). The former is inviolable in holiness and beauty; the latter, given into the charge of his earthly people, is caught up in the disaster caused by their sin (cf., Ps. 74:4–7). In the divine intention the earthly was meant to be the replica of the heavenly (cf., Exod. 25:40). The truth remains the same today: the Lord's earthly people are themselves the temple in which he lives by his Spirit (1 Cor. 3:16), the locus and display of his holiness and beauty. Well may we mourn that our sinfulness, divisiveness, our failure in biblical distinctiveness, and our manifest lack of holiness have marred the image. Who, looking at today's church – denominational or local – can see the likeness of Jesus? And this is not a matter only of denominational failure, though that is all too plain. The Bible knows nothing of our 'denominationalism', and if Isaiah's wording prompts us to put our hand to reform and renovation then its proper focus is the local church to which we each belong. When we look at the merest sliver of a crescent moon we don't say, 'Oh, there's part of the moon'. We say 'Look, there's the moon.' In the same way each local church, however small – or in the eyes of onlookers, insignificant – is meant to be a mirror and image of the whole, an earthly replica of the heavenly reality where Christ is all. We should be able to look at the fellowships to which we belong and say, 'There is The Church', bearing the two outstanding marks of holiness and beauty; obeying the command, 'Be holy because I am holy' (Lev. 19:2), and displaying the beauty of Jesus in all its gatherings, relationships and individual characters.

Day 70   Isaiah 65:1–25

The prayer has now ended. Ruin is anticipated unless the Lord intervenes in power. The Lord's response does not repeat any of the details of the coming of the Conqueror predicted in chapters 59–63, but promises the fruit of his coming in a New Heaven and a New Earth. Everything false will be overthrown and brought to an end; the world-wide people will be gathered and come to the Zion that is yet to be (Rev. 21:23–27).

The Lord's response

The Lord's world-initiative

65:1. I will surely let myself be sought by those who did not ask,
    let myself be found by those who did not seek.
    I am determined to say[1]
    'Behold me! Behold me!'
    to a nation not called by my name.

Provocation and penalty[2]

2.   I have spread out my hands all day
    to a stubbornly rebellious people,
    who walk in the way that is not good,
    following[3] their thoughts:
3.   the people who provoke me, continually, to my face,
    sacrificing in the gardens,[4]
    and burning incense on bricks;[5]
4.   who dwell in the graves,[6]
    and stay overnight in reserved[7] places;
    who eat pig's flesh,[8]
    and soup made from bits[9] of illicit meat in their vessels;

[1]   The main verbs up to this point are treated as perfects of commitment/certainty, matching Paul's understanding of this verse as referring to the Lord's gathering of a worldwide people (Rom. 10:20). This forms an inclusion with 66:18–24.

[2]   In these verses Isaiah uses the corrupt practices of his day to sketch the continuance of religious malpractice right up to the eschaton.

[3]   Lit., 'after'; see 59:13.

[4]   See 1:29.

[5]   Legitimate altars had to be constructed in uncut stone (Exod. 20:25; Deut. 27:5–6).

5. who say,
   'Keep to yourself!
   Do not approach me,
   for I am taboo to you!'[10]
   There is smoke in my nostrils,
   a fire kindling all day!
6. Behold!
   It is written before me!
   I will not keep quiet,
   but rather I am determined to pay in full.
   I will pay in full into their bosom,
7. their iniquities and the iniquities of their fathers all together! –
   Yahweh has said –
   who have burned incense on the mountains,
   and reviled me on the hills.
   And I will measure out their previous activities into
   their bosom.

Blessing for the remnant

8. This is what Yahweh has said:
   Just like new wine is found in a bunch of grapes,
   and someone says,
   'Do not destroy it,
   for there is a blessing in it,'
   even so I will act for my servants' sake,
   so as not to destroy the whole lot.
9. And from Jacob I will produce seed,
   and from Judah one who is going to possess my mountains,
   and my chosen ones will possess it,
   and my servants will make their home there.
10. And Sharon will become a fold for flocks,
    and the valley of Achor[11] a place where herds can lie:
    for my people who have sought me.

Contrasting destinies

11. And as for you who forsake Yahweh,
    who forget the mountain of my holiness,

6   Forbidden spiritism, seeking revelation from the dead; cf., Deut. 18:9ff.

7   Or 'preserved, guarded'. Places kept private, free of interruption, maybe exclusively for the select few.

8   Lev. 11:7; Deut. 14:8.

9   This translation combines the two possibilities of the Hebrew Text here: 'soup of illicit meat' or 'bits of illicit meat'. On 'illicit meat', see Lev. 7:18, translated in NKJV, 'abomination' (sacrificial flesh kept beyond the permitted time).

10   A likely rather than a secure rendering, certainly supported by the essentially elitist religion indicated here.

11   Isaiah has used Sharon to symbolise deterioration (33:9) and messianic renewal (35:2). Achor, in Josh. 7:24–25, was a bright beginning marred. But some day Sharon will be what it was meant to be, and nothing will mar the great new beginning.

who set a table for Luck,
and who fill a drink offering for Destiny:

12. I will destine you to the sword,
and all of you will cower down for slaughter,
because I called and you did not answer,
spoke and you did not hear,
and you did what is evil in my eyes,
and what did not please me you chose.

13. Therefore, this is what the Sovereign, Yahweh, has said:
Behold, my servants will eat, and yourselves,
you will go hungry;
behold, my servants will drink, and yourselves,
you will thirst;
behold, my servants will rejoice, and yourselves,
you will reap shame;

14. behold, my servants will shout aloud out of
goodness of heart,
and yourselves, you will shriek out for pain of heart,
and out of a broken spirit you will howl.

15. And you will deposit your name as a swear-word for my
chosen ones.
And the Sovereign, Yahweh, will put each of you[12] to death,
and his servants he will call by another name.

16. Thus, whoever blesses himself[13] in the land will bless
himself in the God of truth,
and whoever swears an oath in the land will swear
by the God of truth,
for the former adversities will have been forgotten,
for indeed they will have been hidden from my eyes.

All things new: 1. The New Creation[14]

17. For, behold, I am going to create new heavens
and a new earth,
and the former things[15] will not be remembered,
nor will they rise in the heart,

18. but rather be glad and exult for ever in what I am
going to create.

12 'You' is suddenly singular
here, individualising the
divine work of judgment.

13 As in, e.g., Gen. 22:18, the *hithpael*
(reflexive) of the verb 'to bless' has
the developed meaning 'to seek
the blessing one needs for oneself'.

14 Note 'For' at the beginning of
v. 17. This little poem is intended
to explain the individual and
worldwide blessing sketched
in the preceding verses.

15 Including the 'former
adversities' of v. 16.

All things new: 2. The New City and its people

For, behold, I am going to create Jerusalem an exultation,
and its people a delight.

19. And I will exult in Jerusalem,
and delight in my people,
and there will not be heard again in it
a voice[16] of weeping and a voice of screaming.

20. Never again will there be there an infant only days old,[17]
nor an old man who does not fulfil his days
for as a youth one would die a hundred years old –
and the sinner, a hundred years old, will be cursed![18]

All things new: 3. The New Society

Security of tenure

21. And they will build houses – and inhabit them!
And they will plant vineyards – and eat their fruit!

22. They will not build and another inhabit;
they will not plant and another eat,
for like the days of a tree will be the days of my people,
and my chosen ones will make full use of the work
of their hands.

Prosperity in blessing

23. They will not toil for nothing,
nor beget children for terror,
for the seed will be Yahweh's blessed ones,
and their offspring will be with them.

Peace with God, universal harmony

24. And it will be,
before they call I will myself answer;
while they are still speaking I will myself hear.

25. The wolf and the baby lamb will pasture as one,
and like an ox the lion will eat straw.
And as for the snake, dust will be its bread.
They will neither do wrong nor destroy in all the
mountain of my holiness,
Yahweh has said.

16 'Voice' in the sense of 'sound'.

17 Lit., 'an infant of days'.

18 As usual Isaiah is using features
of life as we know it to suggest
the coming bliss. Thus no infant
mortality, no premature death –
indeed a centenarian would be
considered to be in his youth!
But there is no escape for the
sinner: even should he live to be a
hundred the curse will catch him!

Thought for the day: Isaiah 65:1–25

Isaiah assembled an impressive list of charges against those who, he said, were provoking the Lord to anger: all manner of religious defection and disloyalty, abhorrent practices, and, believe it or not, spiritual snobbery and elitism (vv. 2–5). Yet, remarkably, when all comes to all, none of these things are mentioned when the sword arrives to inflict judgment and sin issues in death (v. 12). The real problem, the 'killing' sin, is to have failed to listen to the Word of God: he called and spoke; they refused to respond or hear. How did that voice come to them? Was it in the preaching and writing of the prophets? Was it in the instruction of the priests? Was it the careful counsel of the Wise? (cf., 30:8–11; Jer. 18:18; Mal. 2:7.) Undoubtedly so, and their cardinal sin, the final nail in their coffin, the sin that could not be overlooked, was, as Amos put it (Amos 2:4), spurning the teaching of the Lord, and failing to keep his commandments. The people of God have always been marked out by possession of the Word of God, his revealed truth, and the transition from their very different circumstances to our own day is obvious and easy. The deadly sin of the Lord's people is neglect of his Word – the Bible set aside, or doubted, or half-believed, or denigrated, or left as a closed book gathering dust. How it hurts the Lord when we let a day start without opening the Book (Isa. 50:4)! What loss to us and damage to our souls when the Word of God has not been hidden in the heart to guard us against sin (Ps. 119:11)! Here is a lover who gets a letter from his beloved and says, 'Oh, I can't be bothered with that!' Imagine the feelings of the beloved on finding all those love-letters, oh yes, carefully kept, and, yes indeed, tied round with red ribbon, but the envelopes never opened (Isa. 29:11). What made the people of Berea 'more noble' – as the AV says – in Acts 17:11? They received the Word; they searched the Scriptures daily. Here indeed is true Christian nobility!

Day 71 Isaiah 66:1–24

Isaiah's final chapter continues the contrast between those who are right with God and accepted before him and those who face his final judgment. The chapter is in four sections, with the first and last matching each other and the second and third contrasting with each other. Verses 1–4 and 18–24 focus on the House of the Lord. In verses 1–4 those who tremble at Yahweh's word (vv. 1–2) are contrasted with those who chose not to hear when Yahweh spoke (vv. 3–4). In verses 18–24 a worldwide gathering comes to the House (vv. 18–23), keeping Sabbath, but alongside lies the cemetery of the rebels (v. 24). Verses 5–14 deal with those who tremble at the Word, and verse 15–17 with false worshippers under fiery judgment.

The House and its people: Welcome and refusal

Trembling at Yahweh's Word

66:1. This is what Yahweh has said:

> Heaven is my throne,
> and earth a footstool for my feet.
> Wherever is the house which you will build for me?
> And wherever is the place for my home?[1]

2. All these things my hand has made
> and (so) all these things come into being![2]
> This is Yahweh's Word!
> And for this one I look –
> for one downtrodden and crippled[3] in spirit,
> one who is trembling at my Word.

Refusing to listen

3.[4] One slaughtering an ox, one striking down a man;
> one sacrificing a lamb, one strangling[5] a dog;

---

1 See 11:10, and 'homes' in 32:18. The word (*menuchah*) combines being at rest and being at home.

2 Lit., 'and all these were'. Solomon's question in 1 Kings 8:27 expects (as the context demands) the answer 'Yes'. Isaiah's perspective on the question of the Lord living among his people is to ask wherever such a house could be found. In other words, though the Lord does indeed come to live with his

one offering a gift, pig's blood;
  making a memorial offering of incense, blessing an idol.
  They, indeed, have chosen their own ways,
  and in their abominations their soul has found pleasure.
4. I, indeed, will choose their unforeseen fate,[6]
  and bring on them what they fear,
  because I called and no one was answering;
  I spoke and they did not hear,
  and they did what was evil in my eyes,
  and what did not please me they chose.

Trembling ... or else! ...
5. Hear Yahweh's word,
  You who tremble at his Word.
  Your brothers have said –
  those who hate you,
  who excommunicate you because of my name –
  'May Yahweh be glorified
  so that we may see your joy!'
  But it is they who will reap shame!
6. A voice of uproar from the city!
  A voice from the temple!
  Yahweh's voice paying in full,
  Total requital to his enemies!

Suddenly! Joy for Jerusalem!
7.[7] Before she was writhing in pain she gave birth!
  Before birth pains started coming to her, she delivered a male!
8. Who has heard such a thing?
  Who has seen the like?
  Will the earth be painfully born[8] – in one day?
  Or will a nation be painfully born at a single stroke?
  For, just like that, Zion writhed, gave birth to her sons.
9. Am I one to bring to the point of birth[9] and not to
  cause actual birth?
  Yahweh keeps saying.

3   *Nakeh*, only elsewhere in
    2 Sam. 4:4; 9:3, of a man
    crippled in his feet.

4   Four pairs in which permissible
    acts are linked with impermissible
    ones. Isaiah sets the lawful and
    the unlawful side by side without
    comment. The implication is
    to present a choice between
    obedience and disobedience
    as the end of v. 3 and the
    beginning of v. 4 indicate.

5   Lit., 'necking' a dog. Customarily
    translated 'breaking a neck' but
    examination of instances makes
    this uncertain – and unlikely.

6   Contextually translated
    'capriciousness' in 3:4 – the
    capricious acts of a fickle
    ruler – here seems to point to
    the apparently capricious fate
    which will befall those who
    have chosen their own ways.

People he, as Creator of all, is too
big for the house. The house as
such is meaningless. Everything
depends on being rightly
related to its great Occupant.

7   Isaiah moves from the statement
    of ultimate events (v. 6) to
    affirm that what is impossible
    with humans is possible with
    God – birth without labour,
    children without pain (v. 7), a
    nation created instantaneously
    (v. 8). Because the Lord so wills
    (v. 9) Jerusalem's eschatological
    joy is secure (vv. 10–13), and
    Yahweh's servants will be
    there to enjoy it (v. 14).

Or am I, who cause birth, one to restrain from
bearing a child?[10]
your God has said.

10. Rejoice with Jerusalem and exult in her,
    all who love her.
    Be delightfully glad with her,
    all who were bemoaning themselves over her,

11. that you may suck and be satisfied from her comforting breast;
    that you may drink to the full and luxuriate from the
    nipple of her glory.

12. For this is what Yahweh has said:
    Behold,
    I am going to spread out peace for her, like a river,
    and, like a flooding stream, the glory of the nations.
    And you will suck;
    on the hip you will be carried,
    and on the knees you will be cuddled.

13. Like someone whom his mother comforts,
    so I will comfort you,
    and it is in Jerusalem you will be comforted!

14. And you will see,
    and your heart will be happy,
    and like green growth your bones will blossom.
    And Yahweh's hand will make itself known to his servants –
    and he will be indignant[11] with his enemies.

The equally certain doom

15. For, behold,
    in fire Yahweh will himself come,
    and like a whirlwind, his chariotry,
    with rage to pay back his exasperation
    and with flames of fire his rebuke.

16. For with fire Yahweh will enter into judgment
    even with all flesh with his sword,
    and Yahweh's slain will be many.

17. Those who sanctify themselves
    and cleanse themselves for the gardens,[12]

8 Lit., 'be travailed with' or 'be brought to travail'.

9 Lit., 'cause to break'. See 37:3.

10 Lit., simply 'to restrain'. The verb is used here as an ellipse for the full phrase 'restrain from bearing'. cf. Gen. 16:2.

11 See 10:5.

12 See 1:28–29.

following one in the middle,[13]
who eat pig-meat, and the abomination, and the mouse –
all together they will come to an end.
This is Yahweh's word.

World pilgrimage to Zion
18.[14] And as for me,
  regarding their works and their thoughts,
  it has happened!
  With reference to the gathering of all nations and tongues,
  they will come and see my glory:
19. I will set a sign[15] among them,
  and I will send some of them – escapees[16] – to the nations,
  Tarshish and Pul and Lud, who draw the bow,
  Tubal and Javan,[17] the distant coastlands,[18]
  who have not heard a report of me,
  and have not seen my glory,
  and they will declare my glory among the nations.
20. And they will bring all your brothers,
  from all the nations, as a gift to Yahweh,
  on horses, and in chariots, and in covered wagons,
  and on mules, and on camels,
  to Jerusalem, the mountain of my holiness,
  Yahweh has said,
  just like the sons of Israel bring a gift,
  in a pure vessel to the house of Yahweh.
21. And also from them I will take some
  to be priests, to be Levites,
  Yahweh has said.

The House and the cemetery
22. For like the new heavens and the new earth,
  which I am going to make,
  are going to remain in place[19] before me –
  this is Yahweh's word –
  so your seed and your name will remain in place.

13 The meaning of this phrase is not known. Ezek. 8:7–11 suggests a cult leader or worship leader. 'Following' is 'after'; see 59:13.

14 The Hebrew Text of v. 18 is very abrupt; allusive rather than obvious. Many suggestions have been made for its improvement. The rendering here is as near as we can come to understanding the text as we have inherited it, in its context.

15 See 11:10–12.

16 i.e., immune from the judgment of vv. 15–17.

17 These place names are designedly impressionistic. We are no longer able to identify them with geographical regions: 'no place too remote', 'unknown'. 'Draw the bow' is possibly stated in order to stress that these are real people with real and known characteristics, or possibly that even those who will greet the message with hostility must still be approached.

18 See 41:1.

19 Lit., 'going to stand'.

23. And it will be,
    from month to month, and from Sabbath to Sabbath,
    all flesh will come to bow in worship before me,
    Yahweh has said.
24. And they will go out and look at[20]
    the corpses of the men who were rebelling against me,
    for their worm will not die,
    and their fire will not go out.
    And they will be an object of disgust to all flesh.

---

20 True to the theme of chapters 56–
    66, the redemption and vengeance
    lie side by side. Those who
    enjoy eternal security before
    Yahweh keep in mind ('go out
    and look') the eternal fate from
    which they have been saved.

Thought for the day: Isaiah 66:1–24

Nothing much changes! People in Isaiah's day disbelieved Yahweh's promises of what he was about to do – the New Heaven and New Earth – and mocked those who did believe (v. 3b). That was in, say, 700 BC. In the first century AD Peter warned of scoffers who dismissed the truth of the Lord's Second Coming (2 Pet. 3:3–4), and now, over two thousand years on? Sadly there are thousands who, week by week, recite the faith that 'He will come again in glory', and yet the truth of what they profess has never dawned on them. But even more sadly, there are those for whom the supernatural elements of our Lord coming as they saw him go (Acts 1:11), and of our being caught up to meet him in the air (1 Thess. 4:17), are stumbling blocks, making them current doubters of biblical eschatology. To them (it would seem) a coming kingdom is an acceptable thought but a coming King a problem. Yet, as Isaiah taught (and the New Testament affirms), the coming kingdom too is totally supernatural. Isaiah asked if a world could be born in a day (v. 8); John saw the New Jerusalem descending out of heaven from God (Rev. 21:10), illuminated not by explicable light but by the glory of God and the Lamb (Rev. 21:23). The kingdom is as foreign to 'modern' modes of thought – and to all anti-supernatural notions – as the reality of the Son of man coming in the clouds. Let us be insistent on recovering, teaching, and rejoicing in the great truth of the Lord's return, specially with reference to its awesome reality (2 Pet. 3:10), its triumph, its present moral (2 Pet. 3:11) and churchly (2 Pet. 3:14) implications, and the Christ-centred eternity to which it ushers us (1 Thess. 4:17). But behind this contrast between those who accept and those who reject biblical eschatology lies a fundamental difference: there are those who 'tremble' at the Lord's Word (vv. 2, 5) and those who do not hear when the Lord speaks (v. 4). To face up to this distinction, firmly to choose to live under the authority of the Bible, and to seek to hear, every day, what the Lord our God will say to us (Isa. 50:4) is as central a response to Isaiah's sixty-six chapters as he would have wished!

Some suggestions for further reading and study

What next?

If, as I greatly hope, you get bitten with the Isaiah-bug, it might help you to have a few suggestions for further reading and study.

The best starter is F. D. Kidner's article on Isaiah in *The New Bible Commentary, 21ˢᵗ Century Edition* (IVP, 1994).

You will find contrasting presentations, but equally helpful, in Derek Thomas, *God Delivers, Isaiah Simply Explained* (Evangelical Press, 1991), and (dividing Isaiah into short, manageable chunks) Philip Hacking, *Isaiah* (Crossway Bible Guides, 1994).

Moving on to more substantial commentaries, for looking up verses and passages or for a more leisurely working through of the whole book, Allan Harman, *Isaiah, A Covenent to be kept for the sake of the Church* (Christian Focus, 2005); J. N. Oswalt, *Isaiah,* 2 volumes in *The New International Commentary on the Old Testament* (Eerdmans, 1998); Alec Motyer, *The Prophecy of Isaiah* (IVP, 1993), and *Isaiah* (Tyndale Old Testament Commentaries, 1999).

.

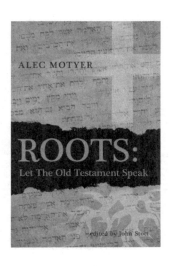

ROOTS: Let the Old Testament Speak
Alec Motyer

"The title, Old Testament, creates difficulties of its own. If it is 'Old' and we are people of the 'New', surely we may properly let it fade away into history? Besides, it seems very unlike the New Testament, even contradictory: all those wars when Jesus is the Prince of peace; all those commandments to obey when we are not under law but under grace. And can the God of the Old Testament be a God of love like the Father, Son and Holy Spirit?"

These are the questions that Alec Motyer, a life-long lover of the Old Testament, seeks to answer starting with the conviction that Jesus is the fulfilment of the Old Testament Scripture. This is for the Christian who wants to know what the Old Testament has to do with the New Testament and why the Christian should read it.

A comprehensive survey of the Old Testament organised around its authors and major characters, the theme of this book is that the Holy Spirit chose, fashioned and equipped the biblical authors to convey distinctive truths through each of them.

ISBN 978-1-84550-506-6

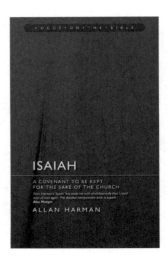

ISAIAH: A Covenant to be Kept for the Sake of the Church
Allan Harman

Isaiah has been called the 'fifth gospel'. Why? Because in it God speaks through his prophet of his people's departure from truth, the need for repentance and the redemption provided by a coming saviour. Isaiah's imagery is some of the most beautiful, and terrifying, in the Bible.

It was written in the 8th century BC at a time of material prosperity. This wealth had brought increased literacy and so God's people could be brought back by a book of 66 chapters to understand a world that had spiritual, as well as physical, dimensions.

This is a key Old Testament book, as well as charting a key change in the life of God's people it provides some of the most important prophecies fulfilled only in the life of Jesus of Nazareth. Its lessons for the contemporary church are particularly apt.

Too often modern commentaries become a discussion between commentators rather than an exploration of what the text has to say to contemporary readers. Allan Harman's methods follow those of Leon Morris and Allan McRae in that he devotes most of his energy to discovering what God is saying through his prophet, rather than what we are saying amongst ourselves.

ISBN 978-1-84550-053-5

PREACHING?: Simple Teaching on Simply Preaching
Alec Motyer

Like many things in life, the skill of good preaching is 95% perspiration and 5% inspiration. Alec Motyer's guide is based on a multitude of sermons over many years of preaching in many different situations, a recipe to help you know your subject and to pull the pieces together into a winning sermon. Preaching is a privilege: let Alec help you reach out and make the best of the gifts God has given you.

ISBN 978-1-78191-130-3

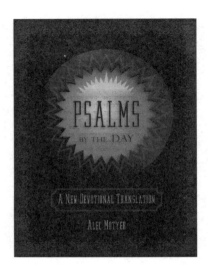

PSALMS BY THE DAY: A New Devotional Translation
Alec Motyer

"...expository without being dry, devotional without being forced. As we get to look over his shoulder, we learn to read the Psalms better for ourselves ... delicious combination-richly full, concisely put."

MARK DEVER,
Senior Pastor, Capitol Hill Baptist Church and President, 9Marks.org, Washington, DC

"This book is an absolute treasure – a life-time of godly scholarship, faithful preaching and pastoral wisdom all in one volume ... a wonderful way to engage freshly with these rich Biblical songs!"

JONATHAN LAMB,
Keswick Ministries, CEO and minister-at-large

"This book is the dream combination: the Psalms presented as a daily devotional by the great Christian scholar ... Everyone who picks up this book will find that they not only learn to read and understand the Psalms as Christian scripture, they may also find their prayer life changed in a profound and dramatic way."

Carl R. Trueman,
Paul Woolley Professor of Historical Theology and Church History,
Westminster Theological Seminary, Philadelphia, Pennsylvania

ISBN 978-1-78191-716-9

TEACHING ISAIAH: Unlocking Isaiah for Bible Teacher
David Jackman

In the period that Isaiah the prophet lived there was immense political upheaval across the ancient near-east. The people of God had a choice – to follow their own human policies or to follow the promises of God. They chose to be unfaithful. The prophet breaks in and calls them to repent asking them to stop violating the covenant. In today's setting this is a message that your hearers will identify with, readily identifying ourselves with the deceitful hearts of the people of Judah, and learn also from their mistakes how our own divided hearts may equally lead us astray. This is not another commentary but a useful resource, which will help the pastor/ preacher, a small group leader or a youth worker communicate a message of grace when speaking from the book of Isaiah. It will give you help in planning and executing a lesson in particular with background, structure, key points and application.

Teaching Isaiah is part of the 'Teaching the Bible' series and is published in conjunction with Proclamation Trust Media whose aim is to encourage ministry that seeks above all to expound the Bible as God's Word for today.

ISBN 978-1-84550-565-3

Christian Focus Publications

Our mission statement –

STAYING FAITHFUL
In dependence upon God we seek to impact the world through literature faithful to His infallible Word, the Bible. Our aim is to ensure that the Lord Jesus Christ is presented as the only hope to obtain forgiveness of sin, live a useful life and look forward to heaven with Him.

Our Books are published in four imprints:

CHRISTIAN FOCUS

popular works including biographies, commentaries, basic doctrine and Christian living.

CHRISTIAN HERITAGE

books representing some of the best material from the rich heritage of the church.

MENTOR

books written at a level suitable for Bible College and seminary students, pastors, and other serious readers. The imprint includes commentaries, doctrinal studies, examination of current issues and church history.

CF4•K

children's books for quality Bible teaching and for all age groups: Sunday school curriculum, puzzle and activity books; personal and family devotional titles, biographies and inspirational stories – because you are never too young to know Jesus!

Christian Focus Publications Ltd,
Geanies House, Fearn, Ross-shire,
IV20 1TW, Scotland, United Kingdom.
www.christianfocus.com